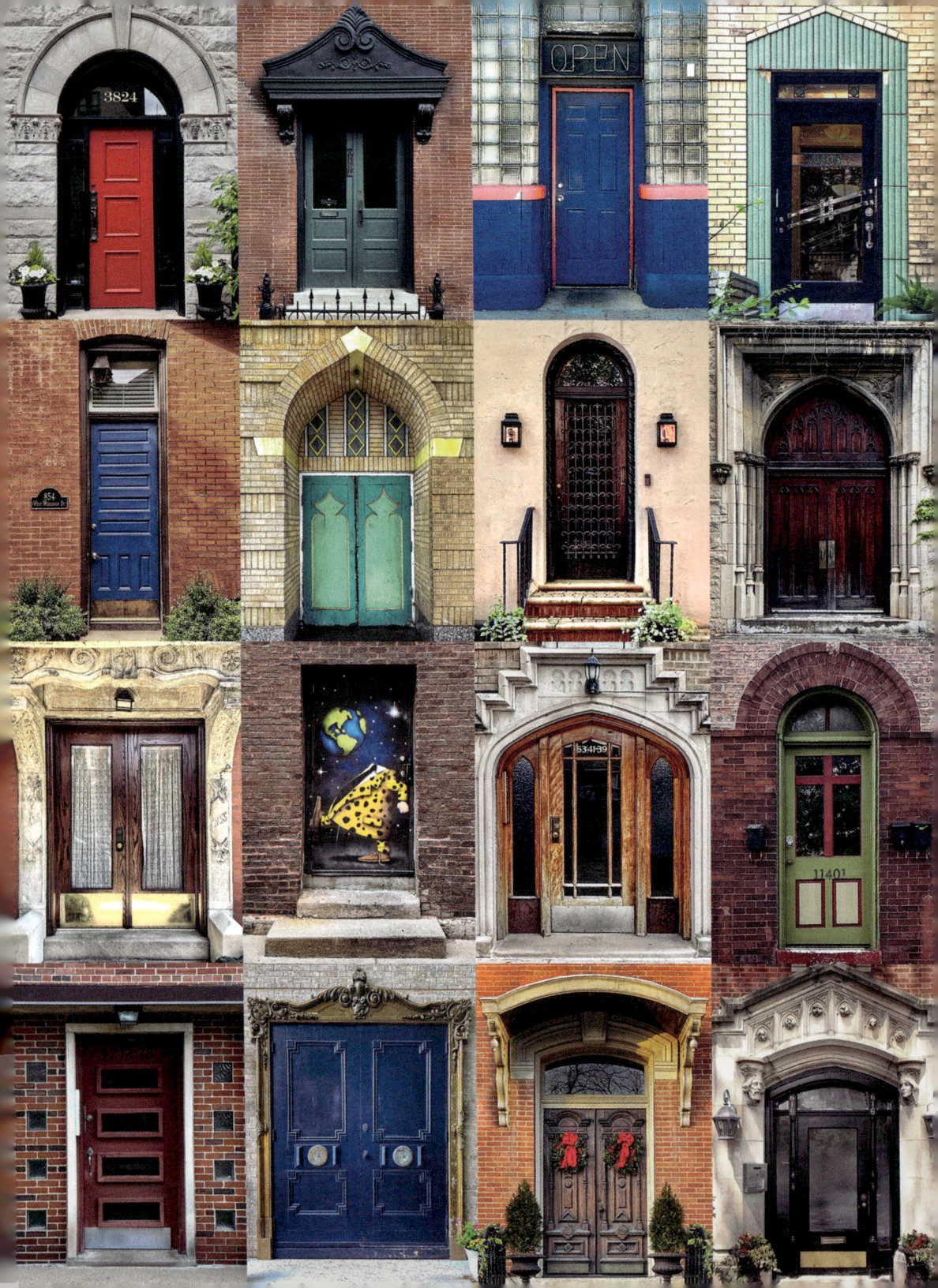

DOORWAYS OF
CHICAGO

RONNIE FREY

TROPE PUBLISHING CO.

This book is dedicated to the late Laurie Fujimori, my best friend and my roommate for five unforgettable years. She could say more in one sentence than most people manage in a lifetime, choosing each word with care. An indigo child, as am I, she had an uncanny gift for reading people, and if a conversation took a wacky or wild turn, she would grin and say, "Waka Waka."

Laurie and I spent countless hours talking about living in the moment. As I read Eckhart Tolle's books, she revisited them through me, though she had seen their truths long before I did. I will never forget the day I celebrated my @doorwaysofchicago account reaching 800 Instagram followers. Laurie smiled, shook her head, and said, "This is going to be huge." When I asked why, she told me, "I've lived in Chicago all my life and I've seen all these buildings, but never the way you show them." She believed in me long before I believed in myself, and she was my biggest fan.

I wish she were here to hold this book in her hands. She would be so proud, and I can almost hear her saying, "That's my roomie!"

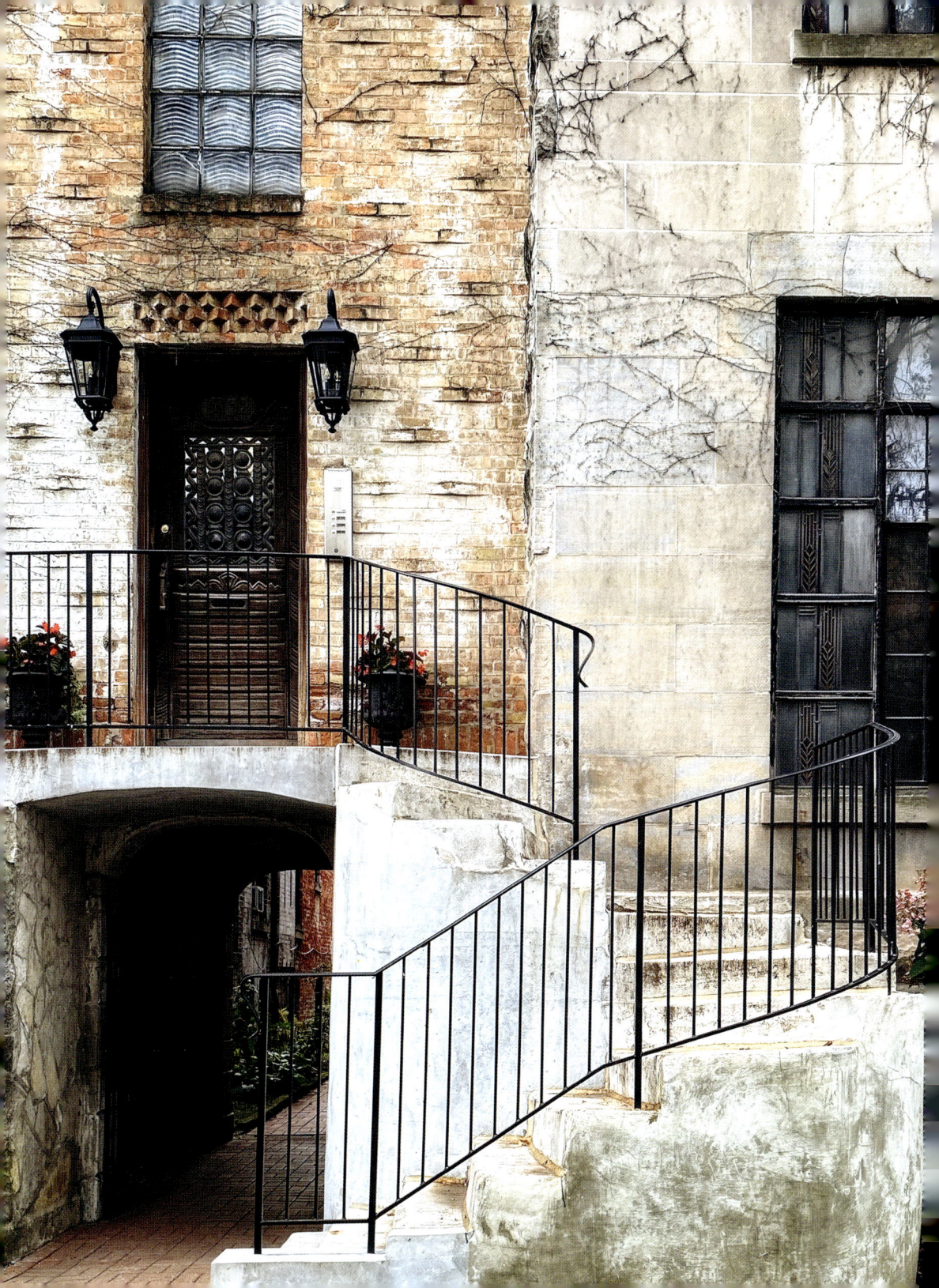

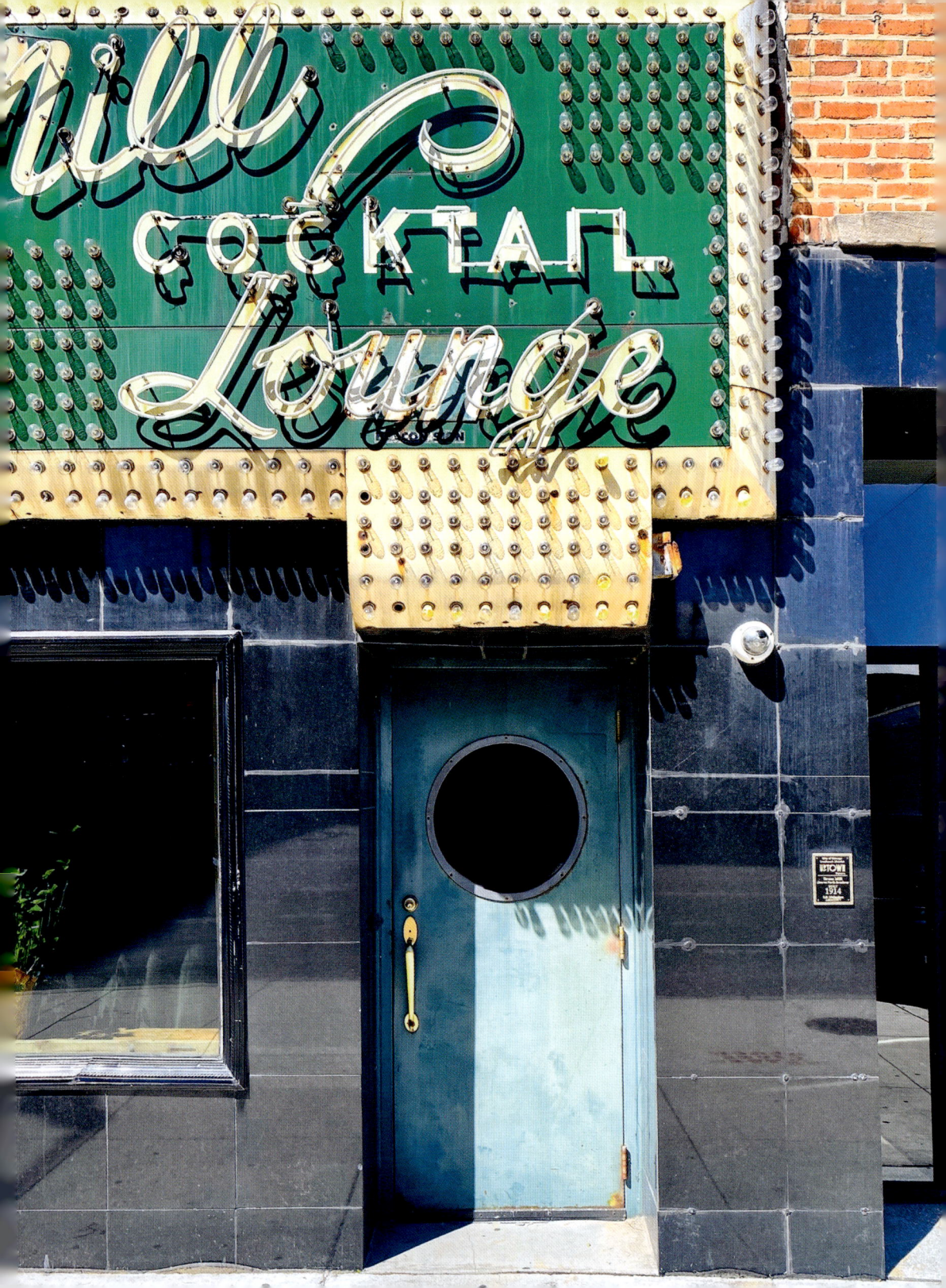

INTRODUCTION

For me, a doorway is a portal into another world. An opportunity to see another moment and envision another's story. Photography pulls me into the present, slows me down, and reveals the extraordinary in the everyday.

Many years ago, while on my first trip to England on a tightly scheduled work trip with no time for sightseeing, I saw a bright blue door while looking out the window of my bus as it wound up a rainy road toward the Royal Citadel in Plymouth. That one vivid door in an austere, prison-like stone wall caught my eye, and something clicked. Ignoring jet lag and stormy skies, I made my way back alone in the pouring rain, umbrella flipping inside out, determined to capture that doorway. That photograph wasn't just a moment. It was a calling that took me on a journey I could never have imagined.

Back in Chicago, I began seeing my city differently. On lunch breaks, I would wander through Chicago's neighborhoods, snapping photos of doorways, cornices, arches, and façades, things I would have just passed without a second glance. Within a few months, @doorwaysofchicago was born, a visual archive of all that makes Chicago one of the most unique and memorable cities in the world.

Doorways of Chicago is my love letter to the city's architecture, history, and soul, and a joyful celebration of the menagerie of scenes we pass by every day. My hope is that these pages inspire you to look closer and see your own streets in a whole new way.

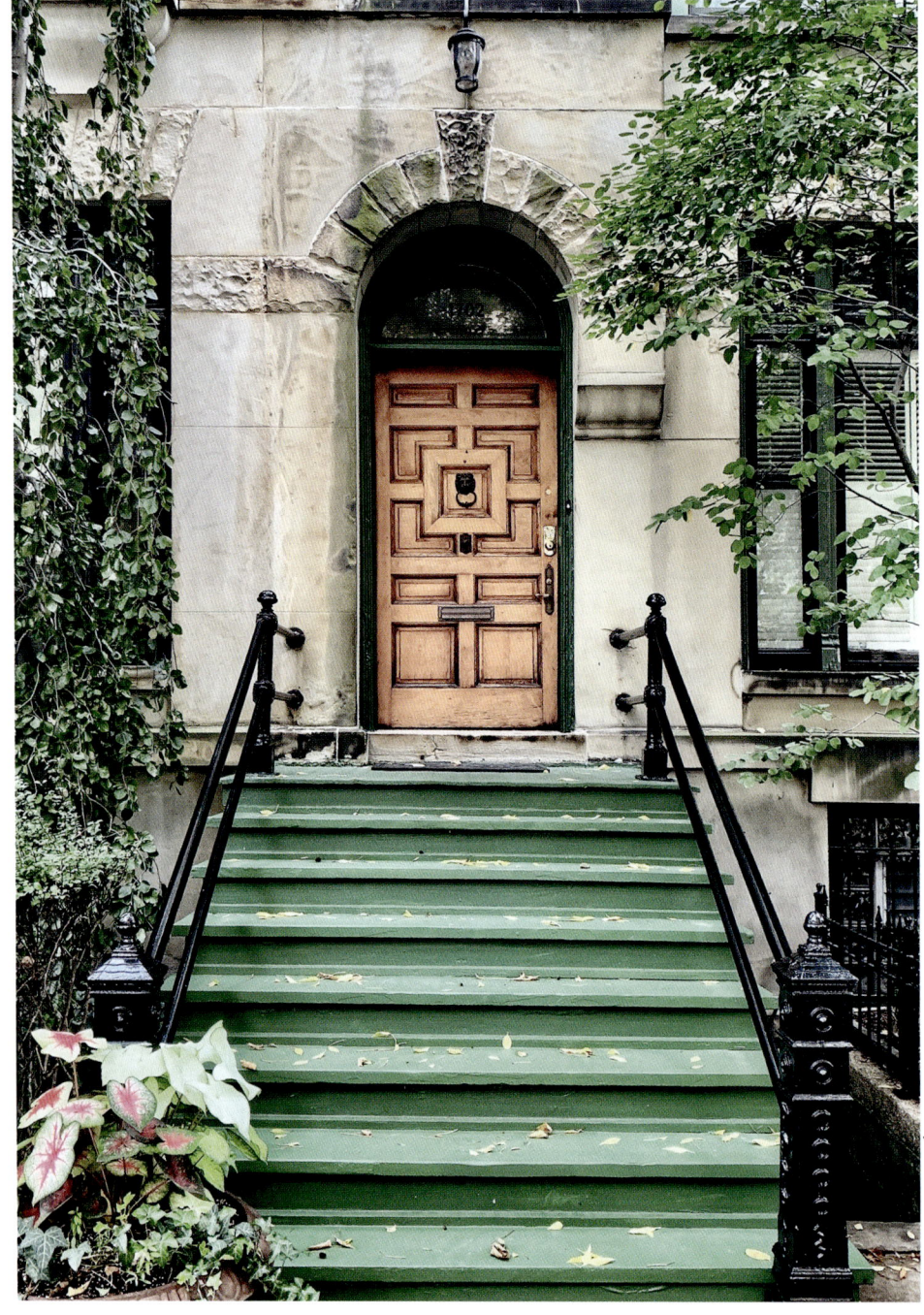

OLD TOWN

Residential

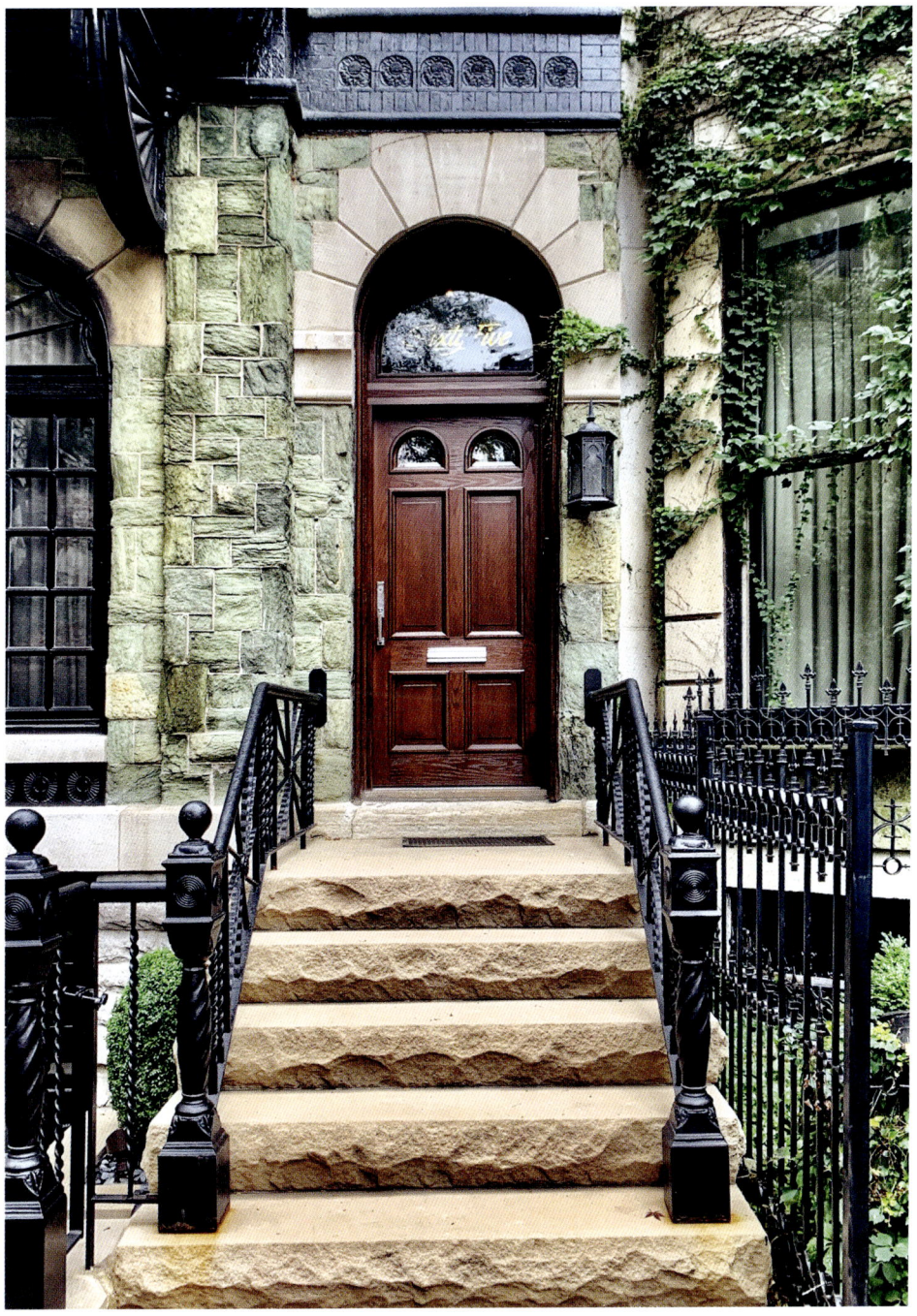

GOLD COAST

Residential

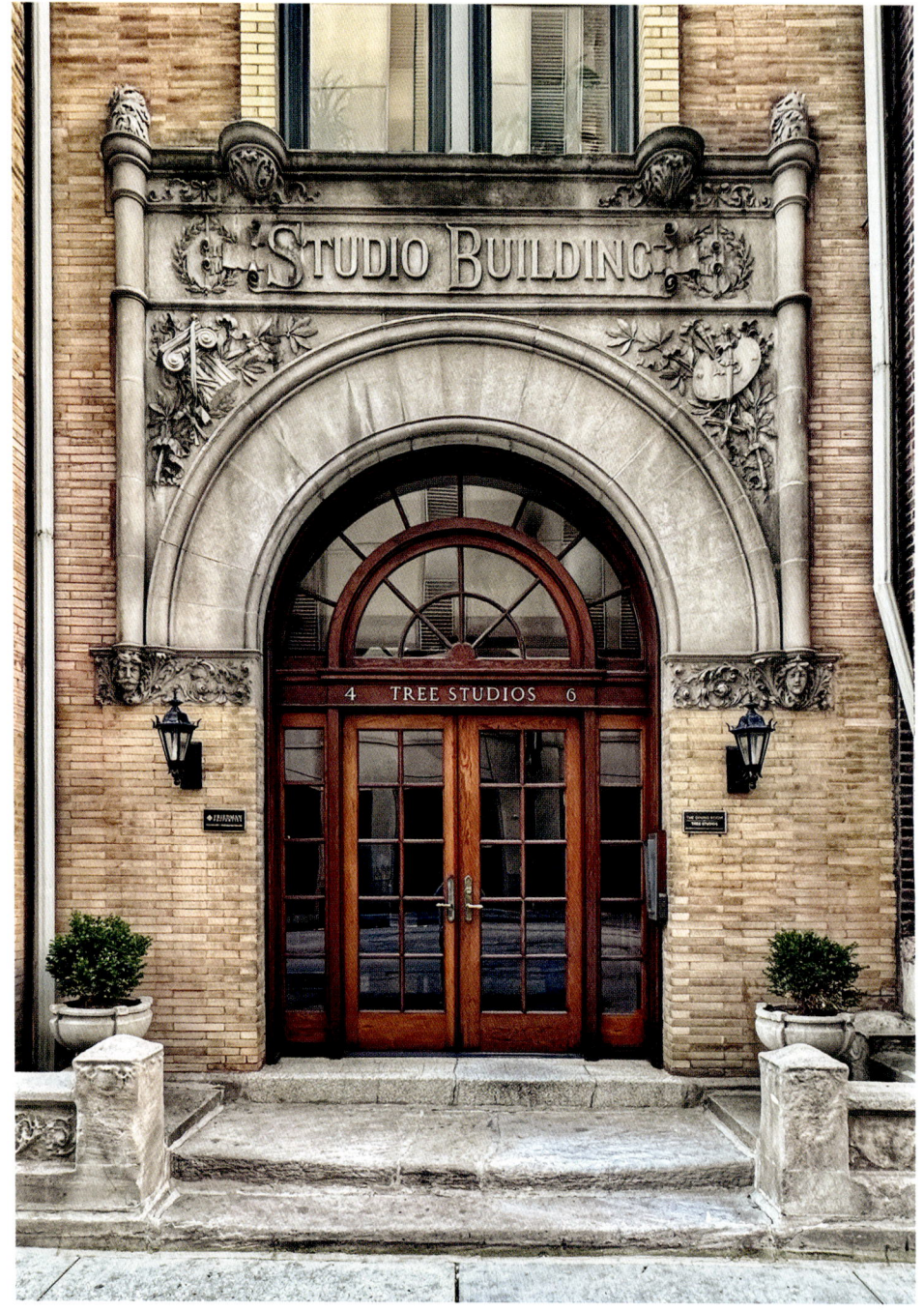

RIVER NORTH

Tree Studios

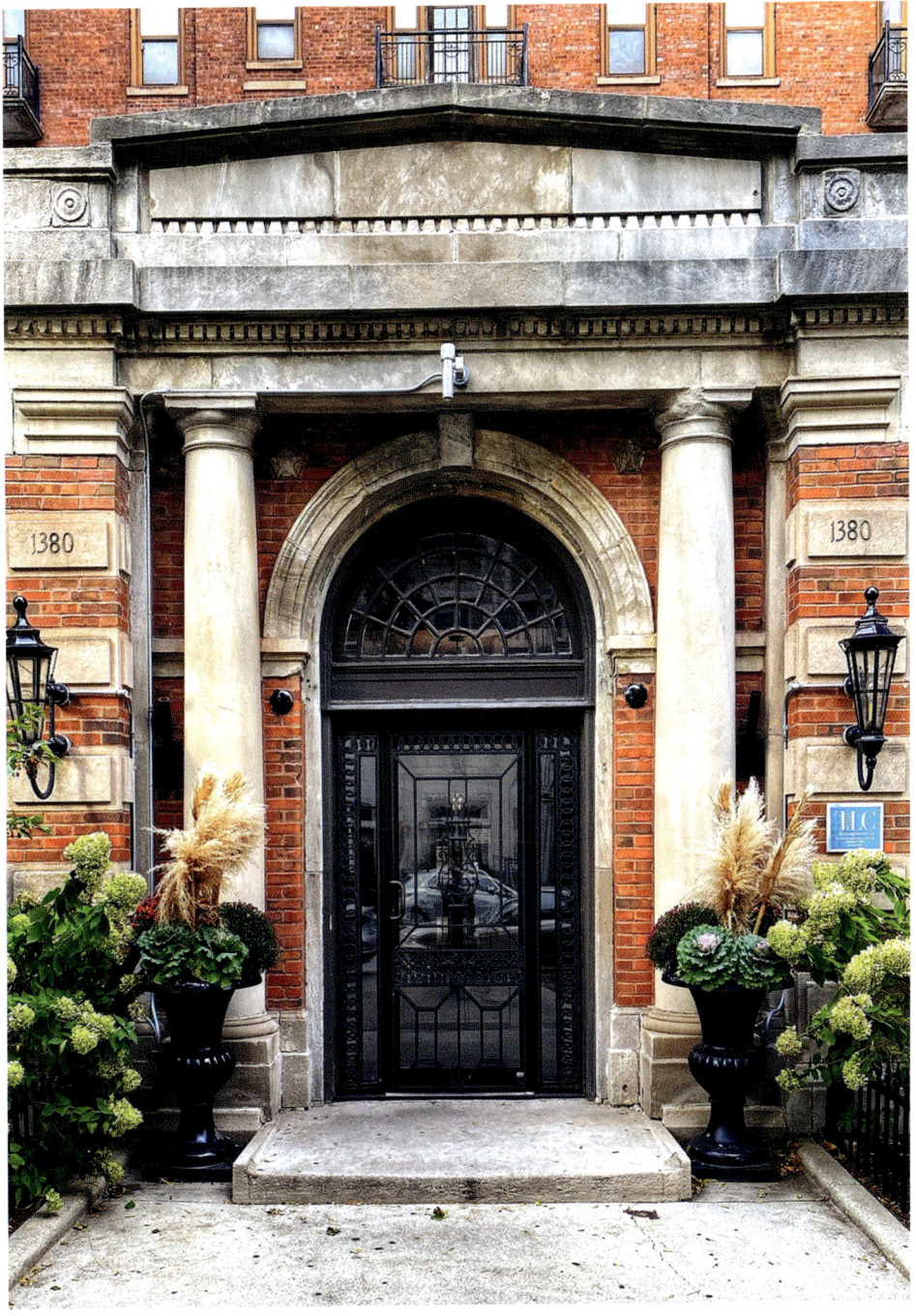

KENWOOD

Residential

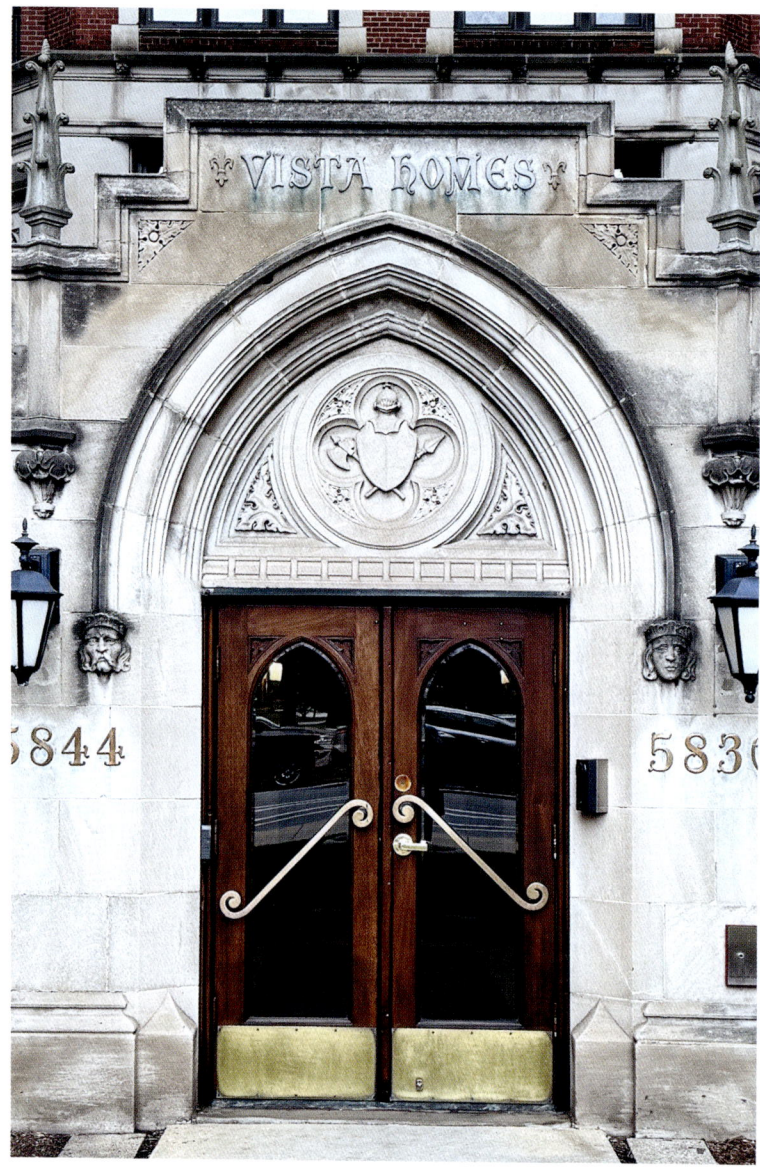

HYDE PARK

Residential

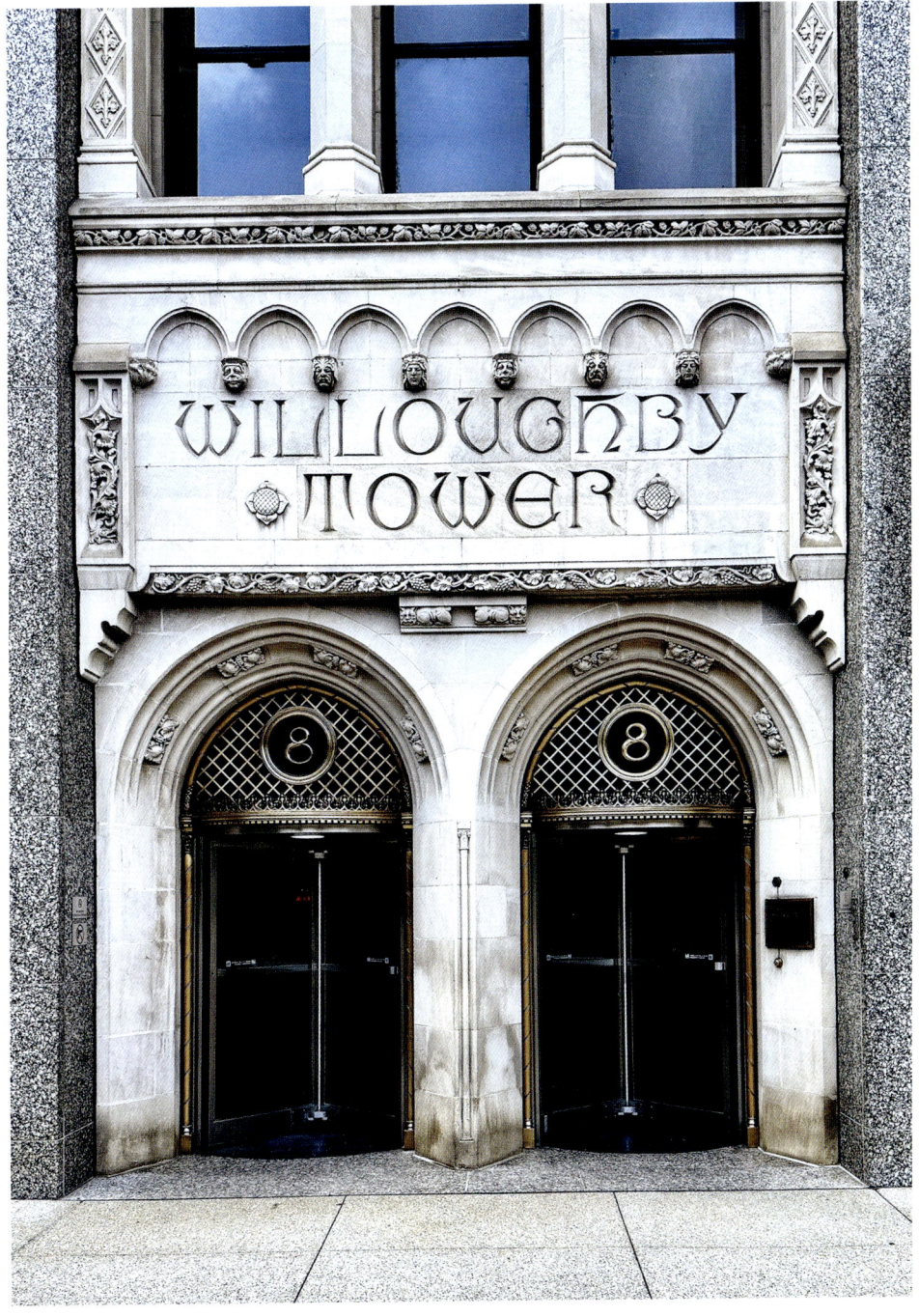

THE LOOP

Willoughby Tower

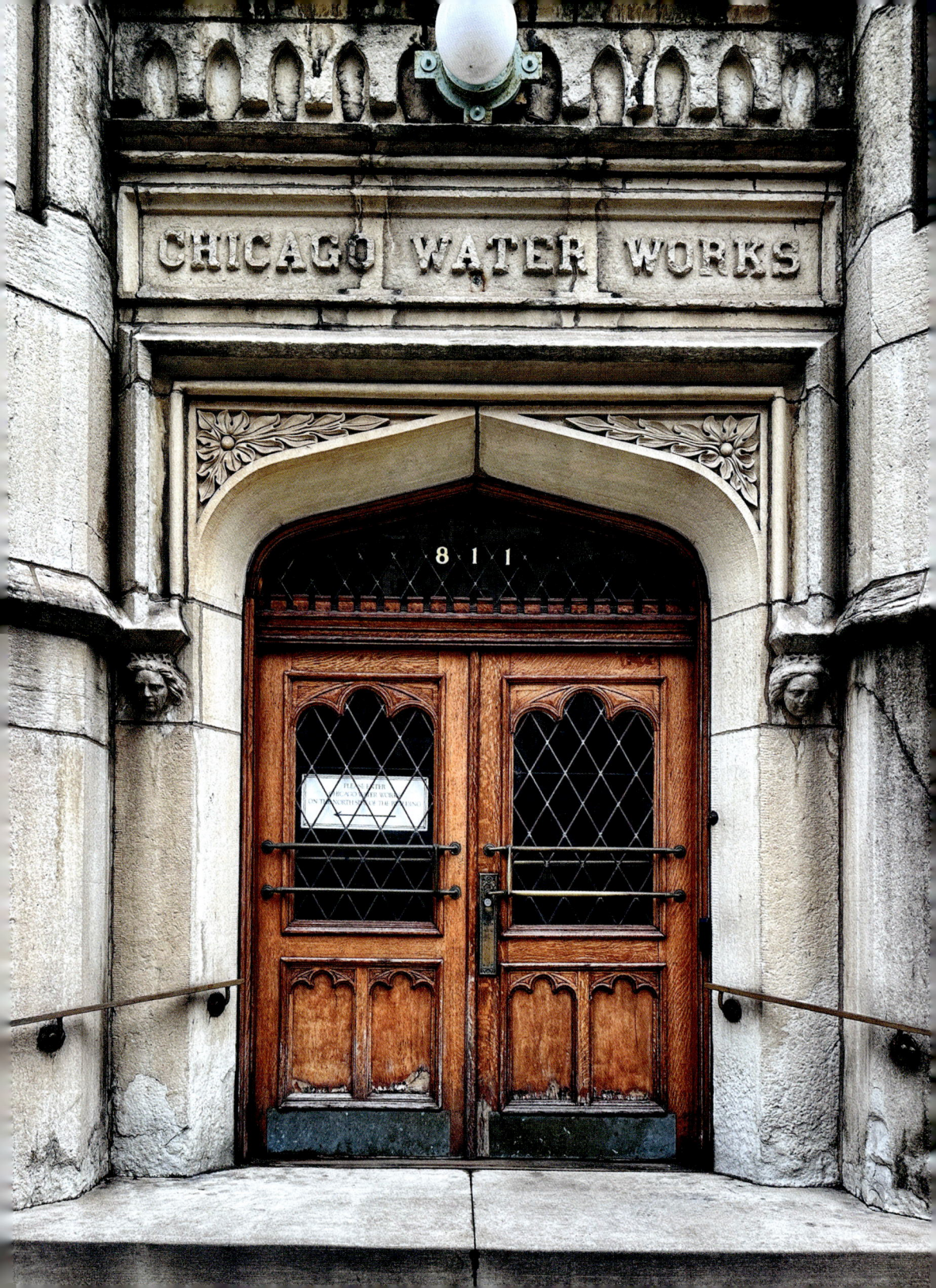

CHICAGO AVENUE PUMPING STATION

Architectural Style: Gothic Revival | Year: 1866

Originally designed and built to receive fresh water via underground pipes from Lake Michigan for a growing city population, the Chicago Avenue Pumping Station is proof that beauty and function are not mutually exclusive.

By the 1860s, Chicago was facing a water crisis. Unable to support its growing population, Chief Engineer Ellis S. Chesbrough looked to Lake Michigan for a solution. While nearshore lake water was too polluted due to run off, Chesbrough designed a water supply tunnel system that ran nearly two miles offshore and brought the lake water back into the city through a pumping station. To accommodate for pressure surges in the water, a standpipe system was added across the street, housed by the now iconic Chicago Water Tower.

Both buildings were built in yellow limestone and feature hallmarks of architect William Boyington's signature Gothic Revival style. Pointed arches, decorative patterns, and tall spires give the Pumping Station and Water Tower a medieval, romantic aura, like a miniature kingdom out of a fantasy movie.

As some of the only buildings in downtown Chicago left standing after the Great Fire of 1871, a devastating fire that burned for two days, killing approximately 300 people and leaving nearly 100,000 homeless, the Water Tower and Pumping Station became symbols of the city's resilience and strength.

Today, the historic Pumping Station is a public landmark and a popular tourist attraction where visitors can step inside and admire its Gothic Revival architecture up close.

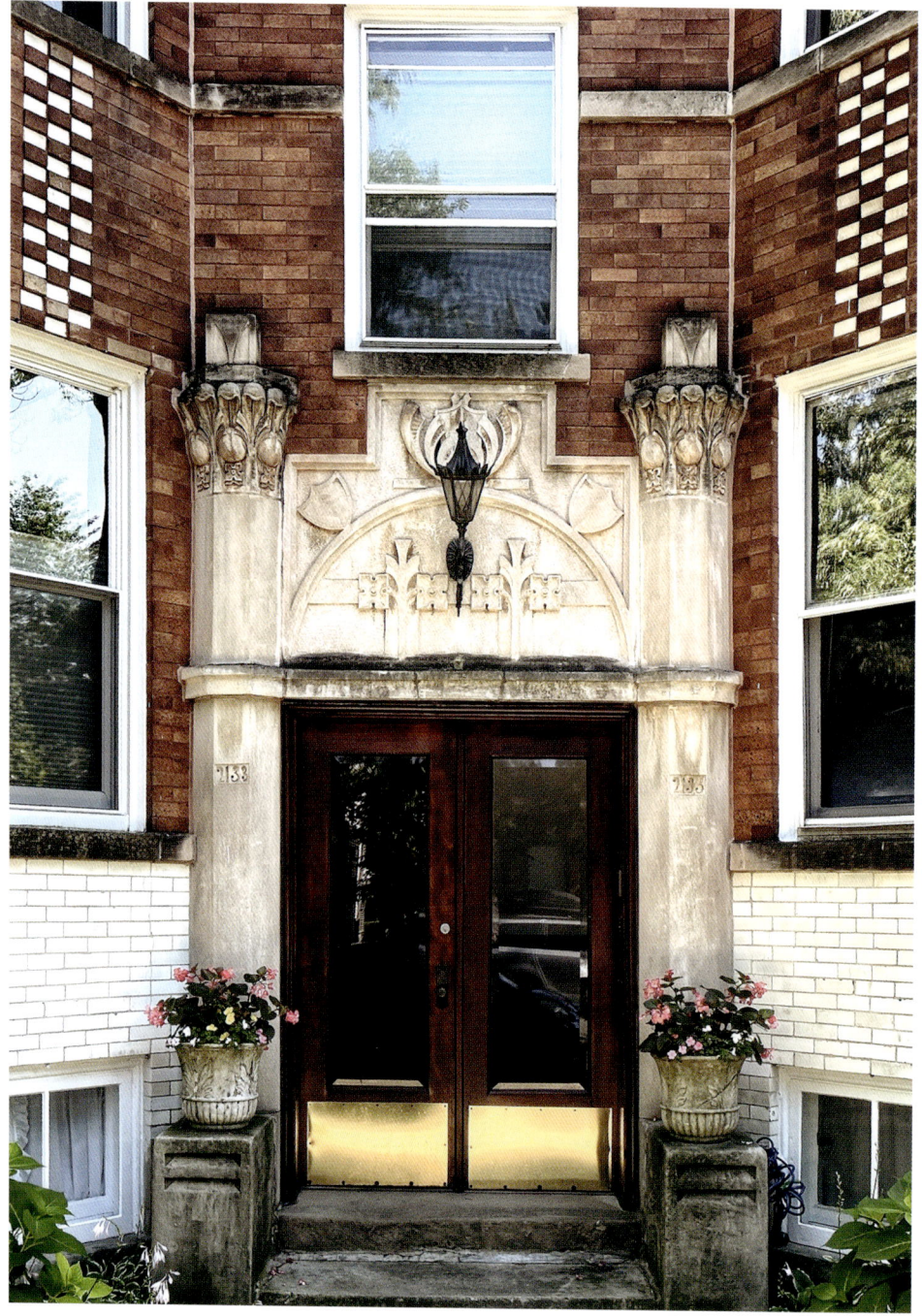

UKRAINIAN VILLAGE

Residential

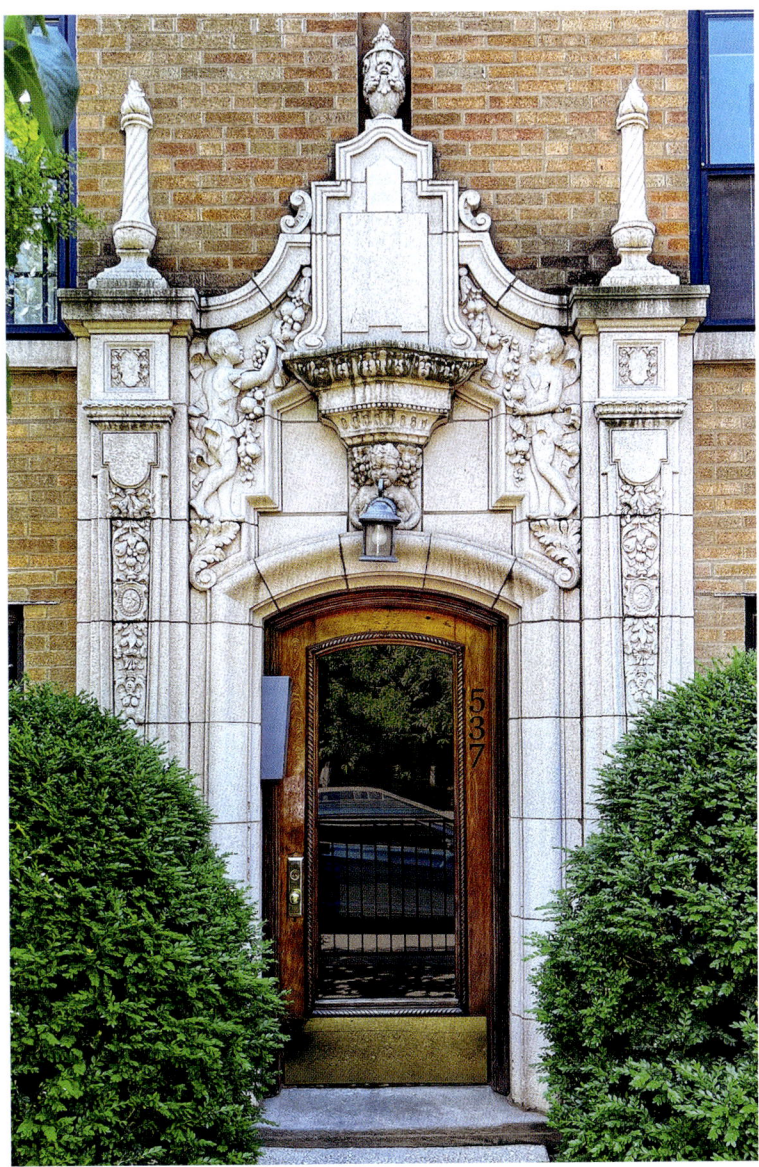

LAKEVIEW

Residential

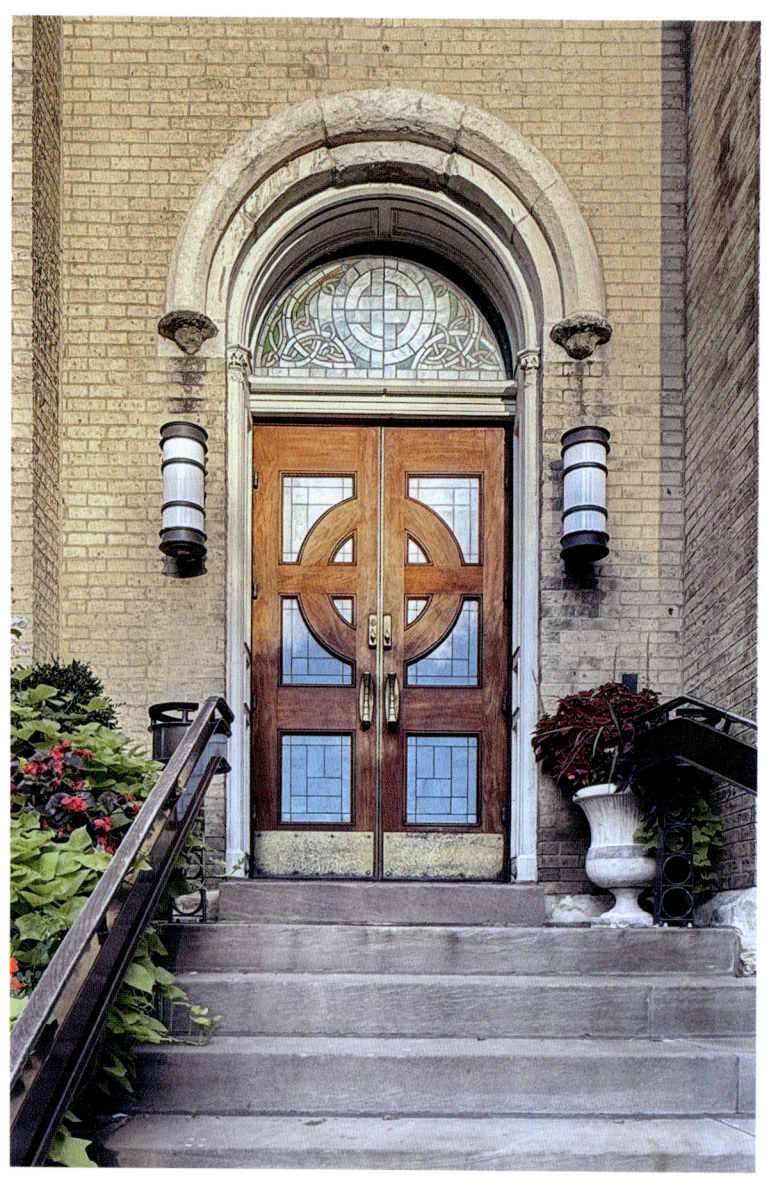

WEST LOOP

Old St. Patrick's Church

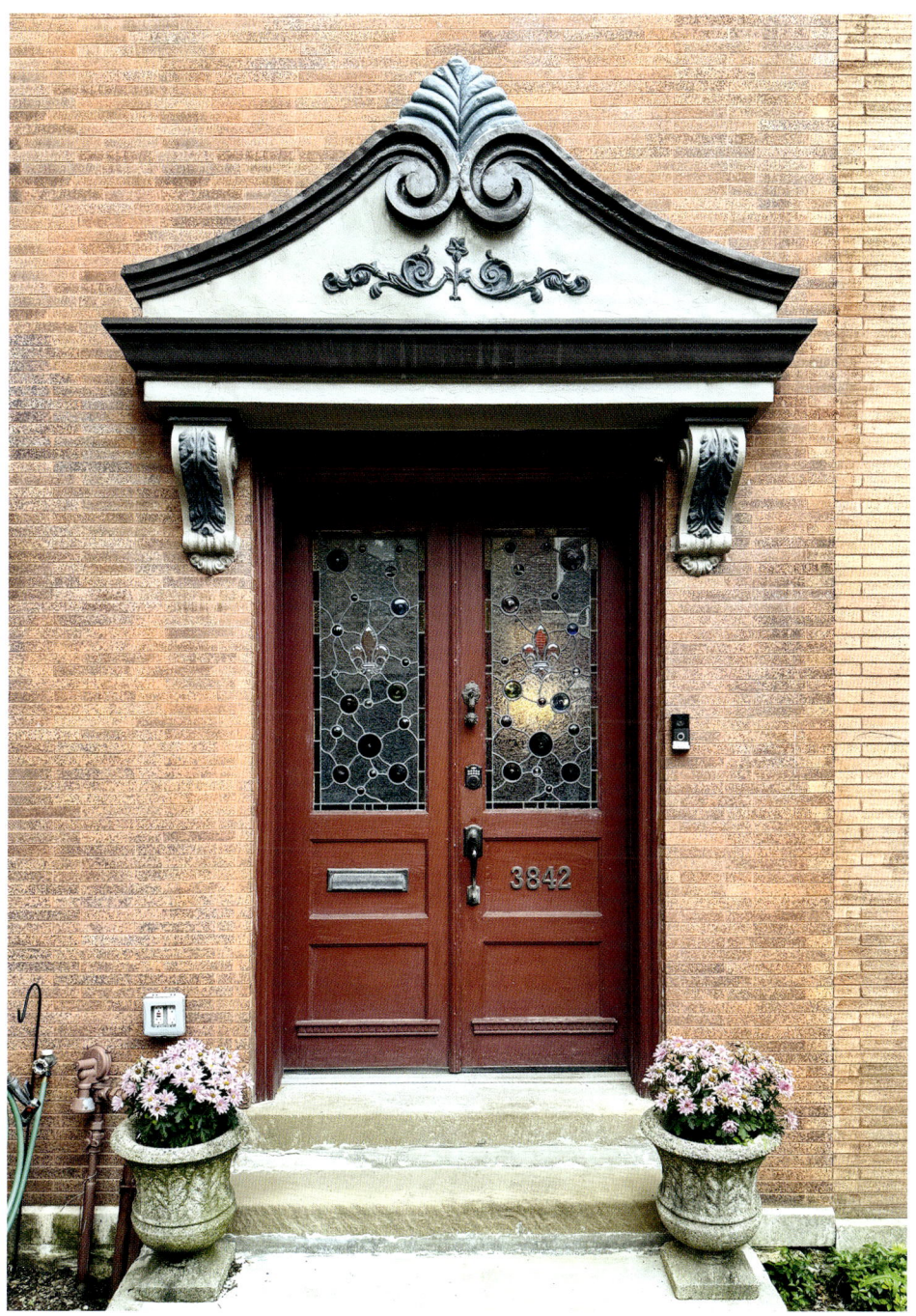

WRIGLEYVILLE

Residential

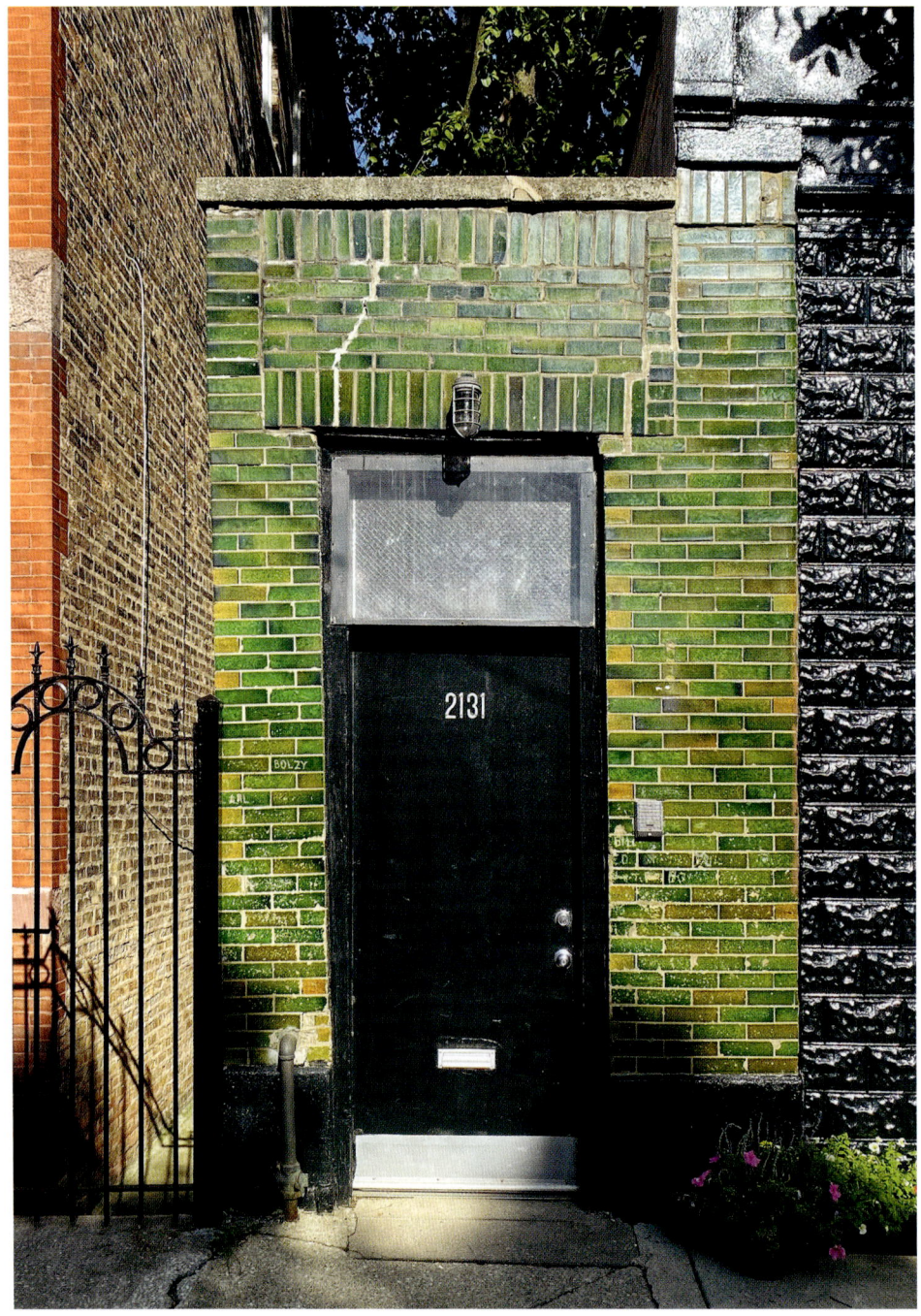

BUCKTOWN

Residential

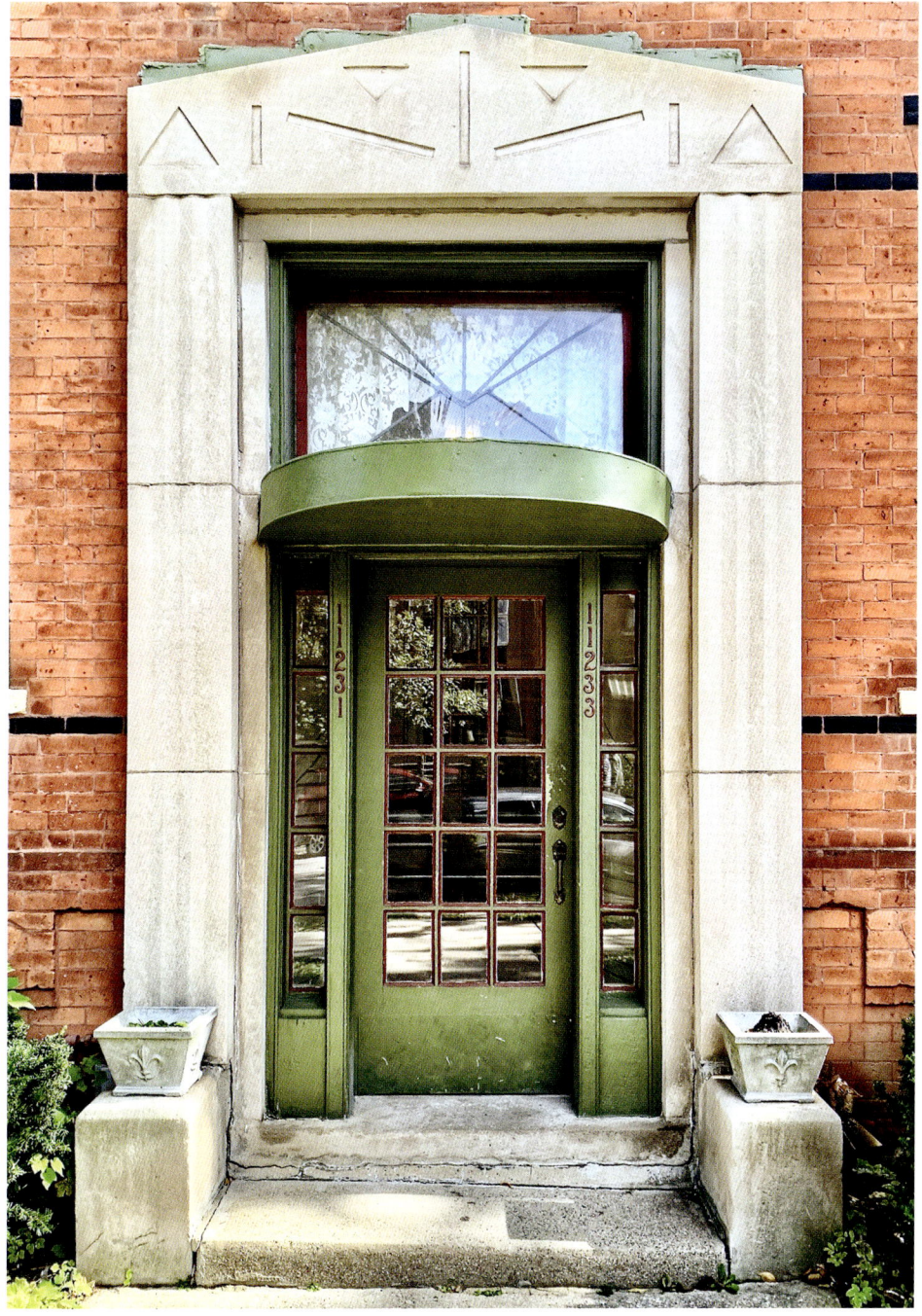

PULLMAN

Residential

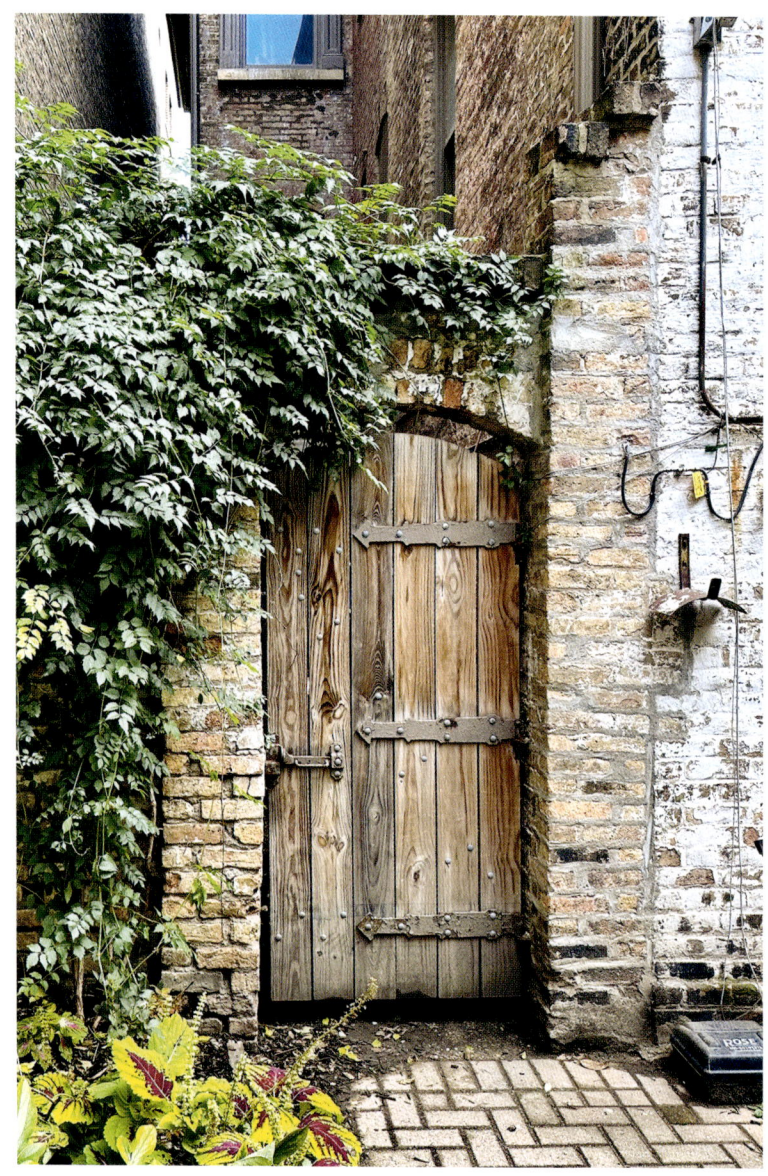

GOLD COAST

Residential

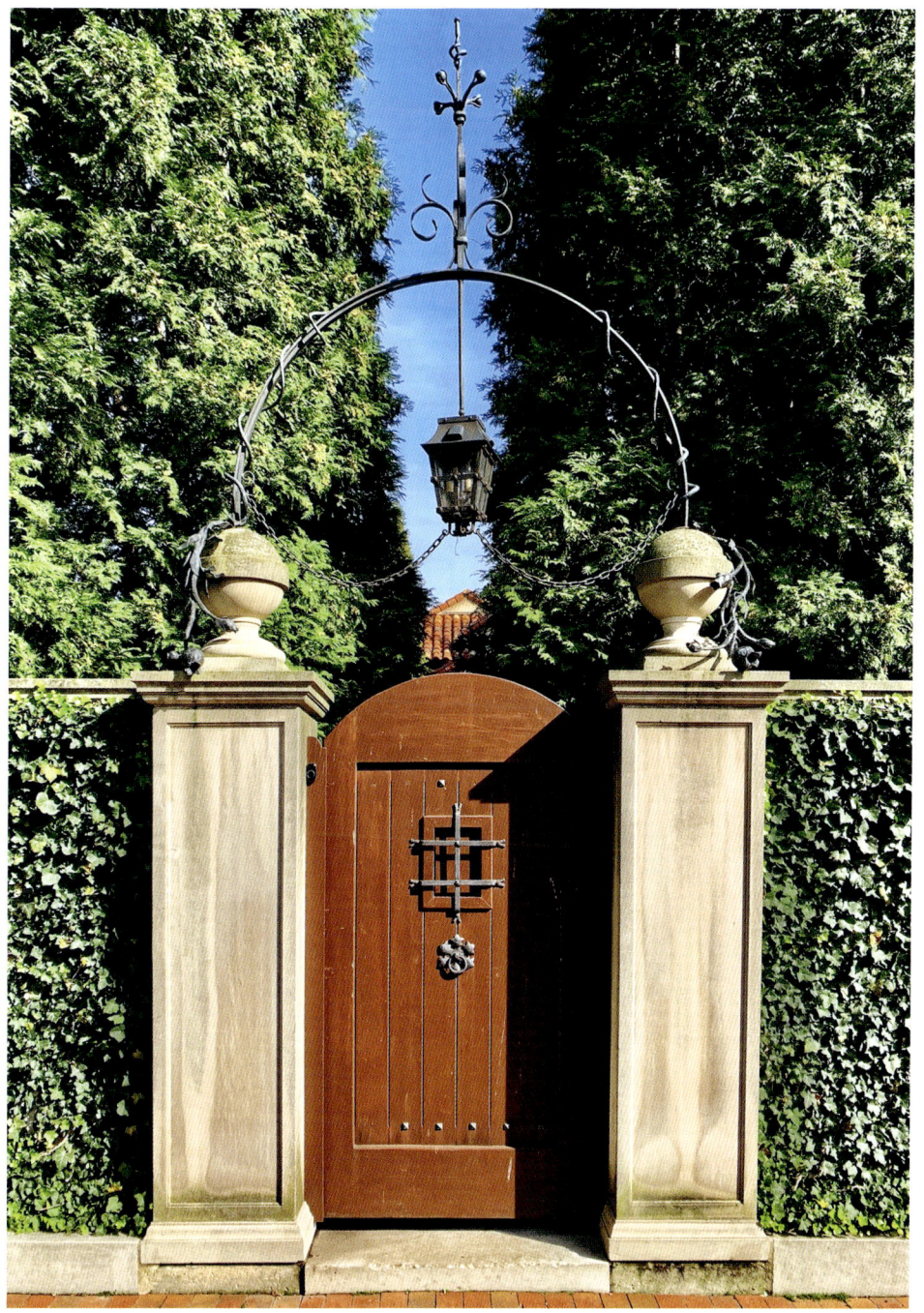

OLD TOWN

Residential

CARL STREET STUDIOS

Architectural Style: Arts & Crafts | Year: 1935

Tucked behind custom-designed iron gates on a quiet stretch of West Burton Place sits one of Chicago's most magical architectural ensembles. Originally a three-story Victorian mansion on the once named Carl Street, the home was reimagined beginning in the late 1920s by architect Edgar Miller and developer Sol Kogen.

Inspired by artist colonies in Paris, Miller and Kogen, who met while students at the School of the Art Institute of Chicago, worked to transform the building into Carl Street Studios, a creative enclave made up of multiple studio units within a single gated complex. Miller led a team of artisans, including many of his former classmates at the Art Institute, and the talented Jesús Torres, to create a communal space where no two rooms, walls, or doors were alike.

Each doorway was hand-carved, with custom handles, lock plates, and mailboxes that turned everyday elements into sculptural delights. Hand-fired ceramic and mosaic tiles weren't limited to the interiors, they spilled onto the sidewalk, offering a vivid preview of the artistry inside. Plagued by financial obstacles throughout its evolution, materials were often salvaged and repurposed from demolished buildings. Every unique detail reveals a blend of influences, from Old World folk traditions to Chicago's Arts and Crafts movements.

While its private courtyards and expressive façades weren't meant to be mass-produced, it did inspire similar enclaves in the area, establishing Old Town as an artistic hub. Nearly a century later, Carl Street Studios remains a secret architectural love letter to Chicago, hidden away and daring you to find it.

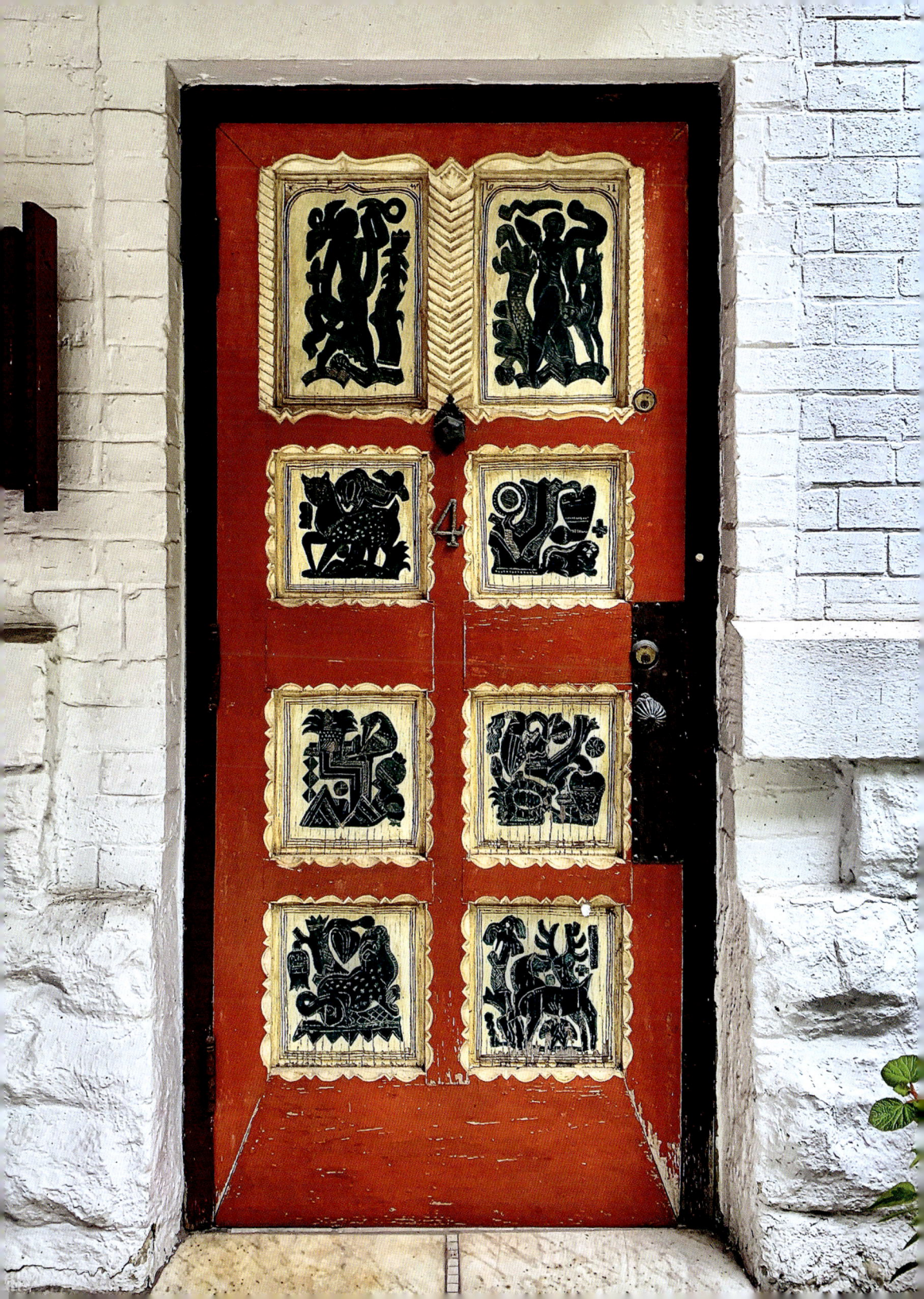

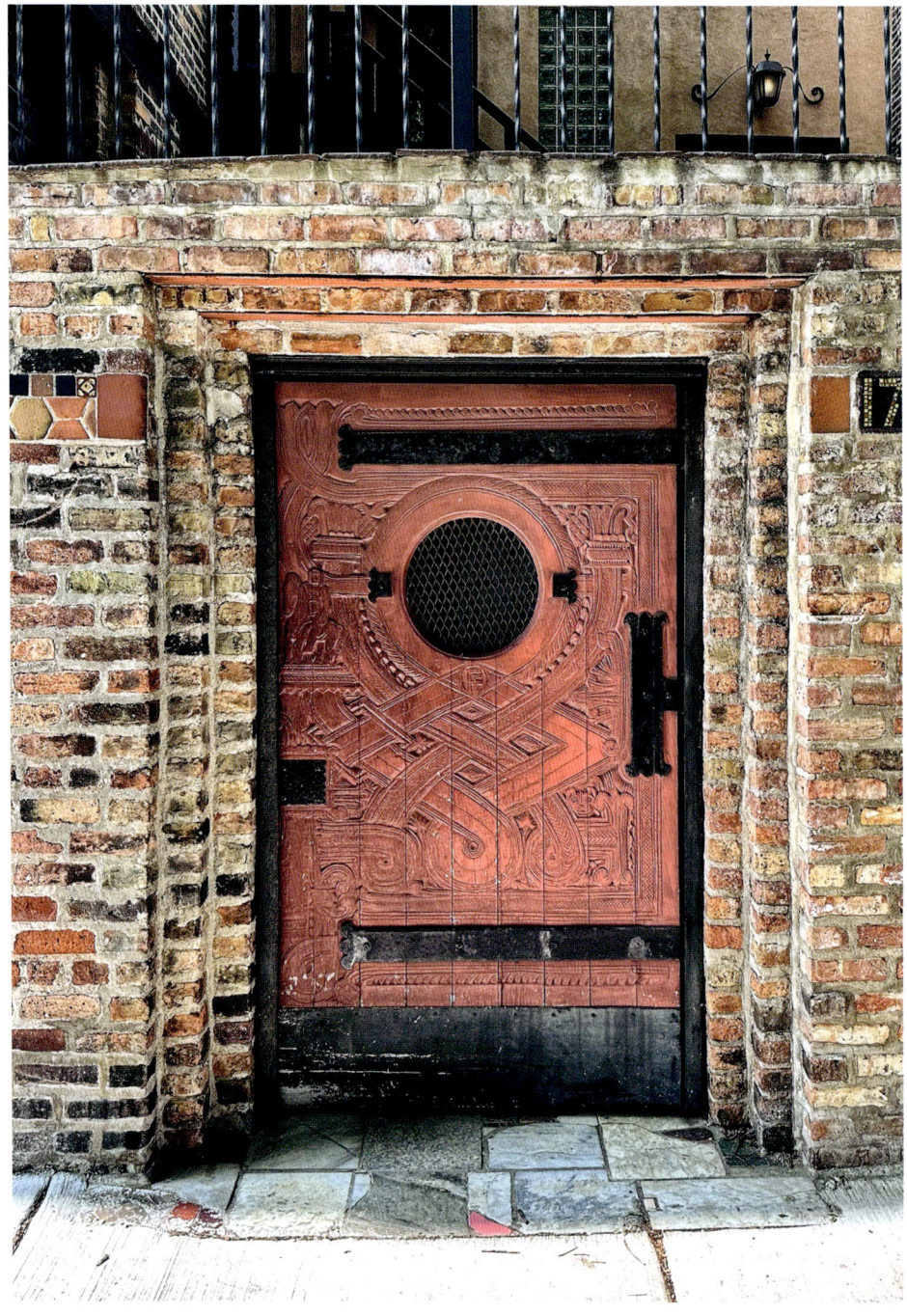

OLD TOWN

Residential

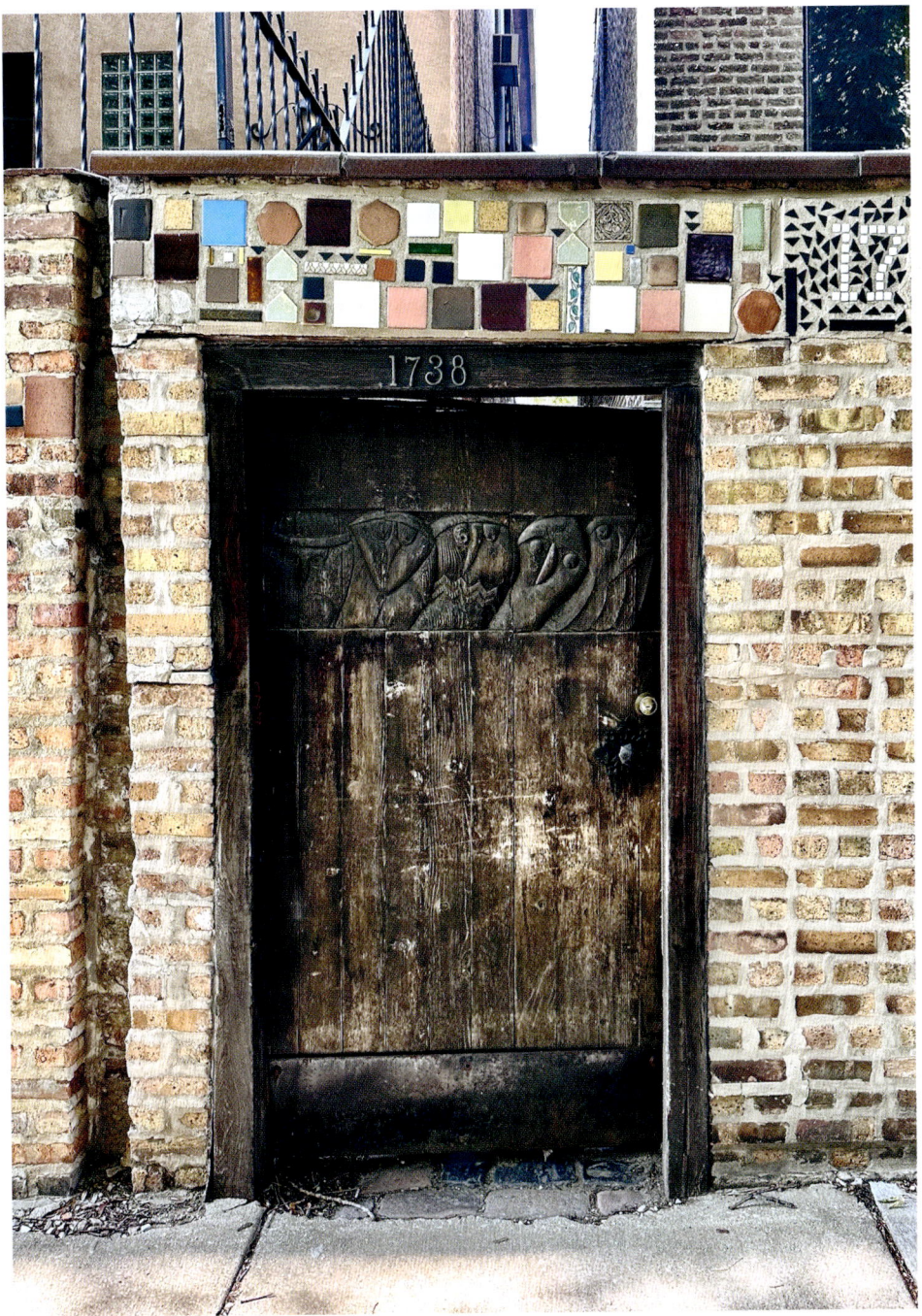

OLD TOWN

Residential

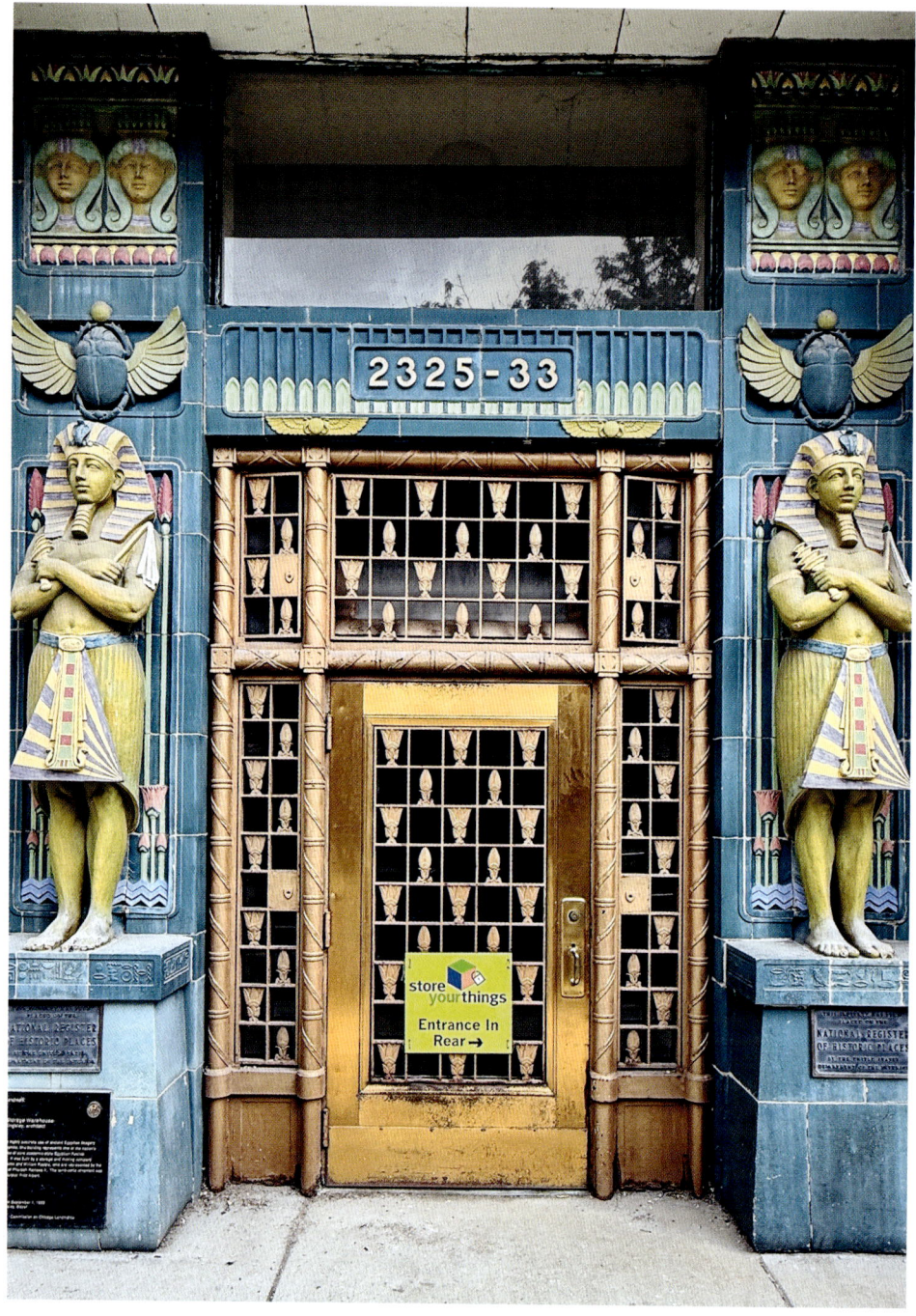

2325-33

LINCOLN PARK

Reebie Storage Warehouse

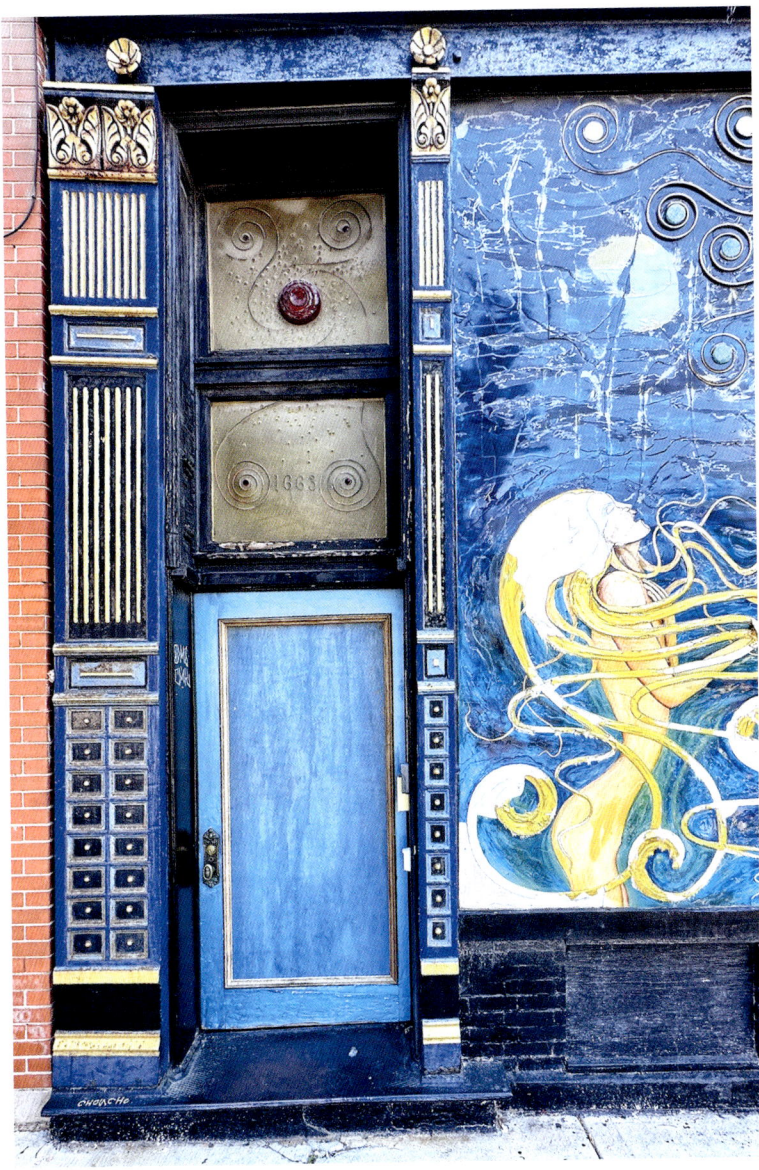

PILSEN

Residential

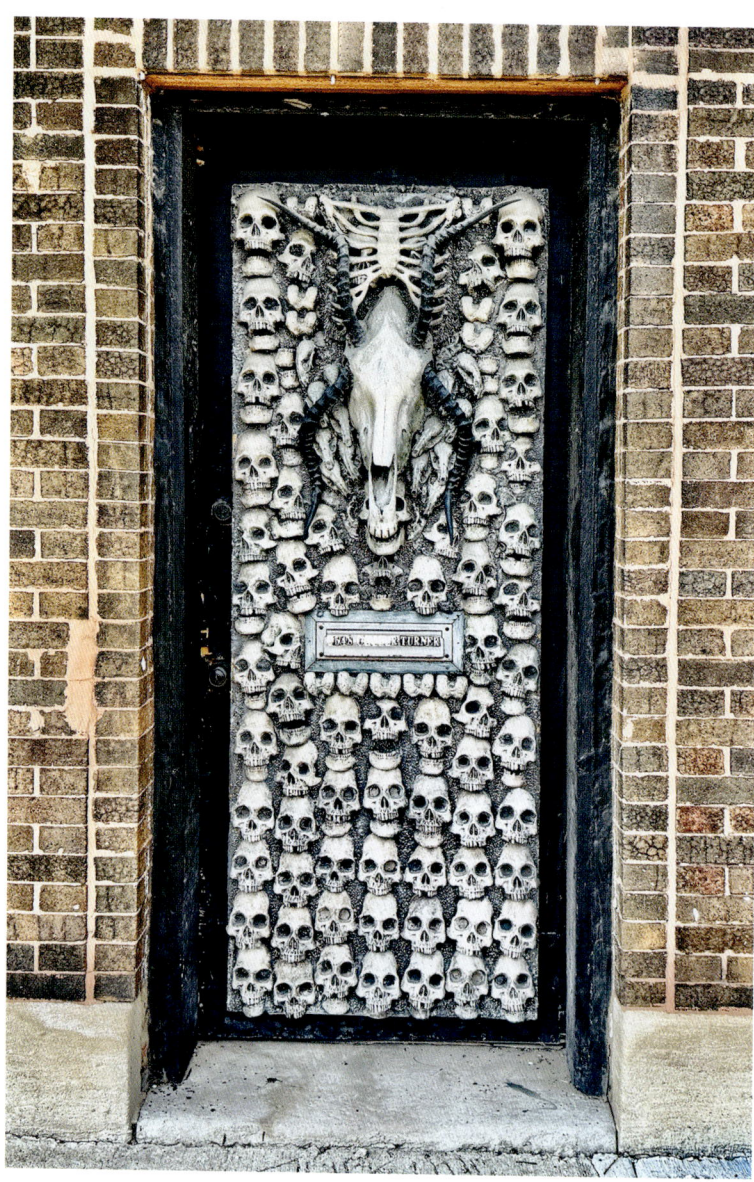

UKRAINIAN VILLAGE

Residential

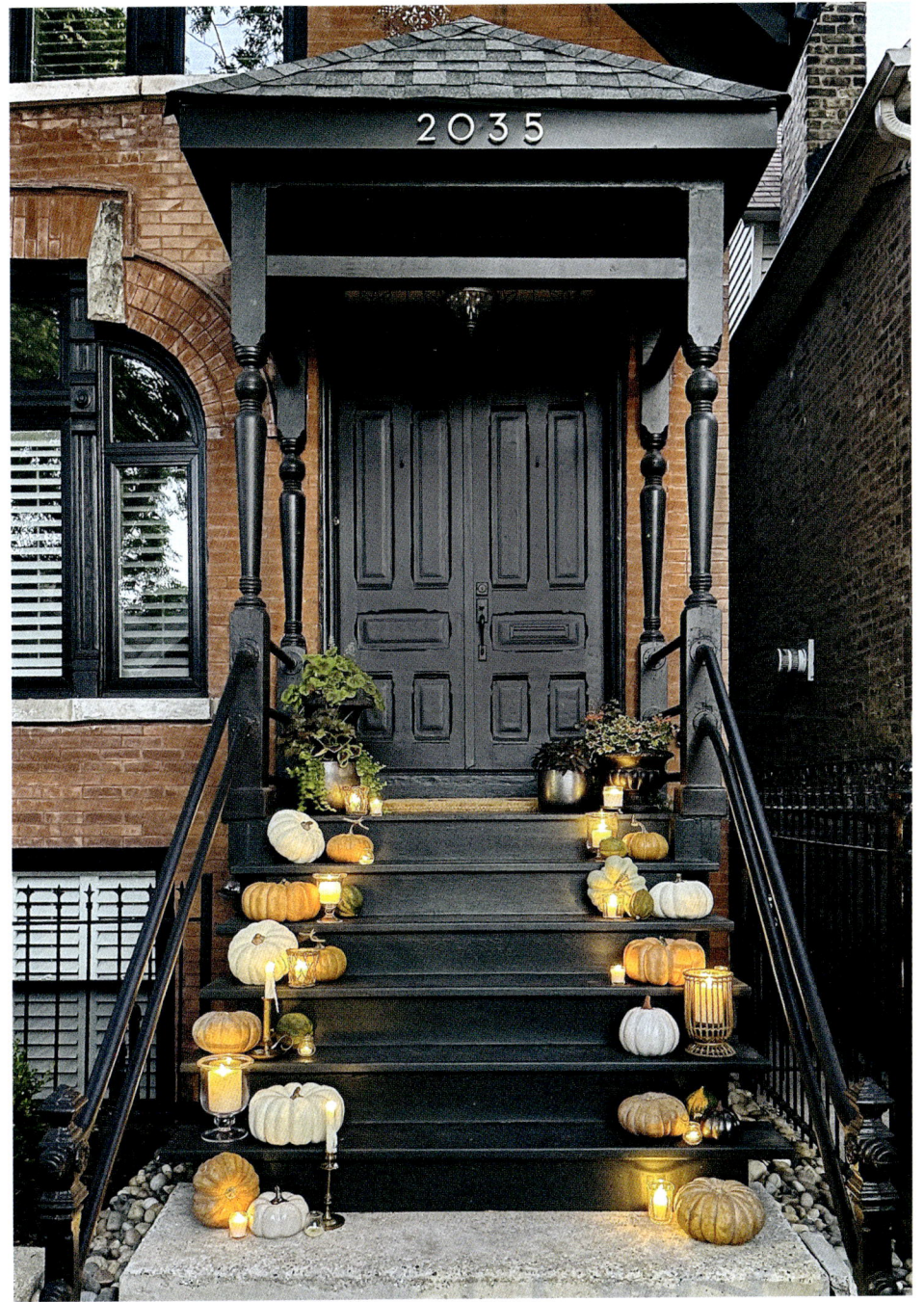

UKRAINIAN VILLAGE

Residential

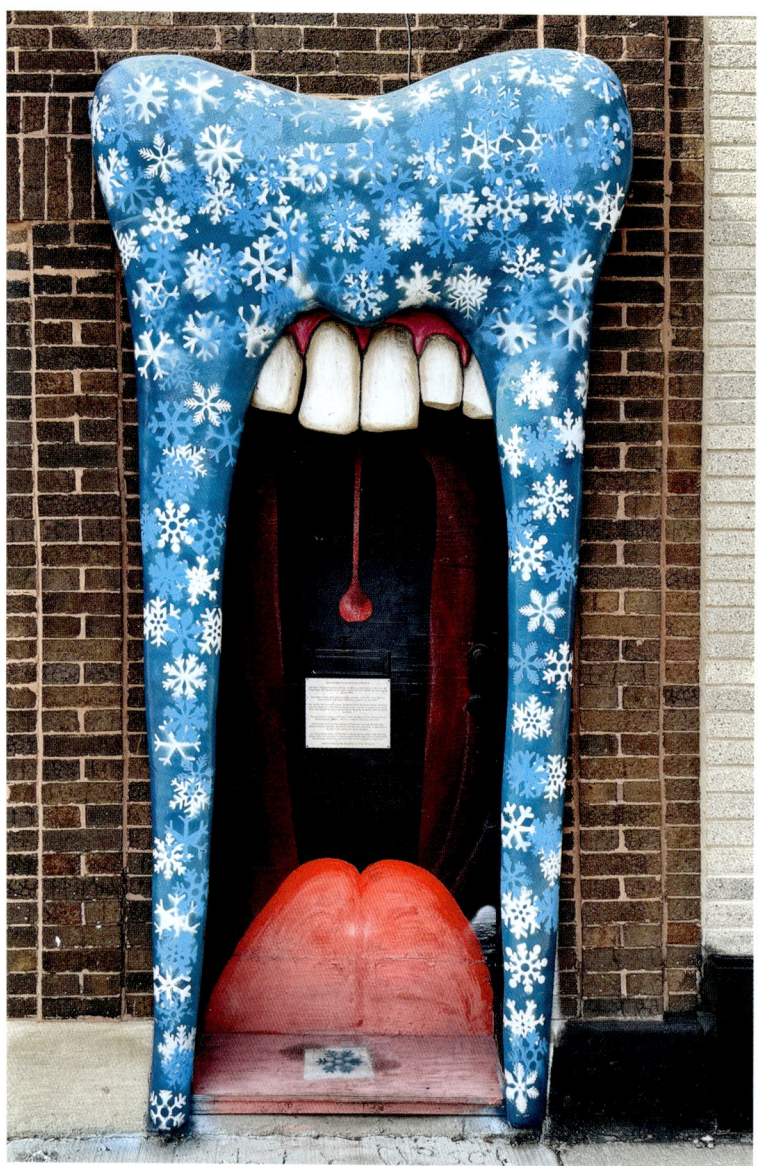

UKRAINIAN VILLAGE

Residential

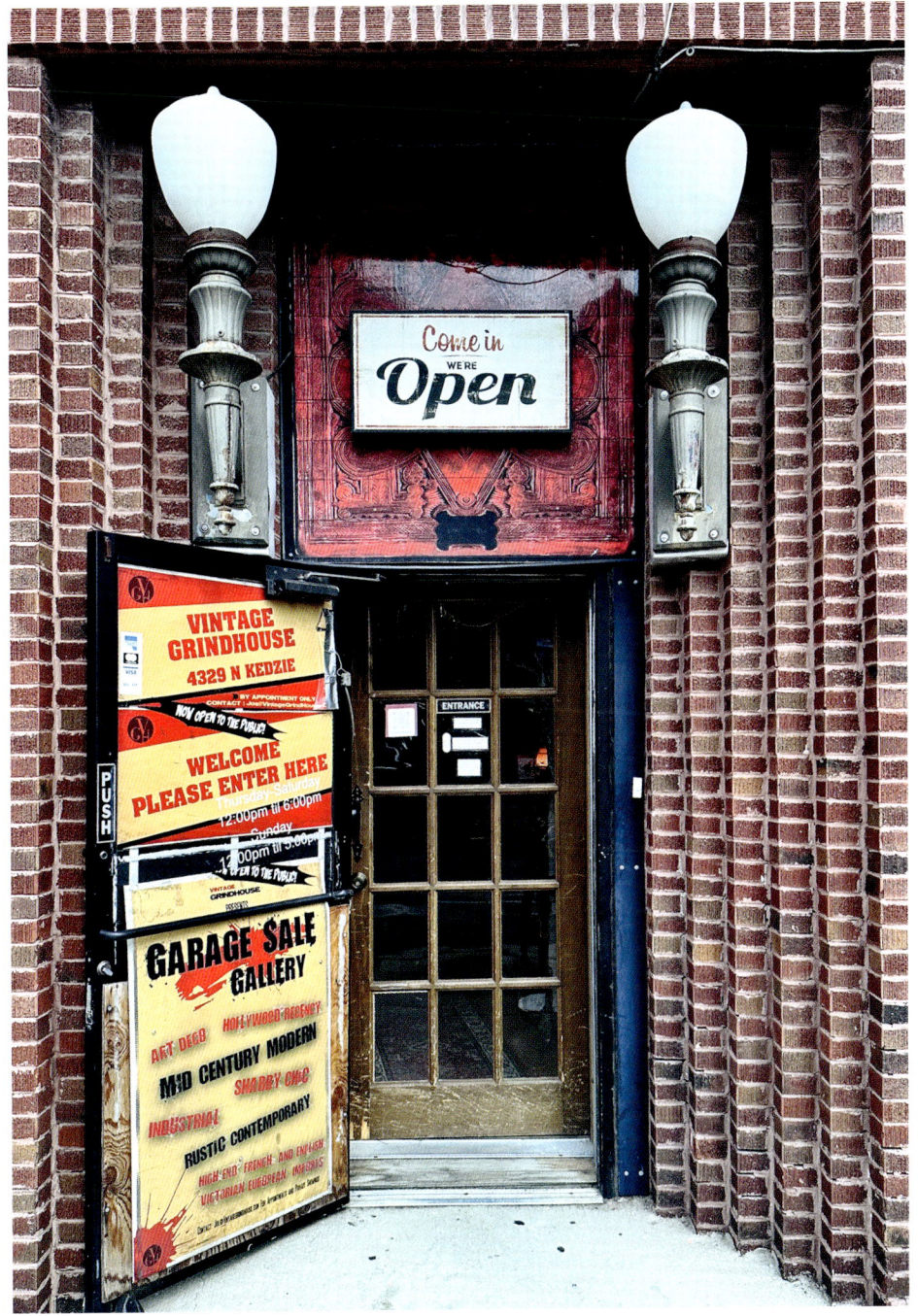

IRVING PARK

Vintage Store

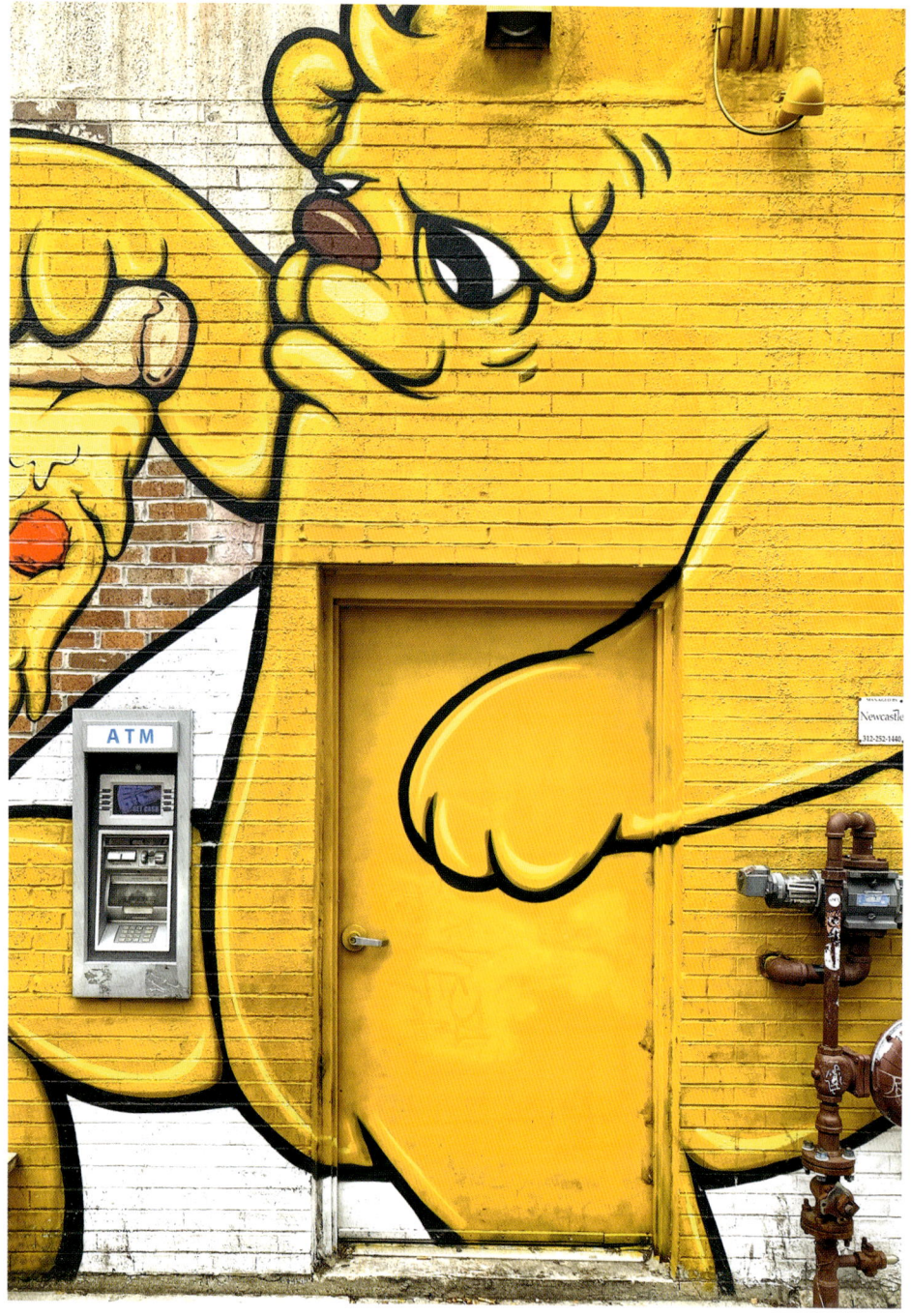

WEST LOOP

Restaurant

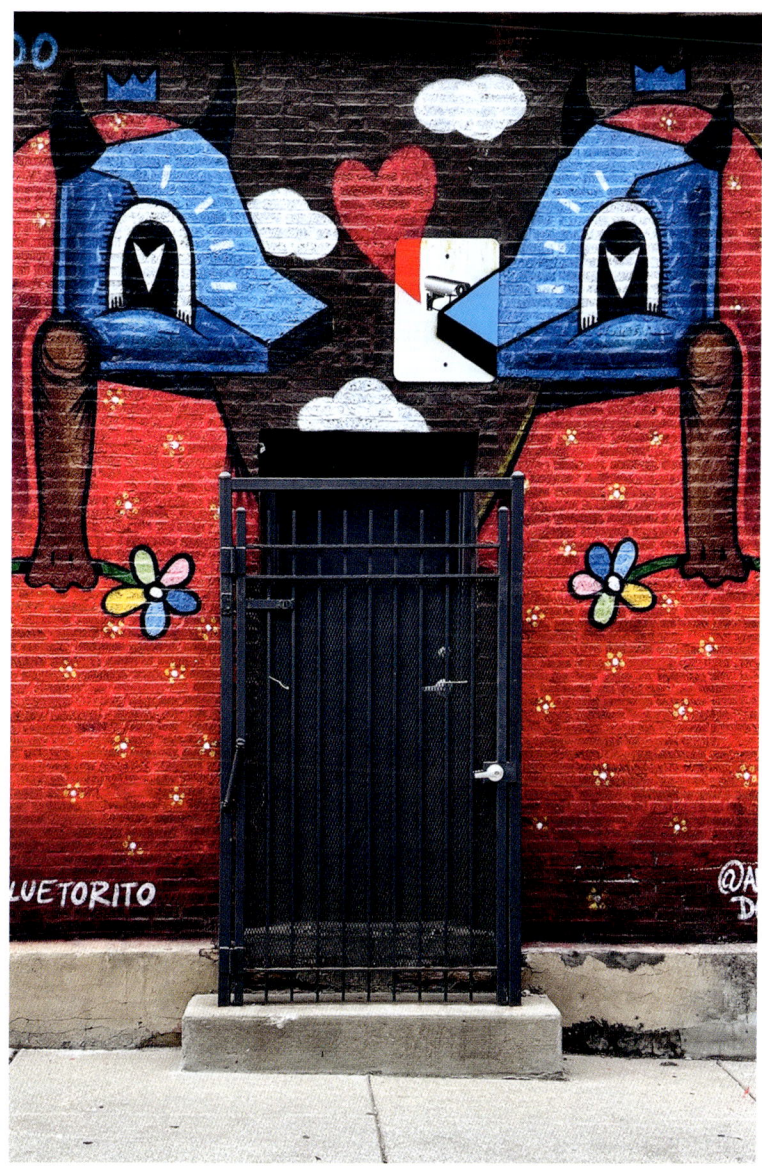

UPTOWN

Clifton Avenue Street Art Gallery

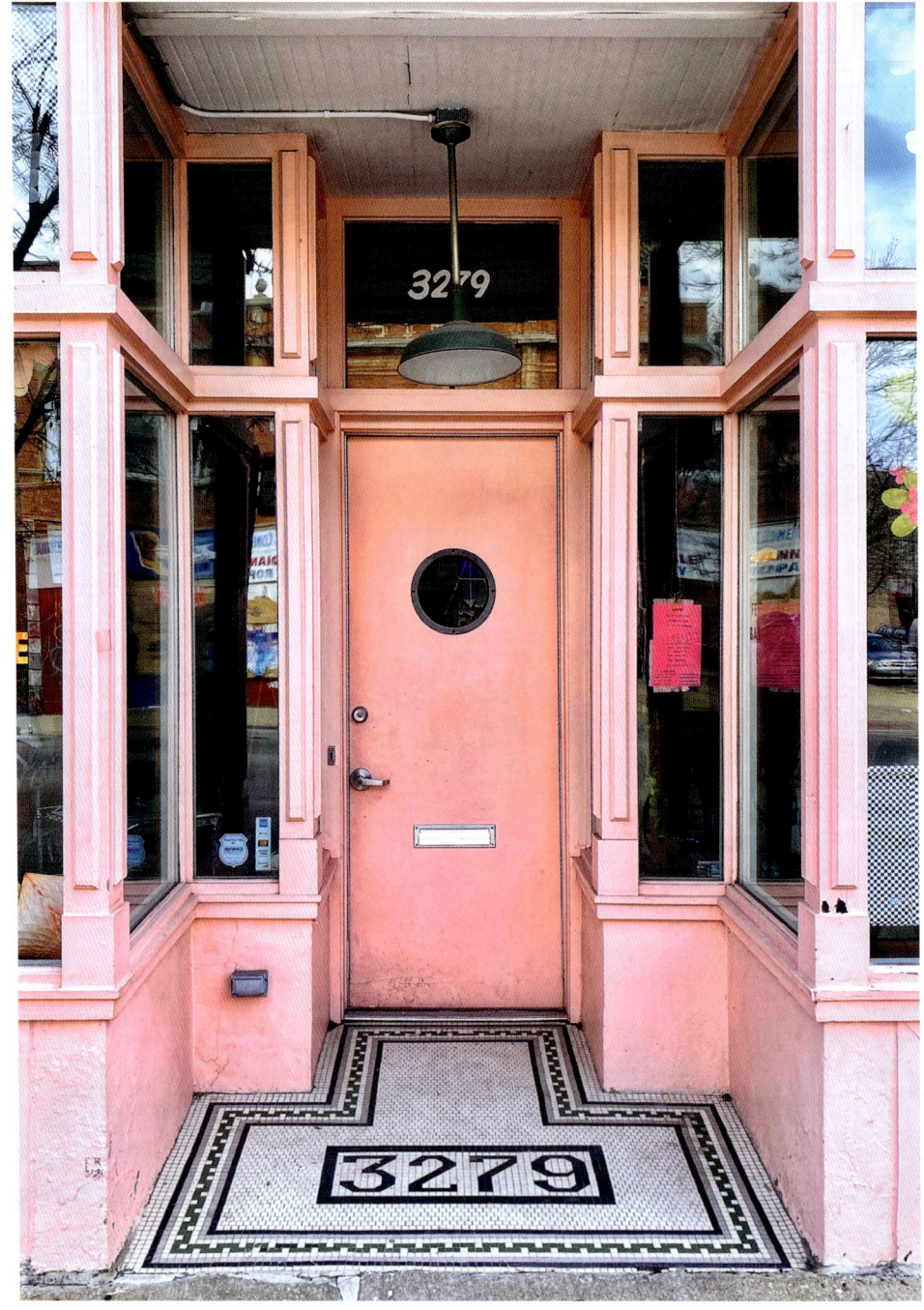

LOGAN SQUARE

Retail

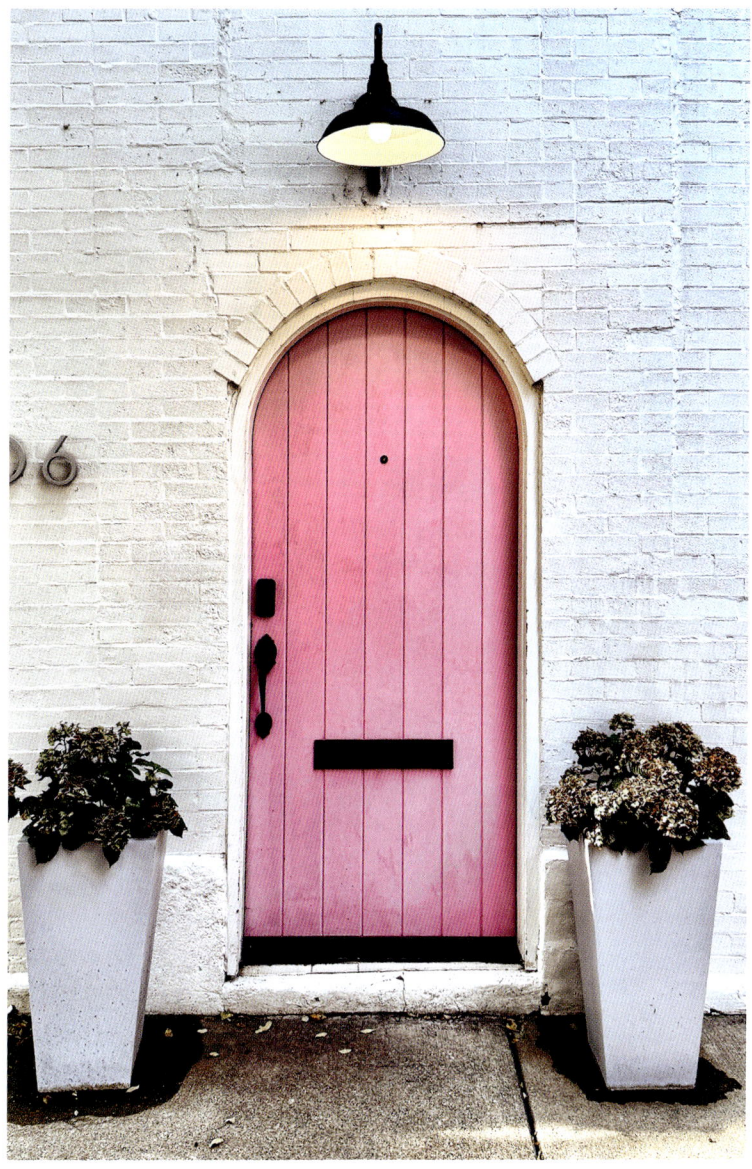

WEST TOWN

Residential

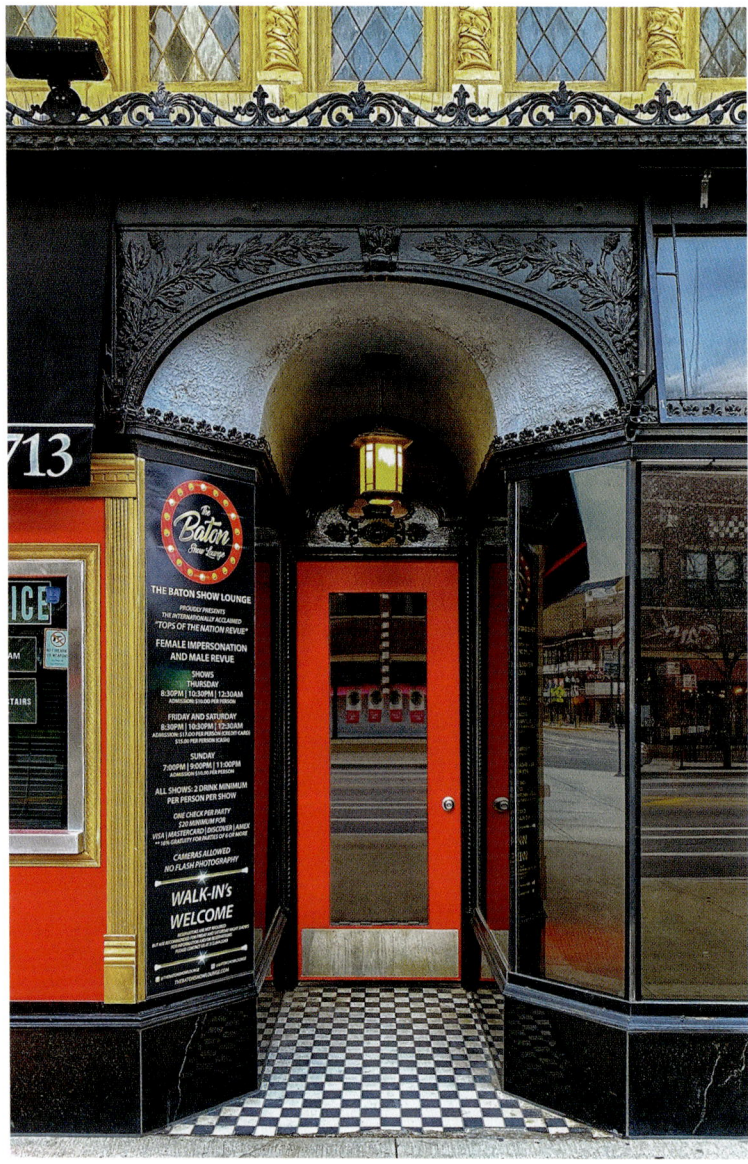

UPTOWN

Nightclub

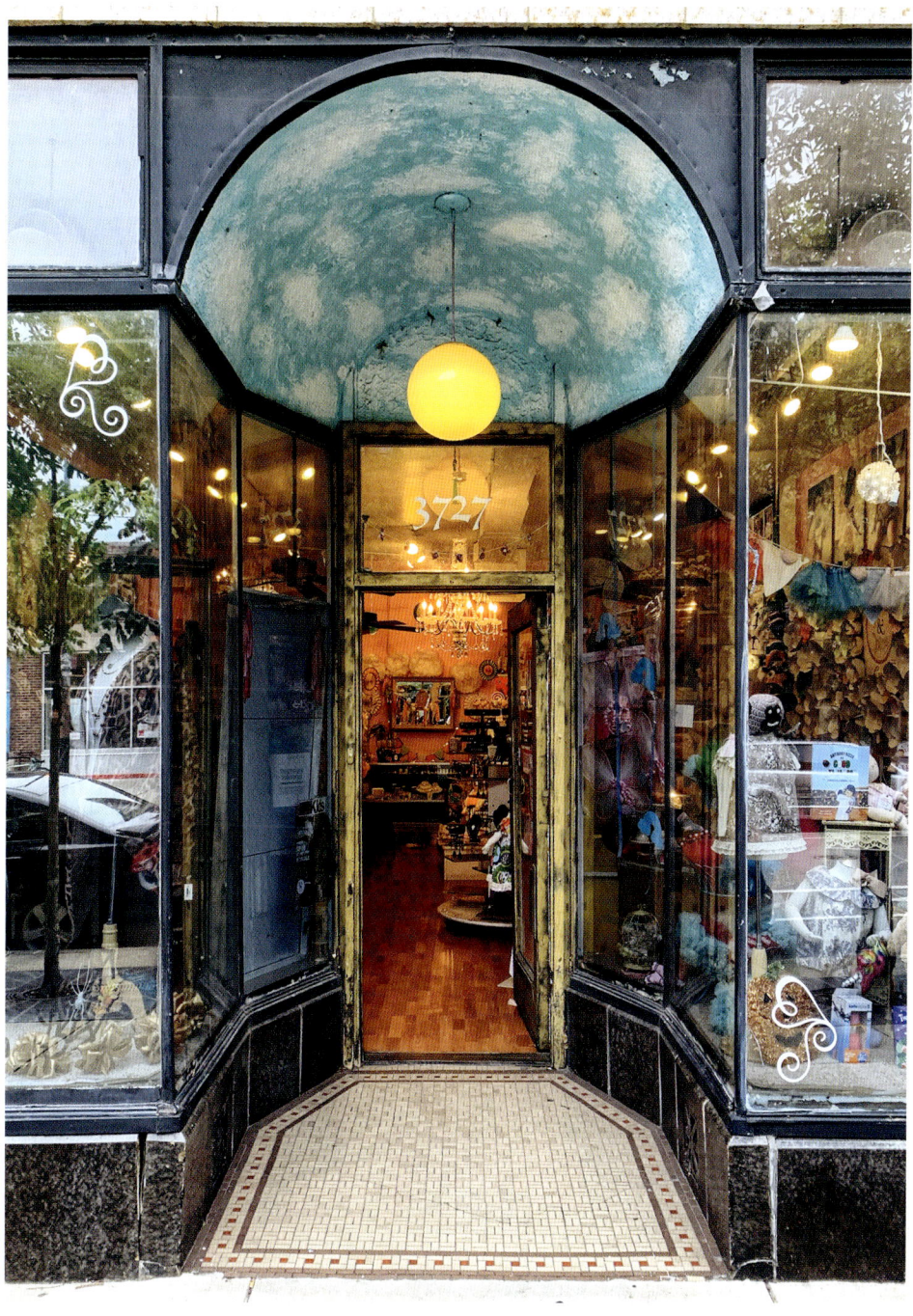

WRIGLEYVILLE

Retail

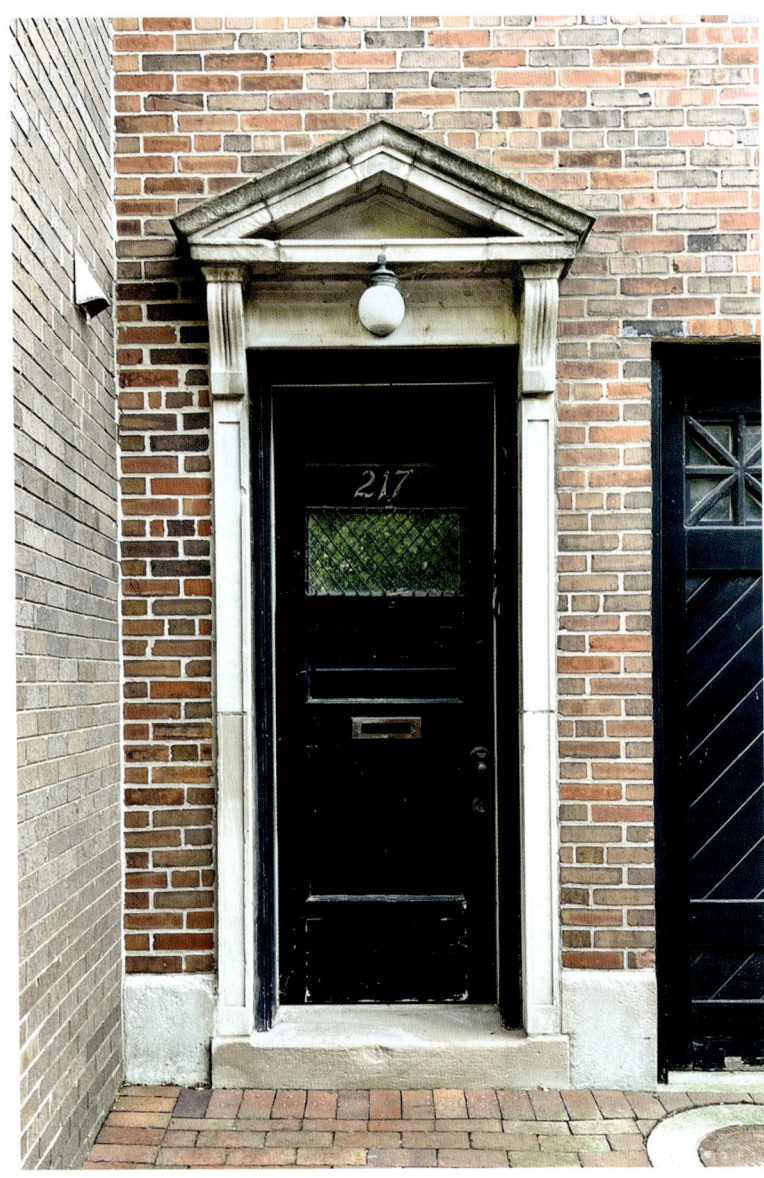

OLD TOWN

Residential

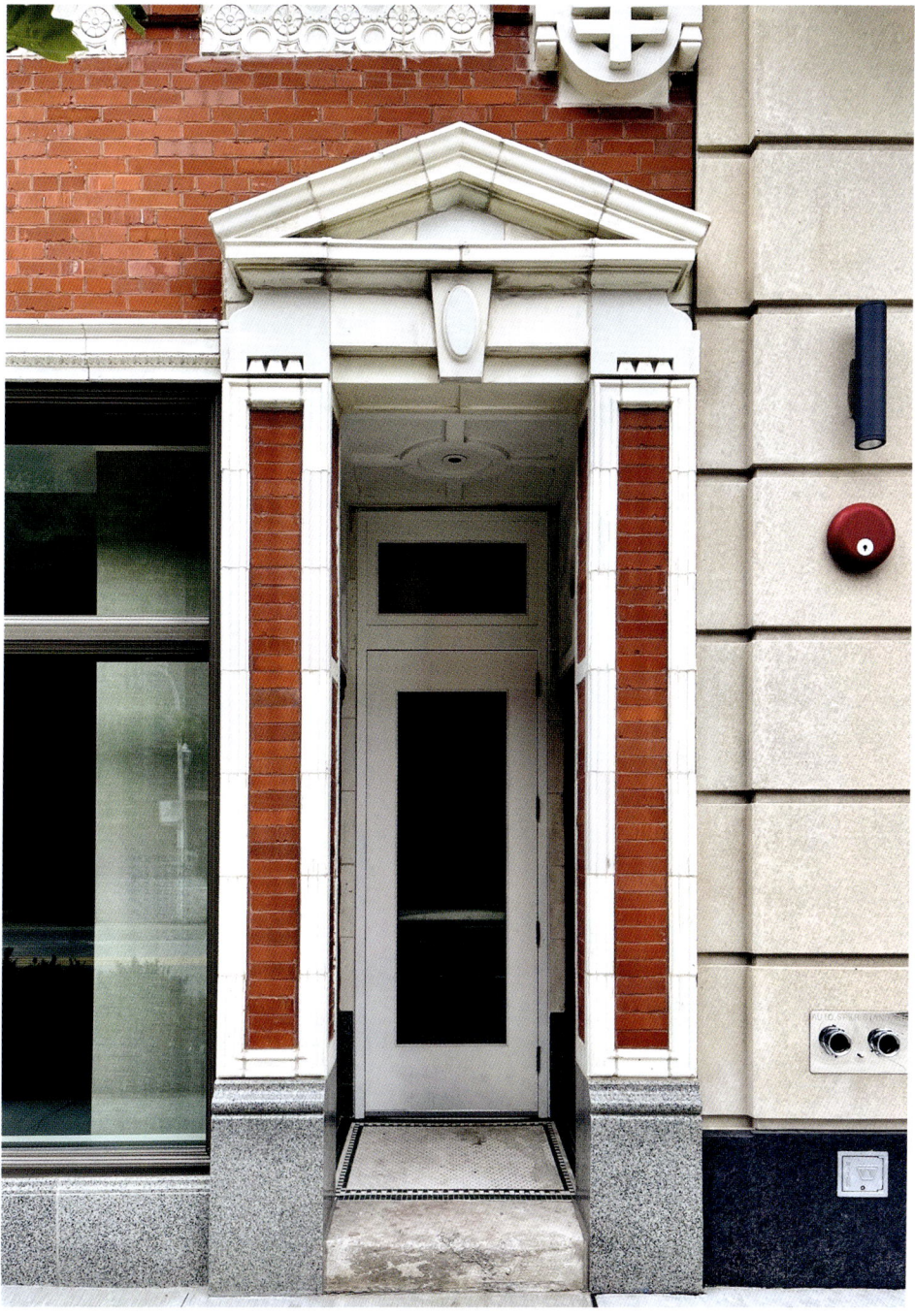

OLD TOWN

Residential

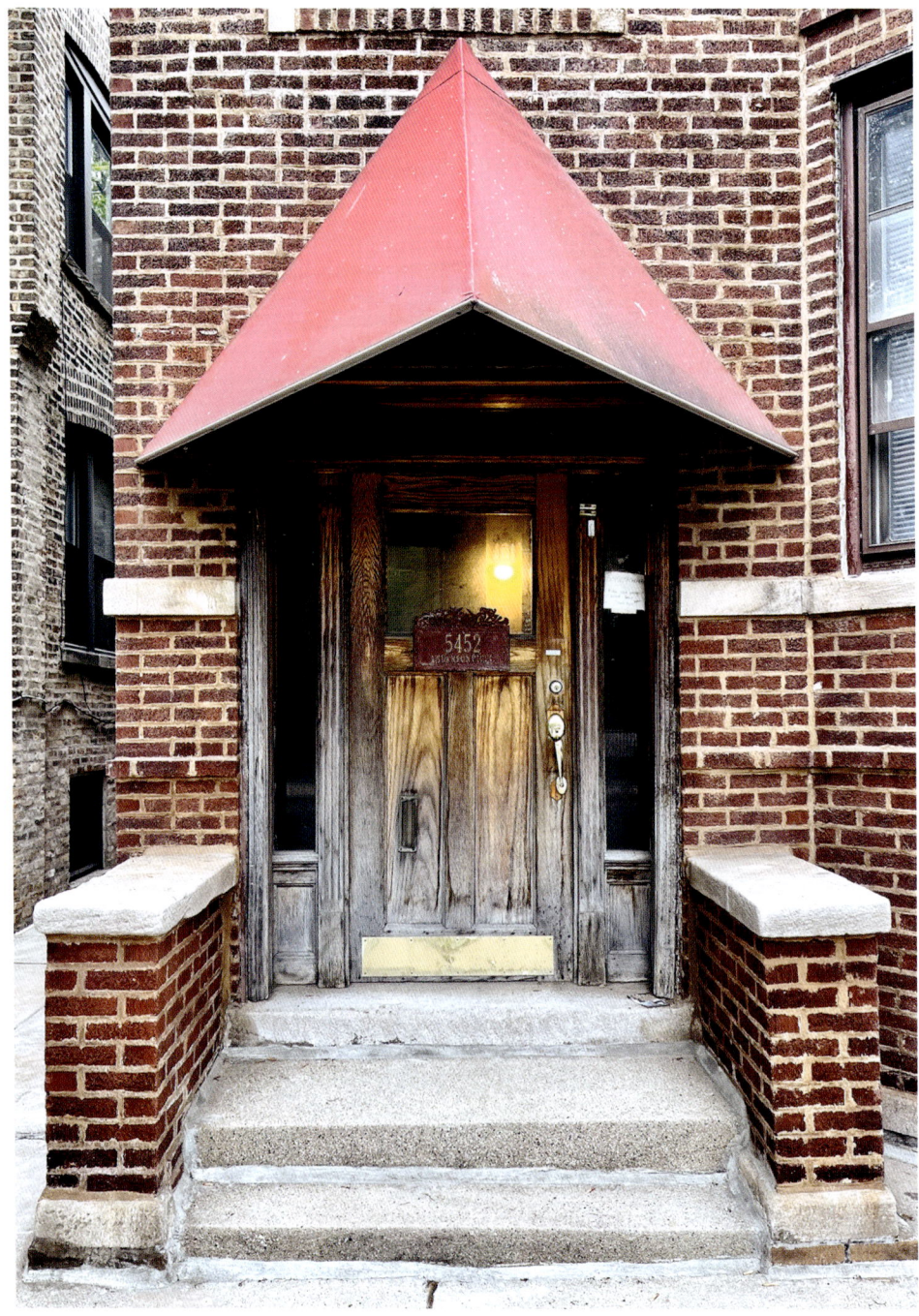

ANDERSONVILLE

Residential

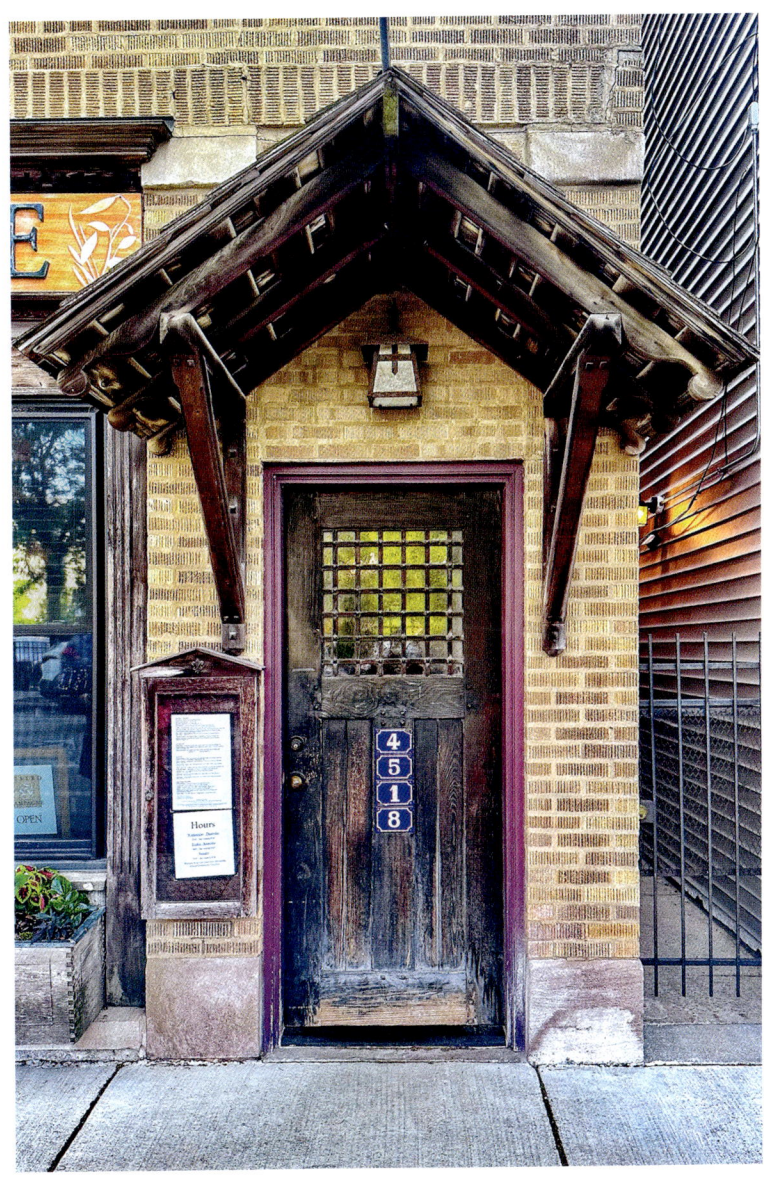

LINCOLN SQUARE

Restaurant

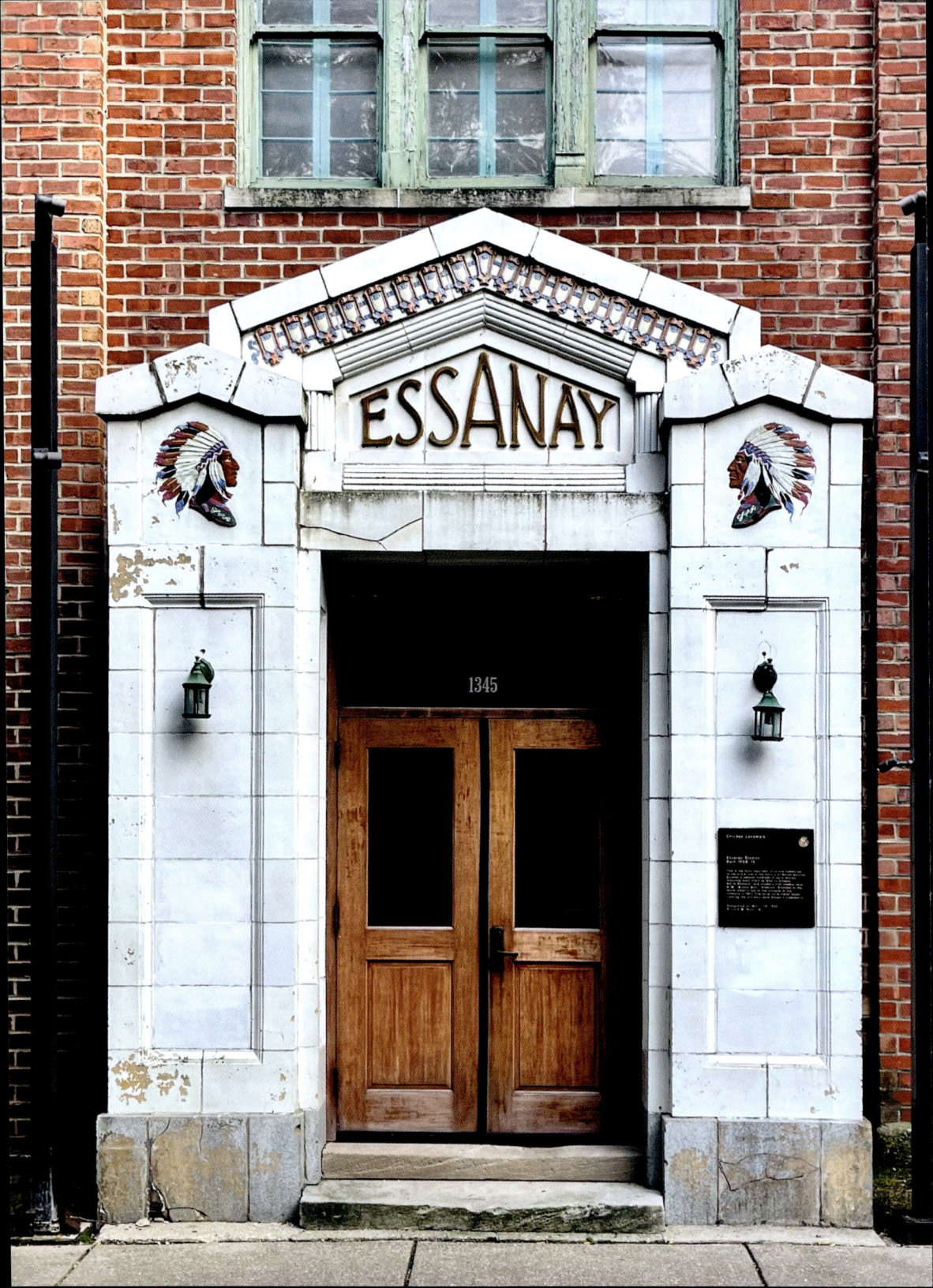

ESSANAY STUDIOS

Architectural Style: Arts & Crafts | Year: 1908

The door to Essanay Studios is an unexpected gateway to classic early cinema in Chicago's Uptown neighborhood. Established in 1907 and named after the last initials of its founders, George Spoor and Gilbert Anderson (S & A), Essanay produced hundreds of 1-2 reeler, black and white silent films in their Chicago studio.

Both men made vital contributions to the film industry, before, after, and during their time at Essanay. In 1894, Spoor debuted "The Magniscope," the first 35mm movie projector used for large audience displays, marking a pivotal moment in motion picture history. Anderson helped pioneer the Western genre, performing as Broncho Billy, cinema's first cowboy hero. Their films also featured iconic stars of the time, including Charlie Chaplin and Gloria Swanson.

The terracotta Indian heads on either side of the doorway is Essanay's logo, referencing their iconic Western films. The logo itself was designed by Spoor's sister Mary Louise, an illustrator for Rand McNally children's books. This detail was shared with me by her granddaughter, who joined me on one of my tours, a serendipitous connection that brought the story full circle!

Changes in the movie industry, the loss of Chaplin as the company's star performer, and disputes between Anderson and Spoor led to the dissolution of the company in 1918, but this doorway endures as a reminder of Chicago's vital role in the early days of motion pictures. Today, the building is part of St. Augustine College, and its main meeting hall is named the Charlie Chaplin Auditorium.

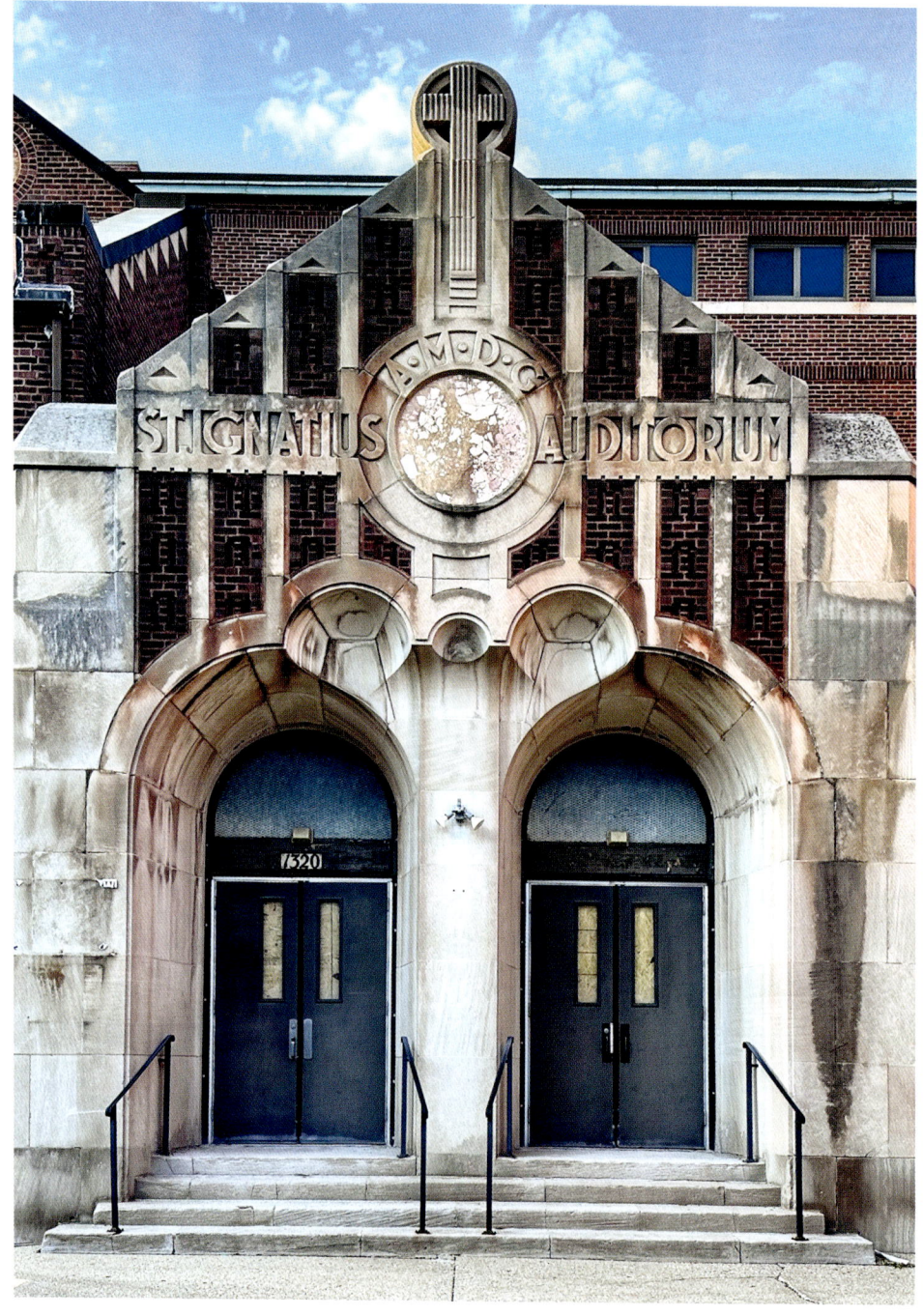

ROGERS PARK

Former St. Ignatius Church

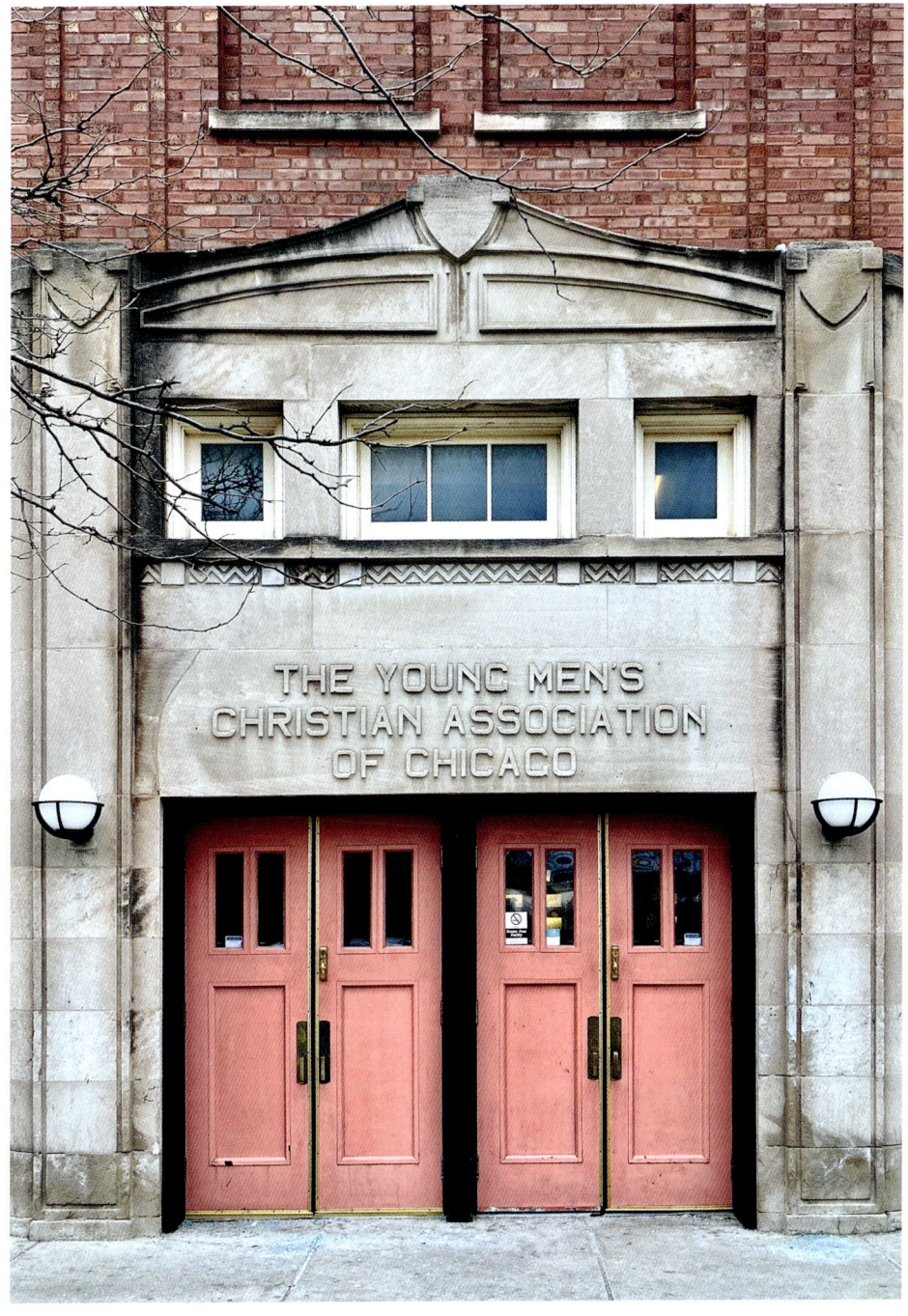

BRONZEVILLE

Wabash Avenue YMCA

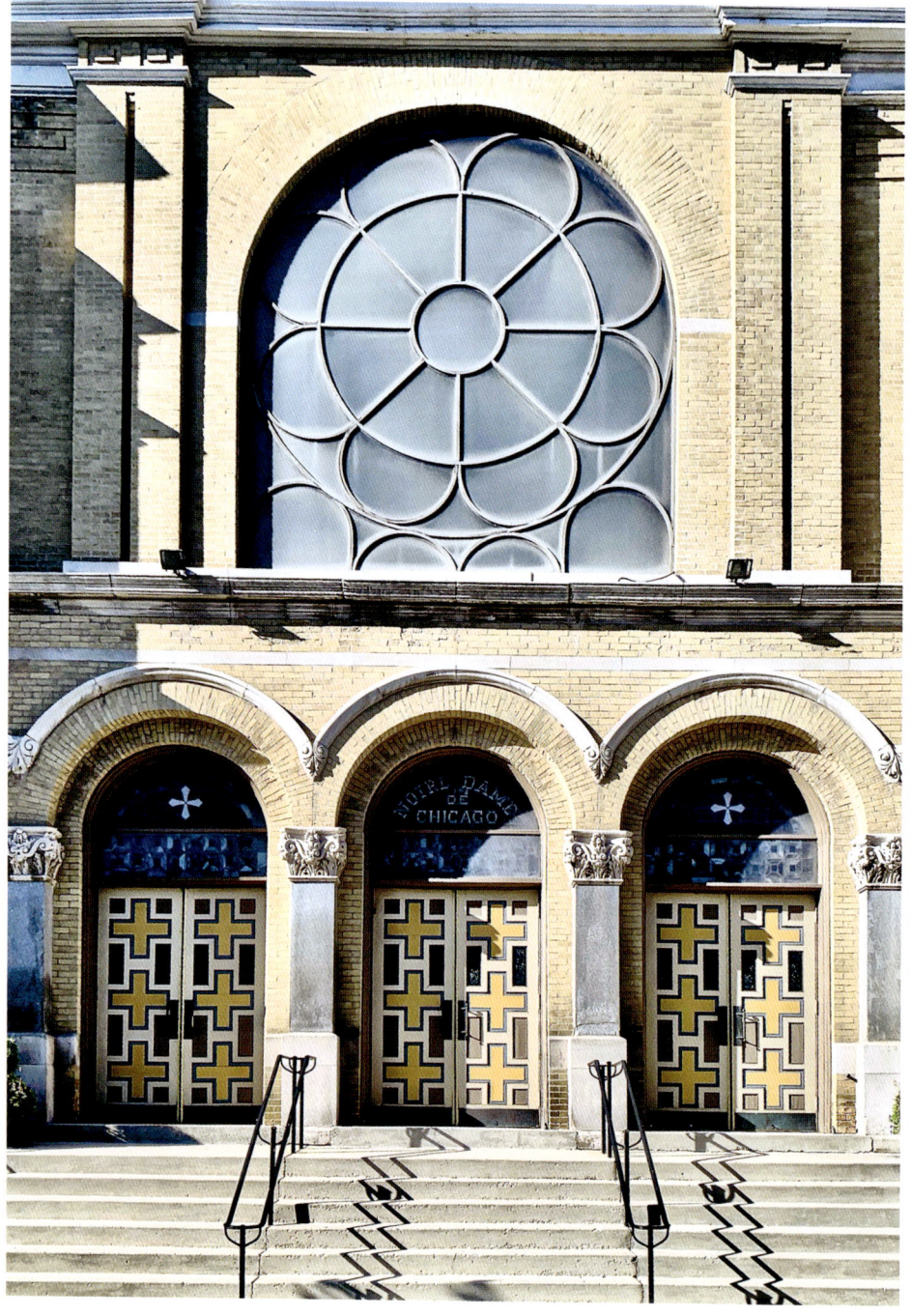

LITTLE ITALY

Notre Dame de Chicago Church

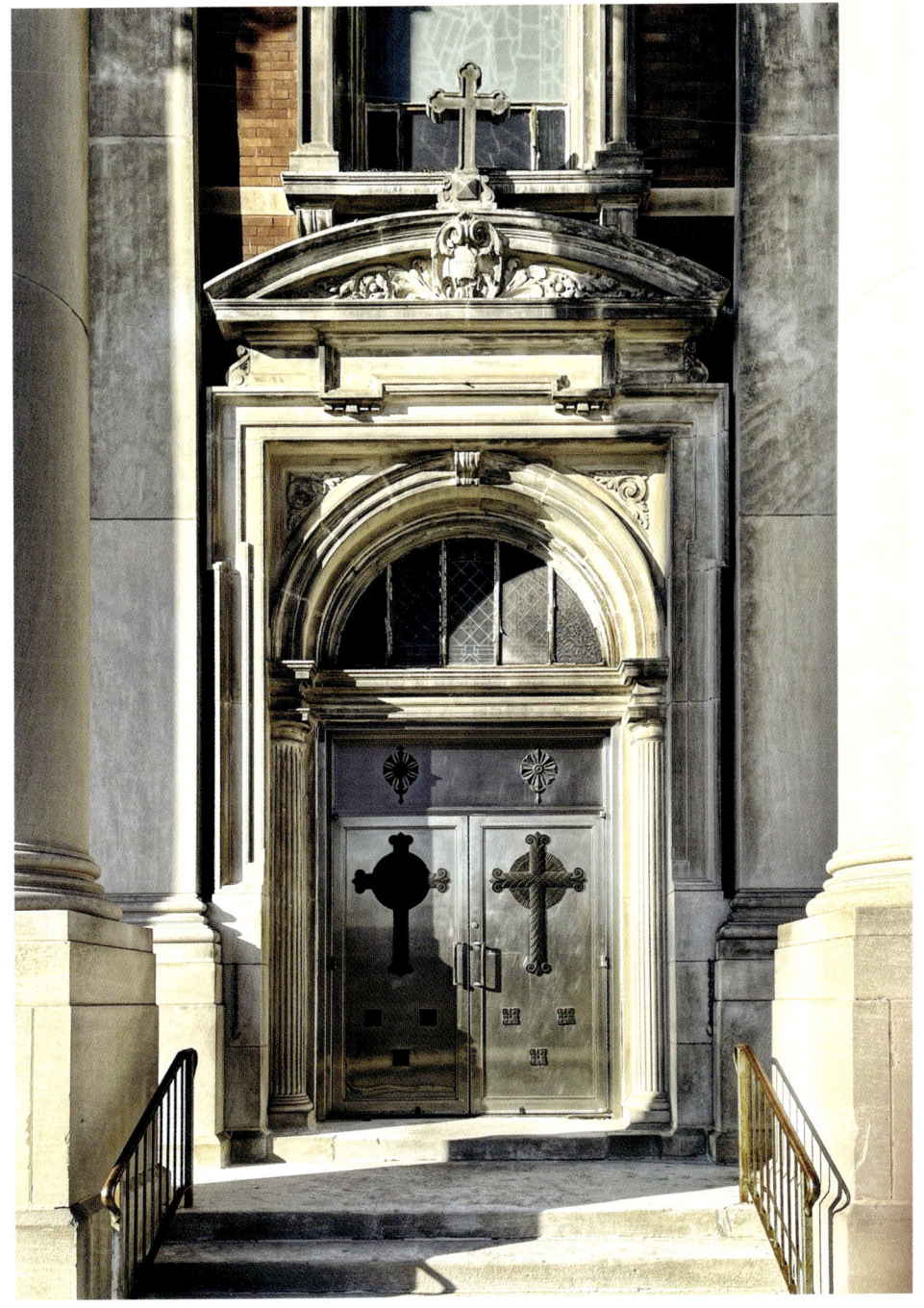

PILSEN

Former St. Adalbert's Catholic Church

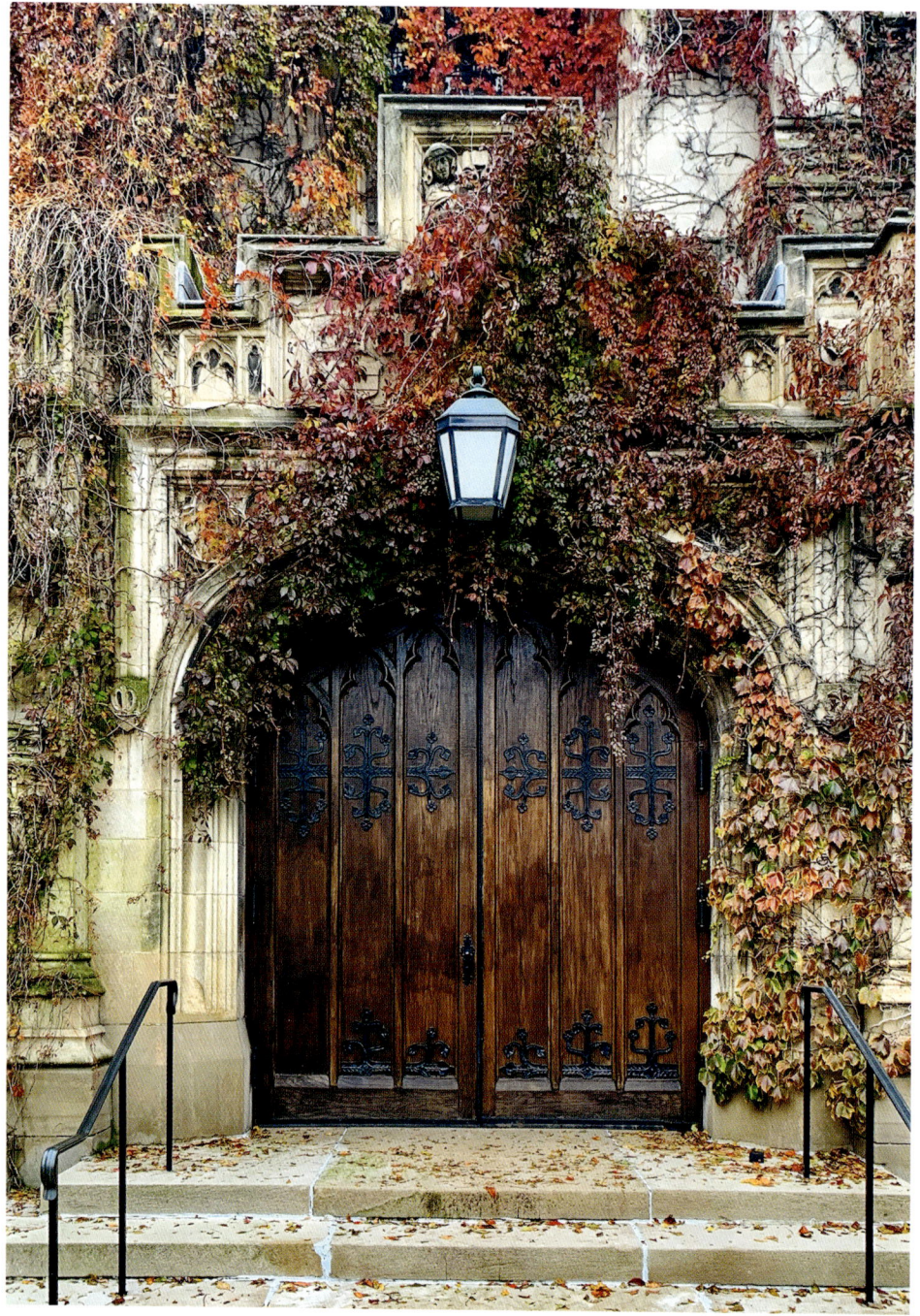

HYDE PARK

University of Chicago

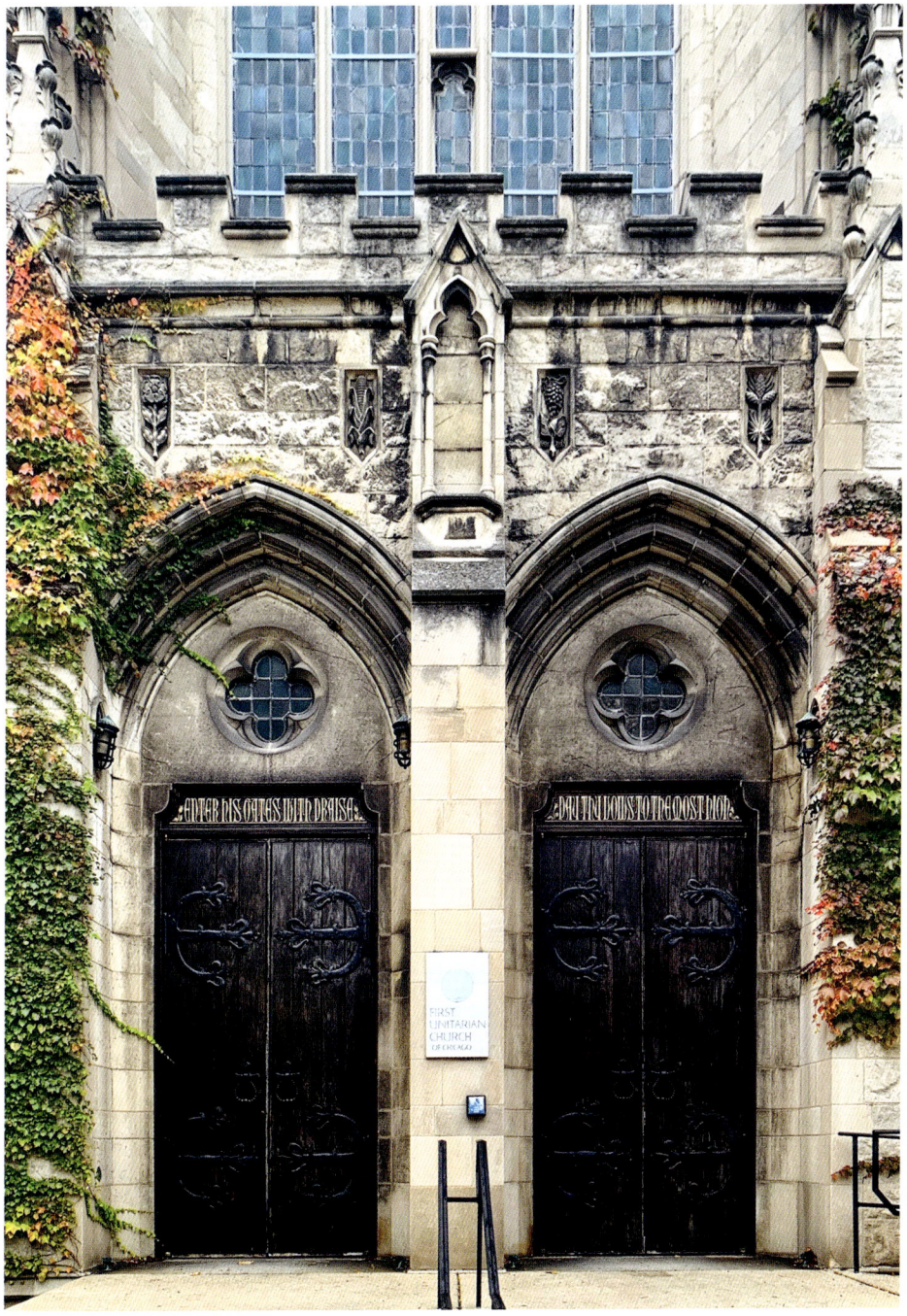

HYDE PARK

First Unitarian Church of Chicago

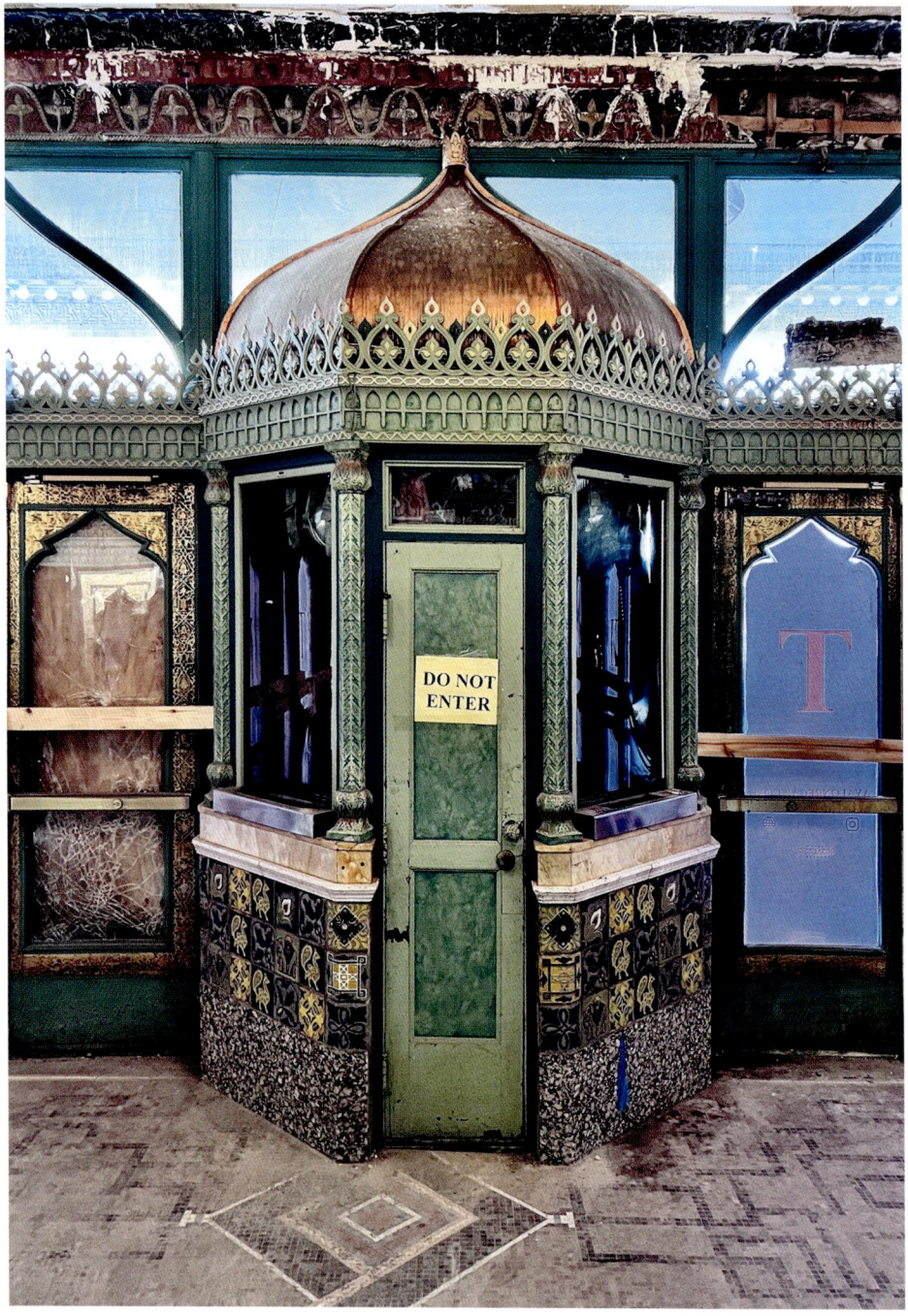

AVALON PARK

Avalon Regal Theater

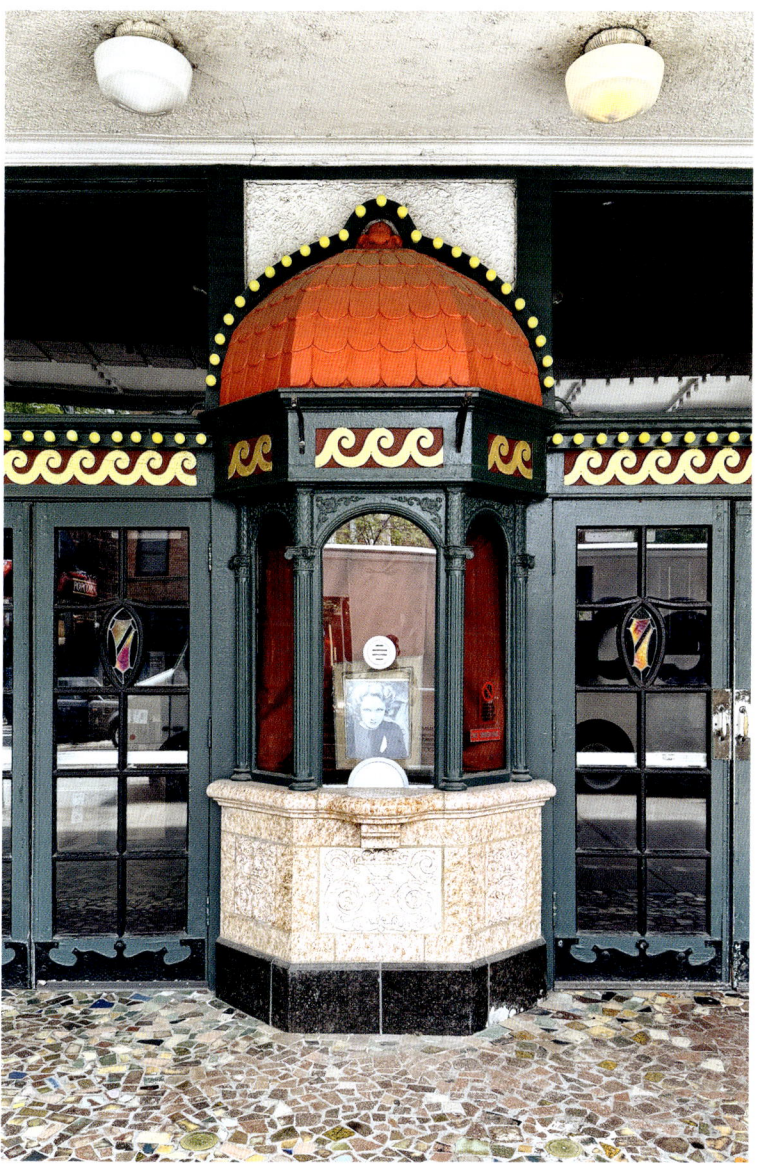

WRIGLEYVILLE

Music Box Theatre

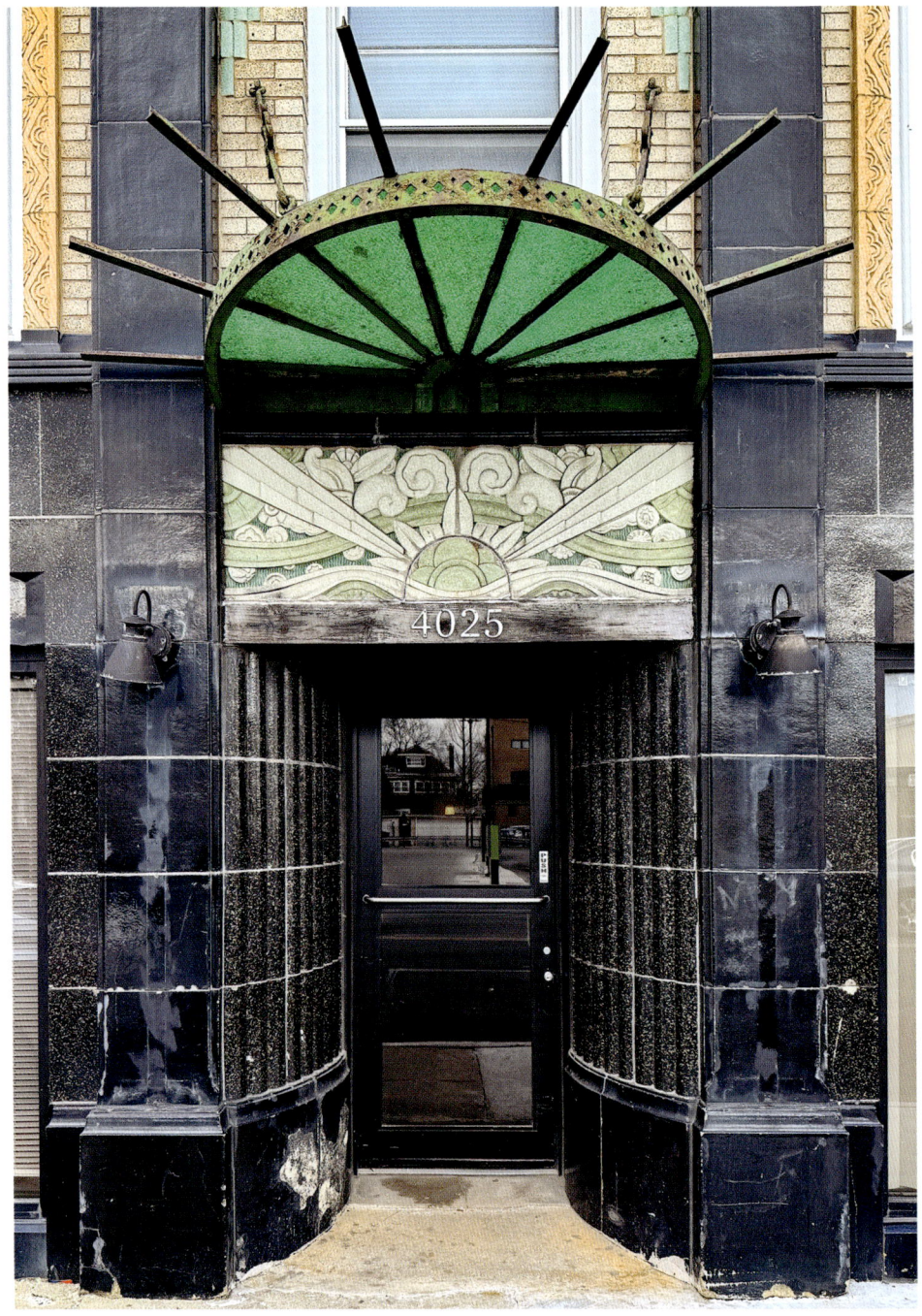

IRVING PARK

Residential

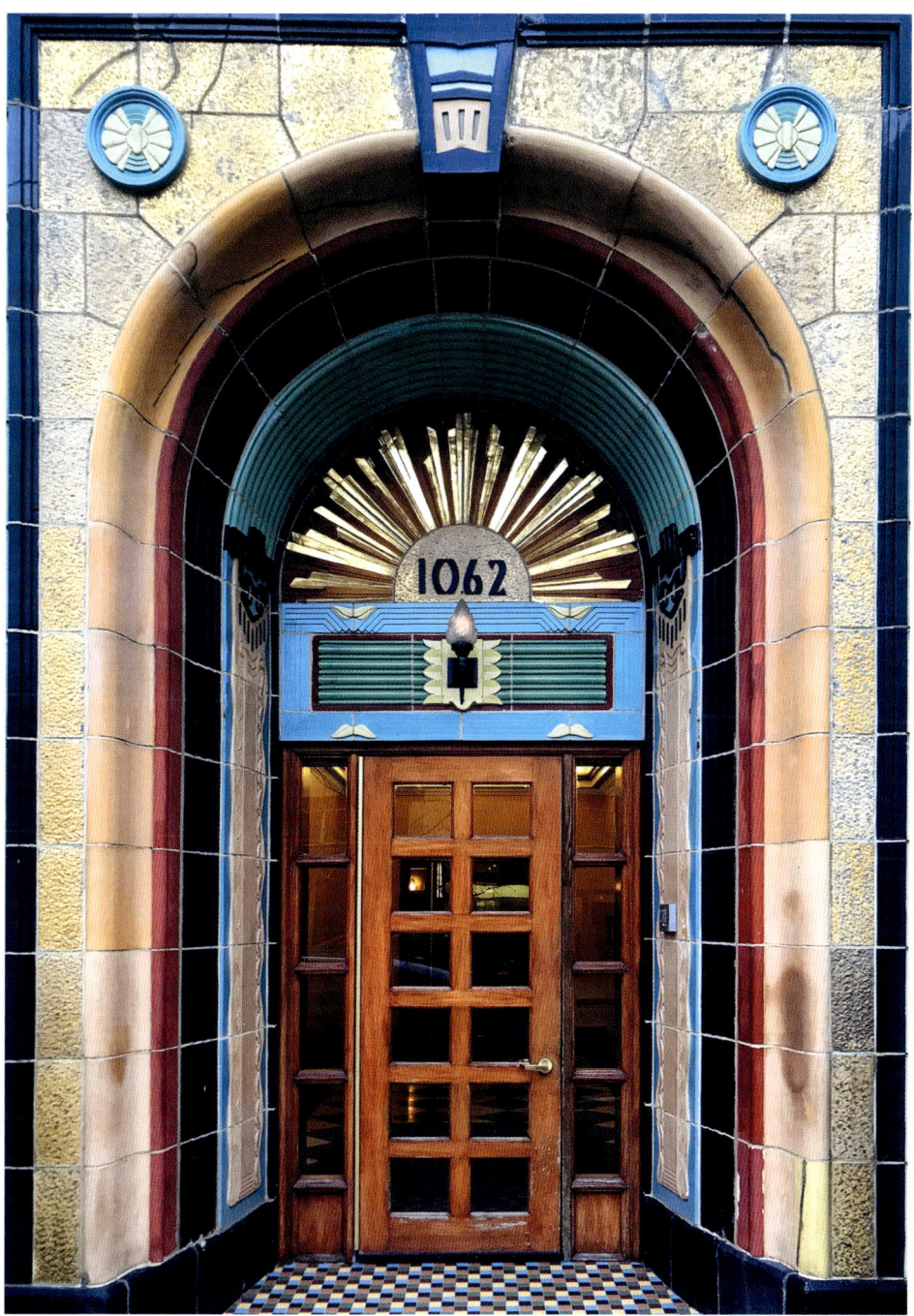

EDGEWATER

Residential

ELIZABETH M. CUDAHY MEMORIAL LIBRARY

Architectural Style: Art Deco, Romanesque Revival | Year: 1930

The dramatic doorway of the Elizabeth M. Cudahy Memorial Library, Loyola University's original library, was designed by Chicago architect Andrew Rebori in 1930. In contrast to the classical style of other buildings on the University's campus, Rebori designed the library in the Art Deco style. Known colloquially by students as the "green doorway," the doorway's bold hue is due to the metal's patina.

Named in honor of Elizabeth M. Cudahy, the building was a gift from her husband, Edward A. Cudahy, a wealthy meatpacking magnate. Edward also helped fund a remarkable mural inside the main reading room. The mural, painted by Chicago legend John Warner Norton, is a sweeping map-style fresco depicting Jesuit missionary activity across the Great Lakes and Mississippi River Valley.

Step back outside, and the doorway itself also tells a story of curiosity and discovery. A remarkable sunburst sits atop the wrought iron doors, symbolizing the rising light of education and wisdom. Perched high above the sun's rays, a limestone owl keeps watch, a classical nod to Athena, the Greek goddess of wisdom. An inscription on the owl's crest reads AMDG, standing for *Ad Majorem Dei Gloria*. This translates to "For the Greater Glory of God," the Jesuit motto that echoes throughout Loyola's campus.

Additions to the library in 1969 and 2008 rendered the original entrance redundant, but in 2009, a new tradition of walking through the original doors as part of First Year Convocation and Senior Week began. Despite only being used ceremoniously, this passageway still stands as a symbol of education and intellectual curiosity.

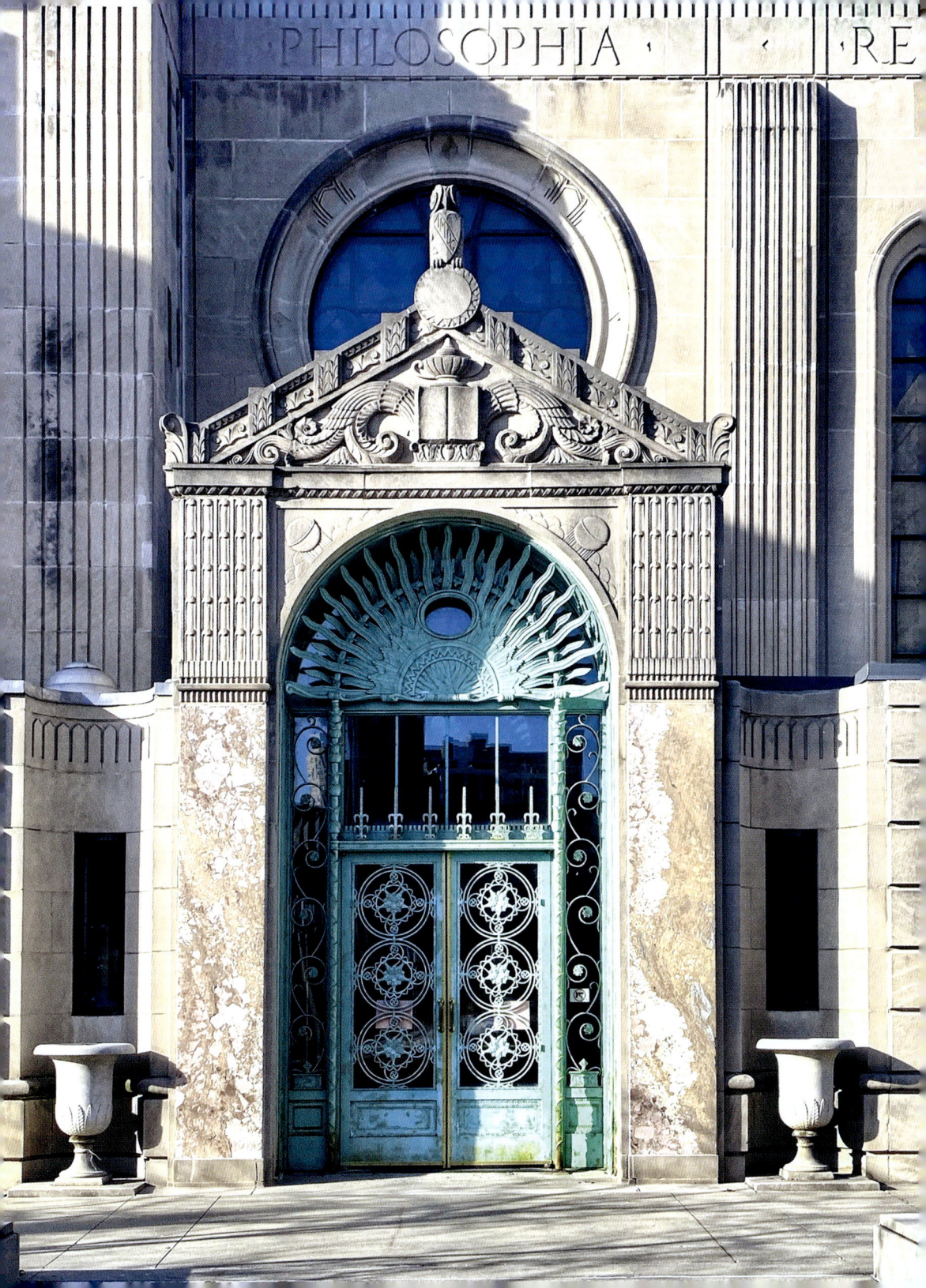

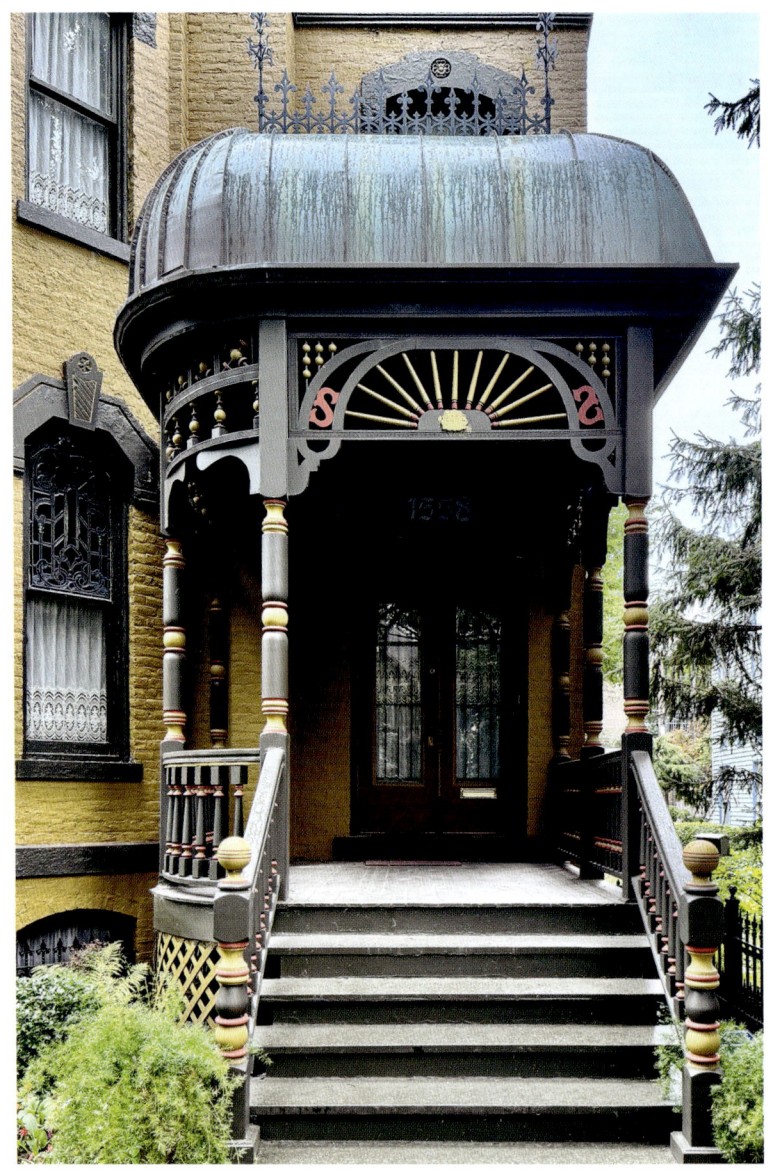

WICKER PARK

Residential

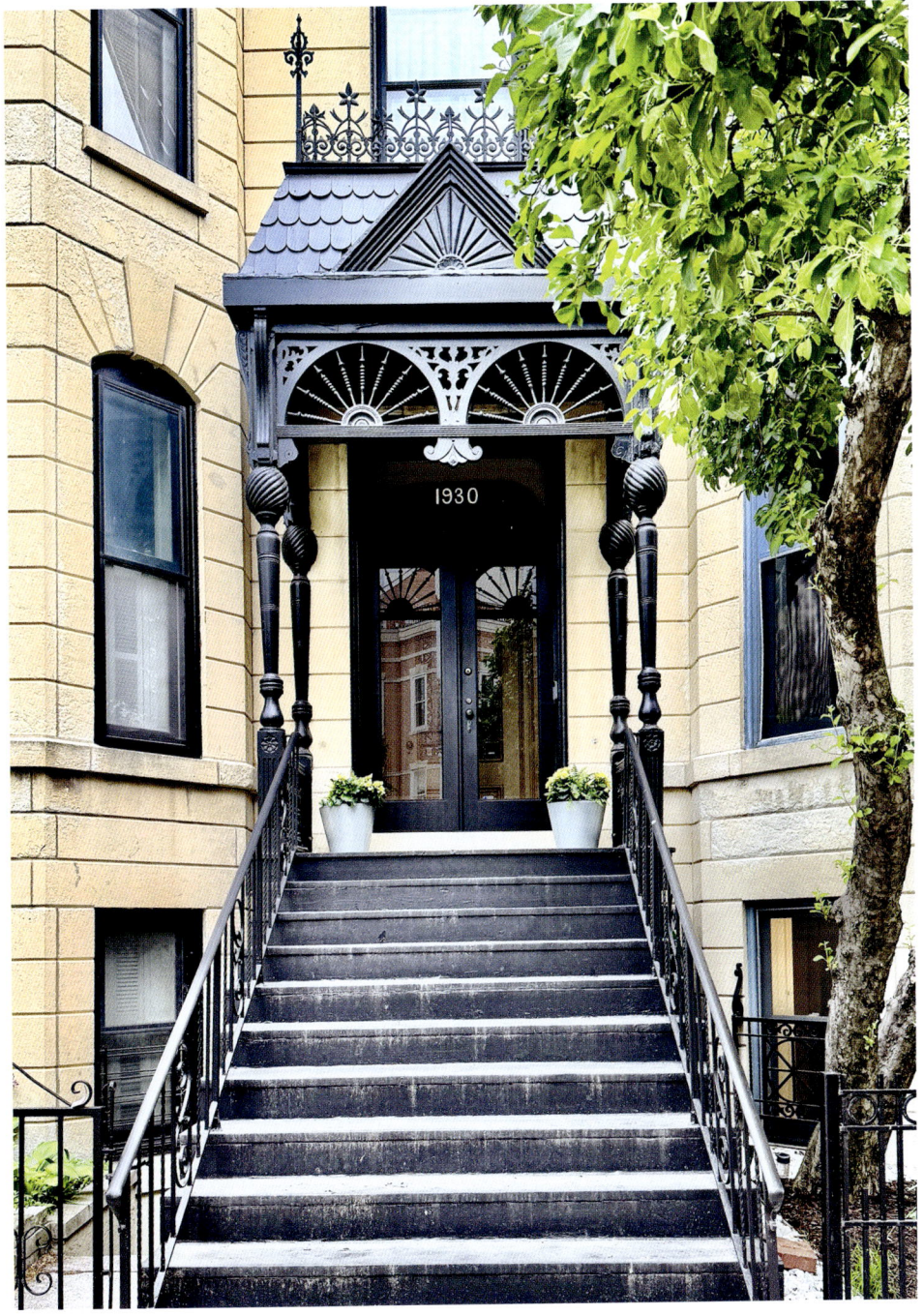

LINCOLN PARK

Residential

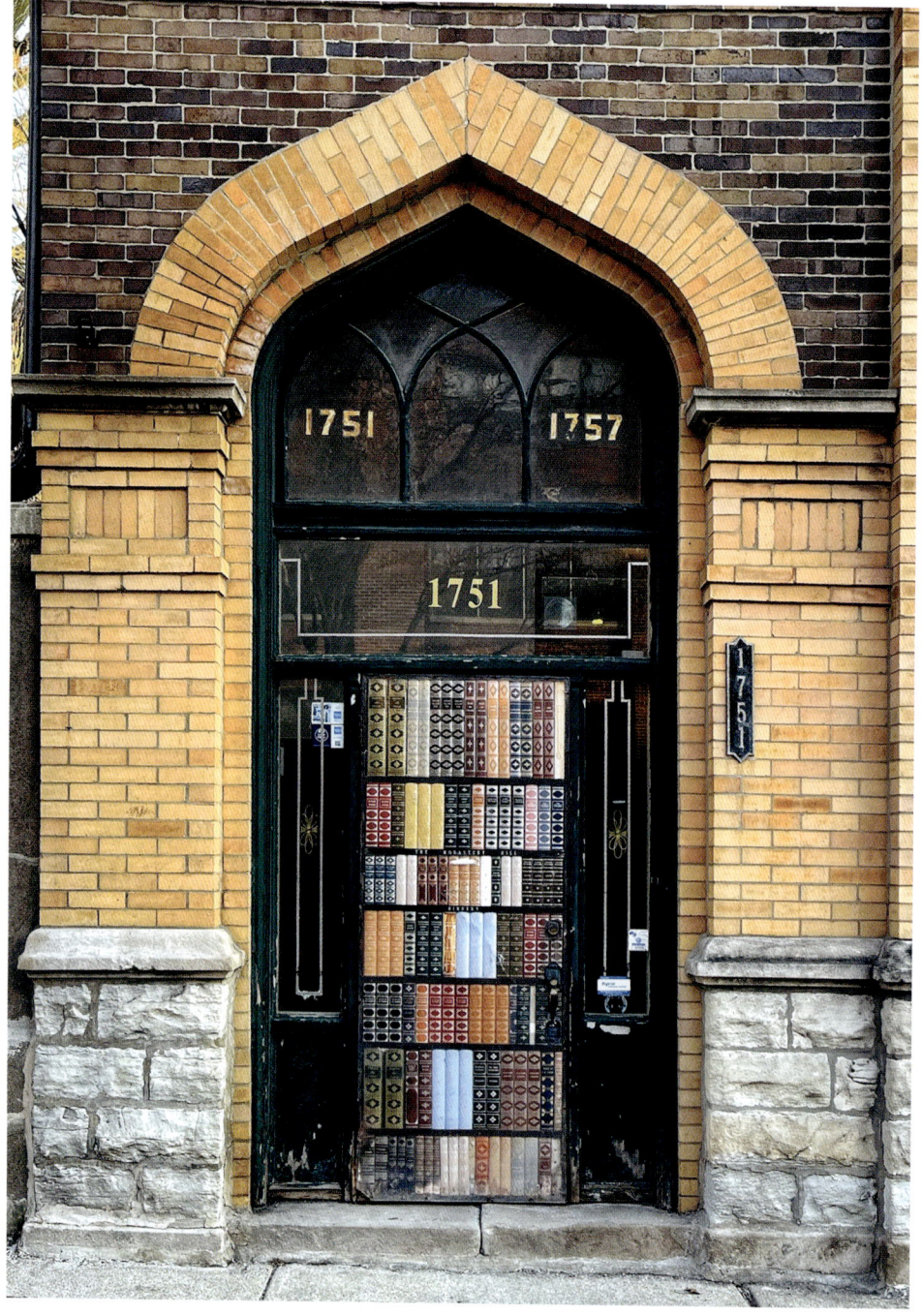

ROSCOE VILLAGE

Monastery Hill Bindery

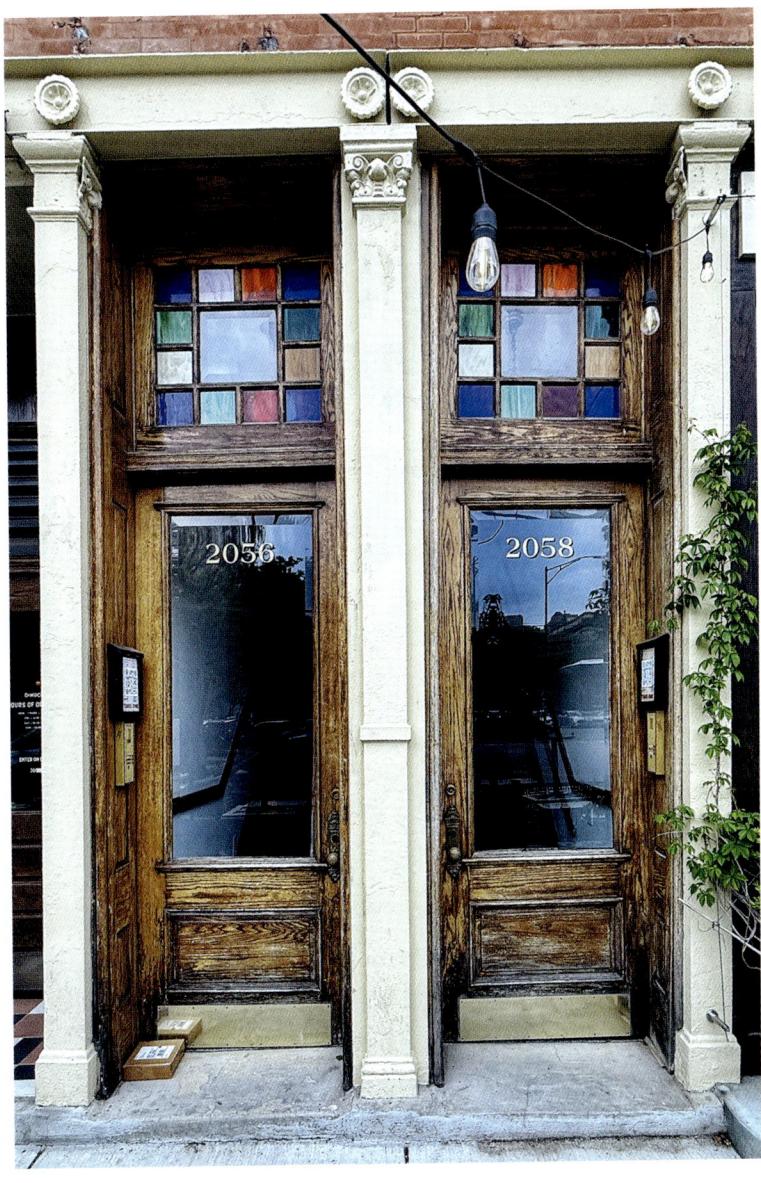

LINCOLN PARK

Residential

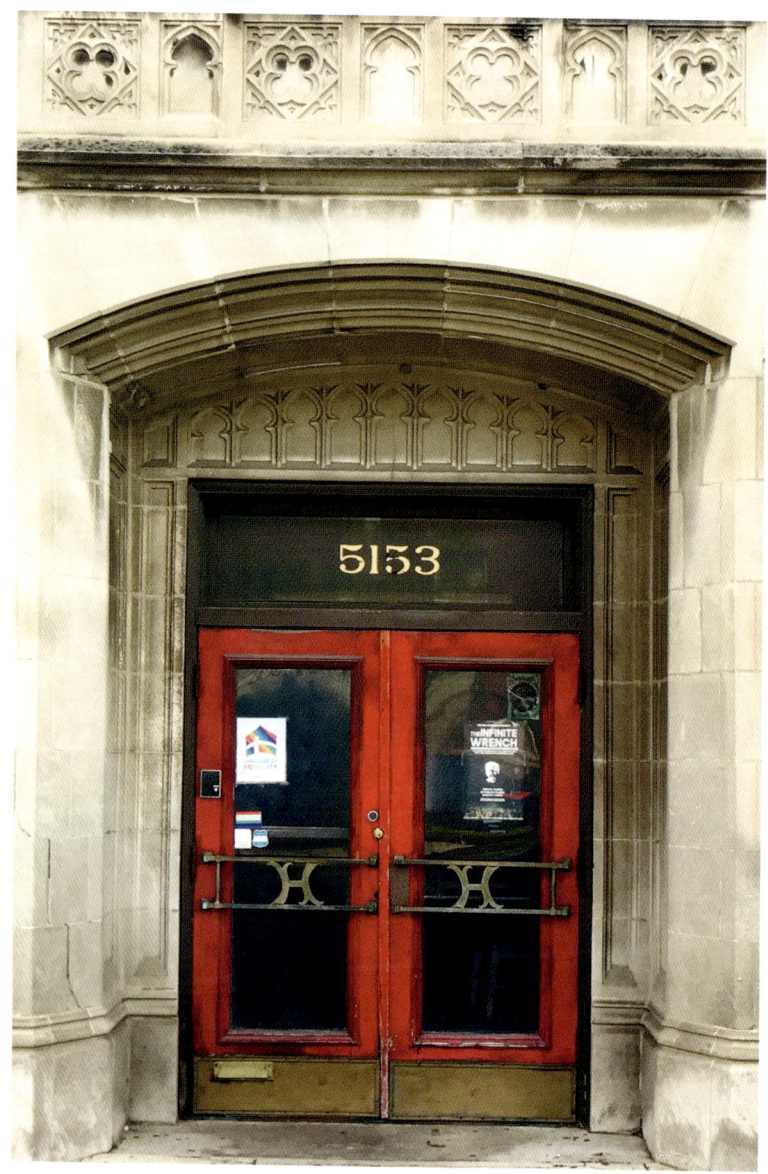

UPTOWN

The Neo-Futurists Theater

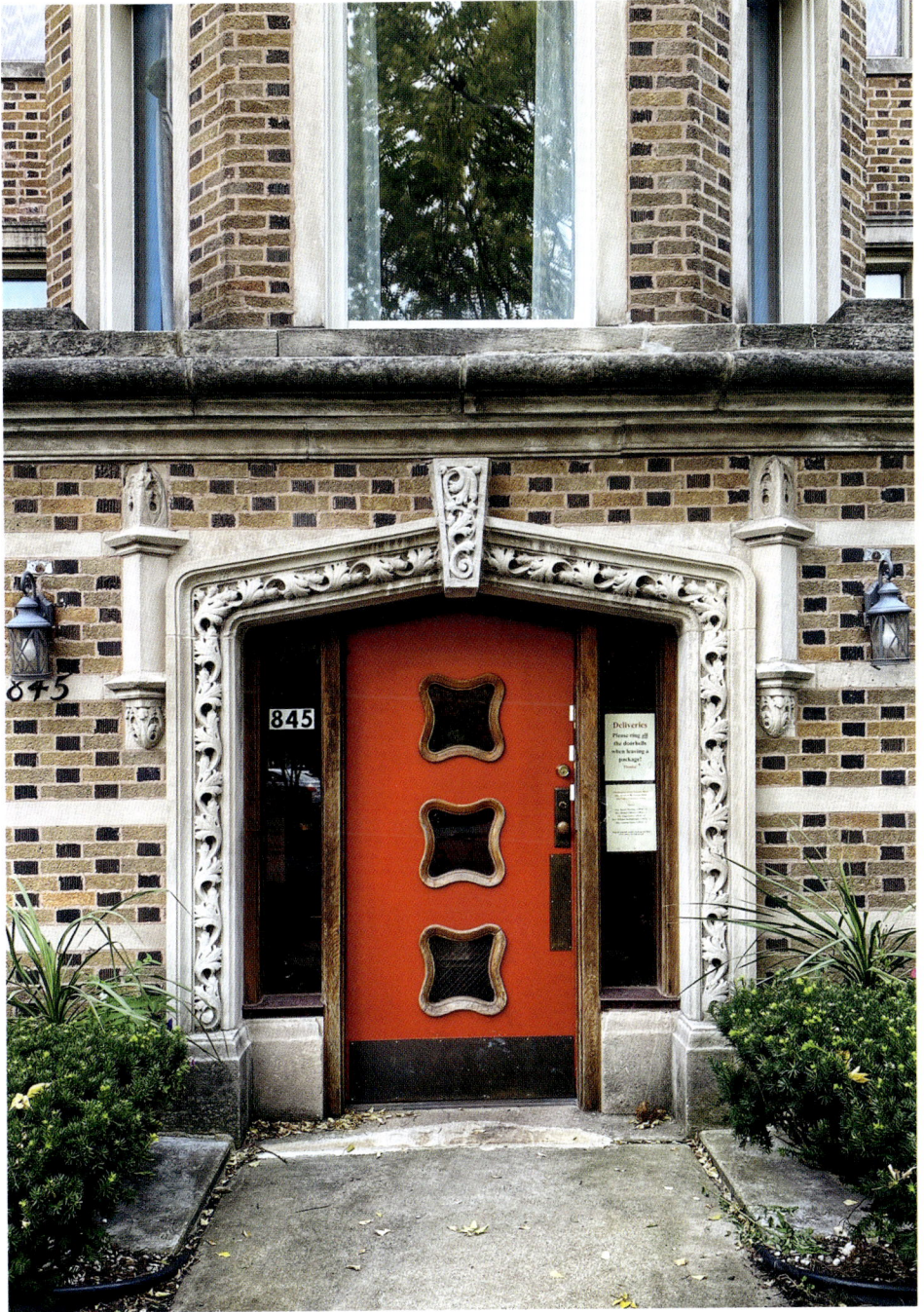

HYDE PARK

Residential

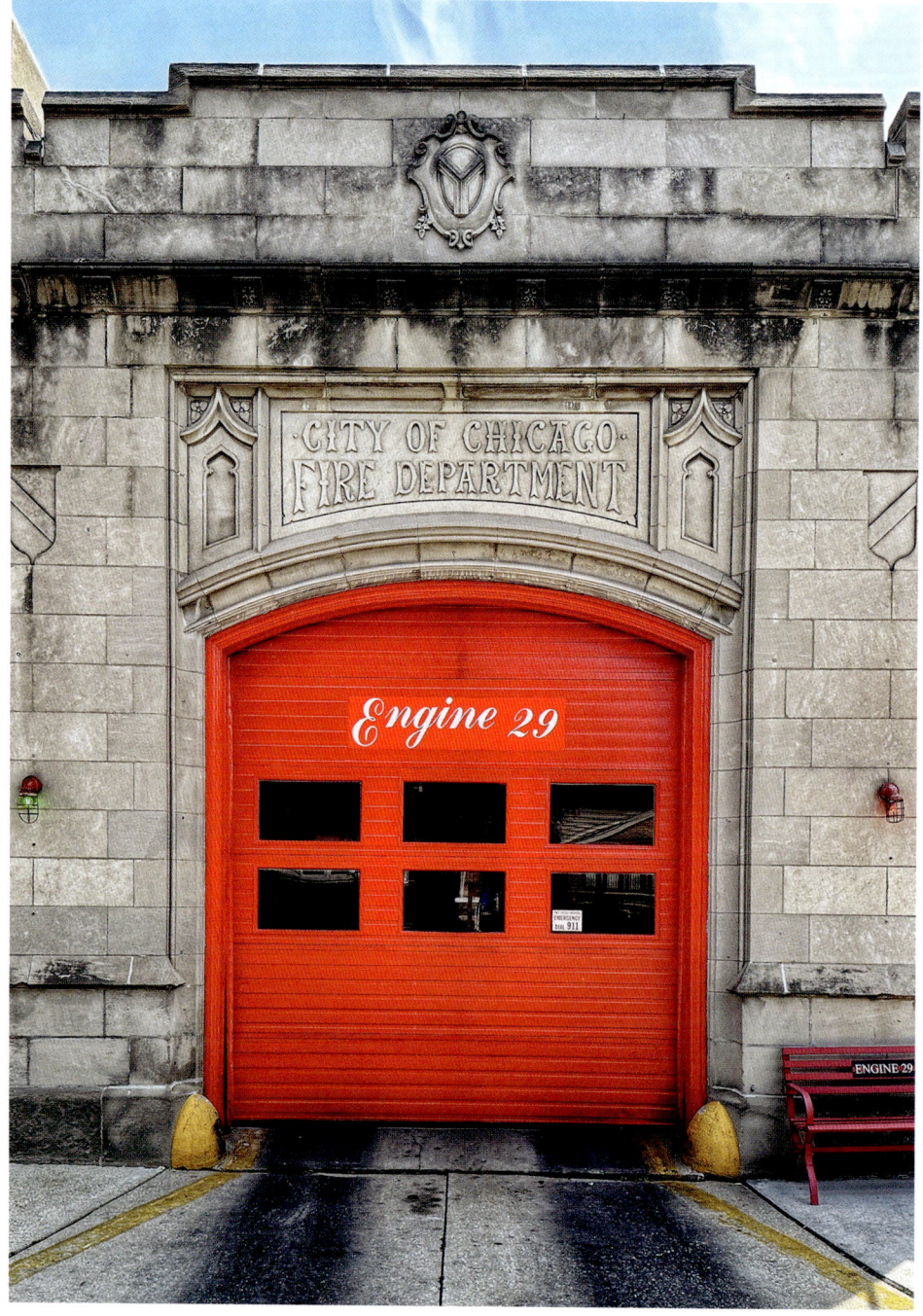

BRIDGEPORT

Chicago Fire Department Engine 29

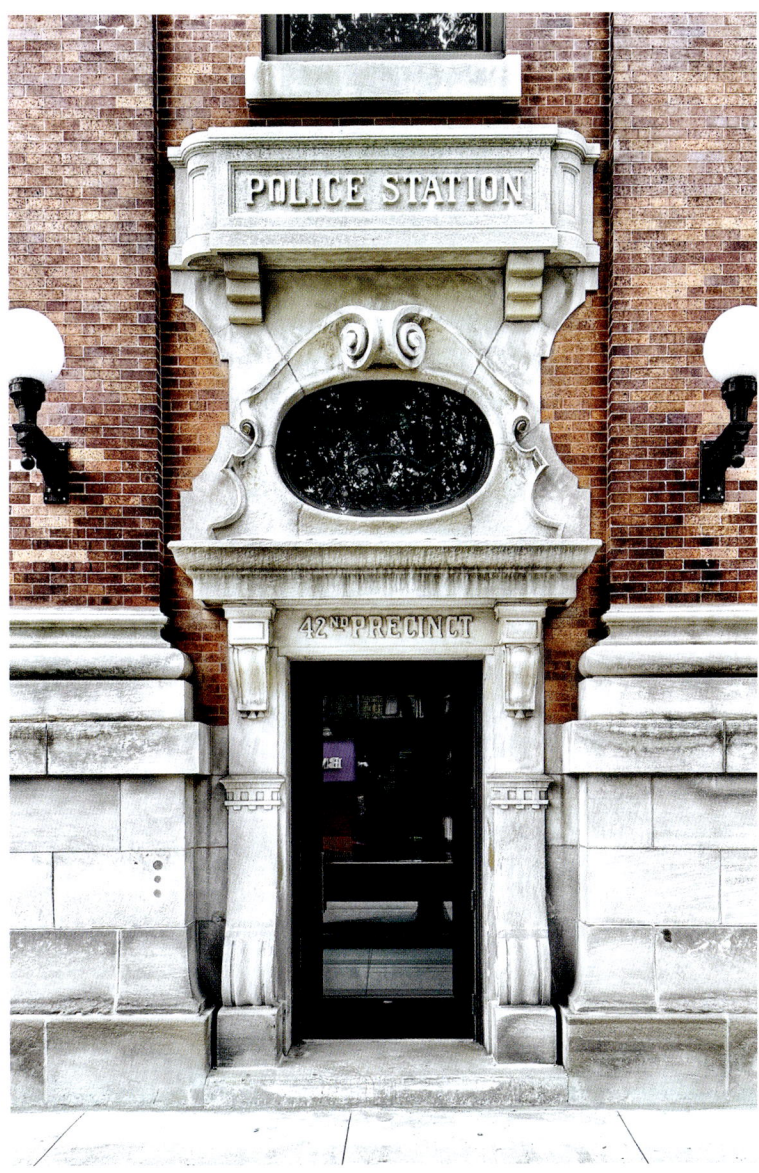

LAKEVIEW

42nd Precinct/Town Hall Police Station

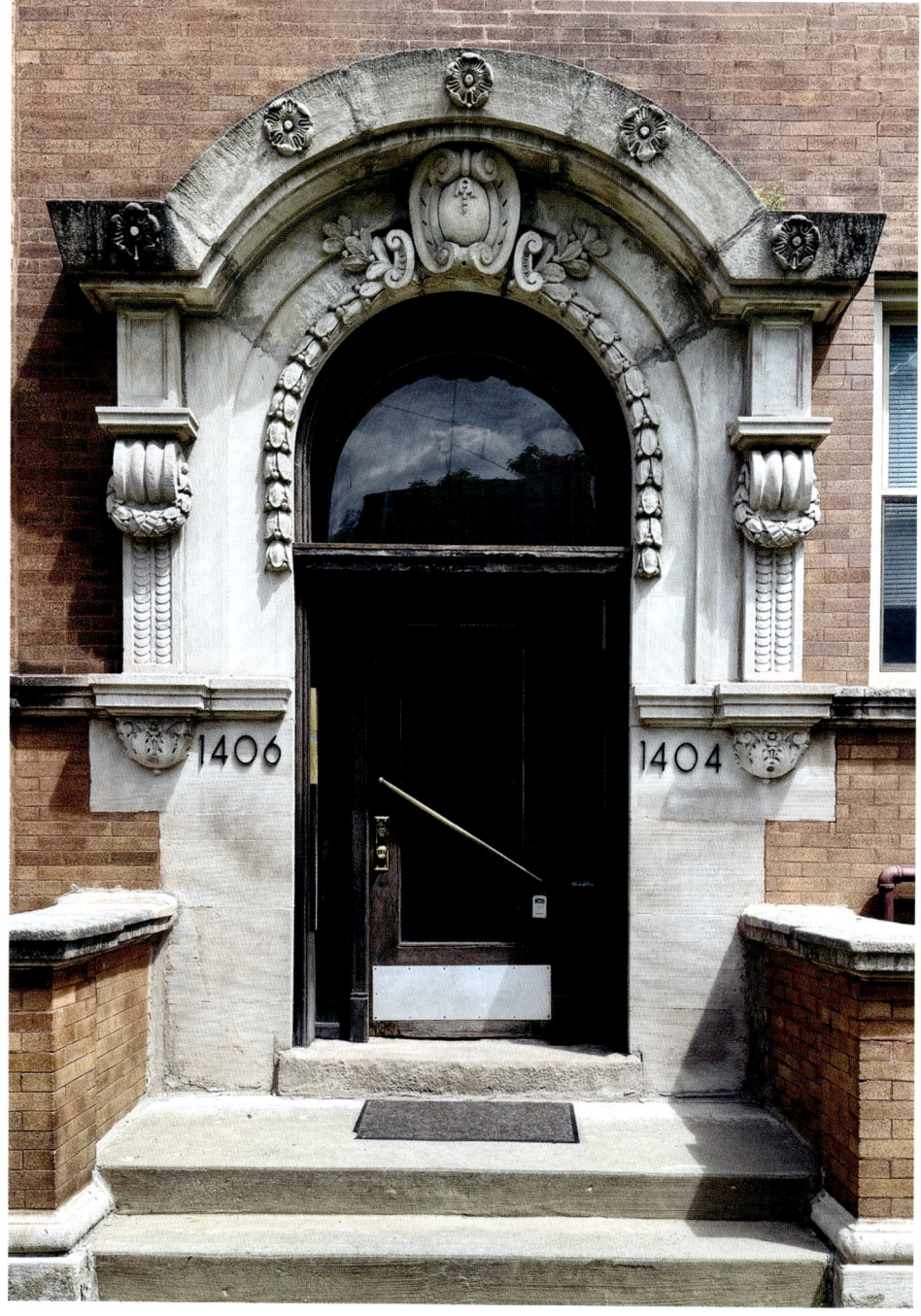

EDGEWATER

Residential

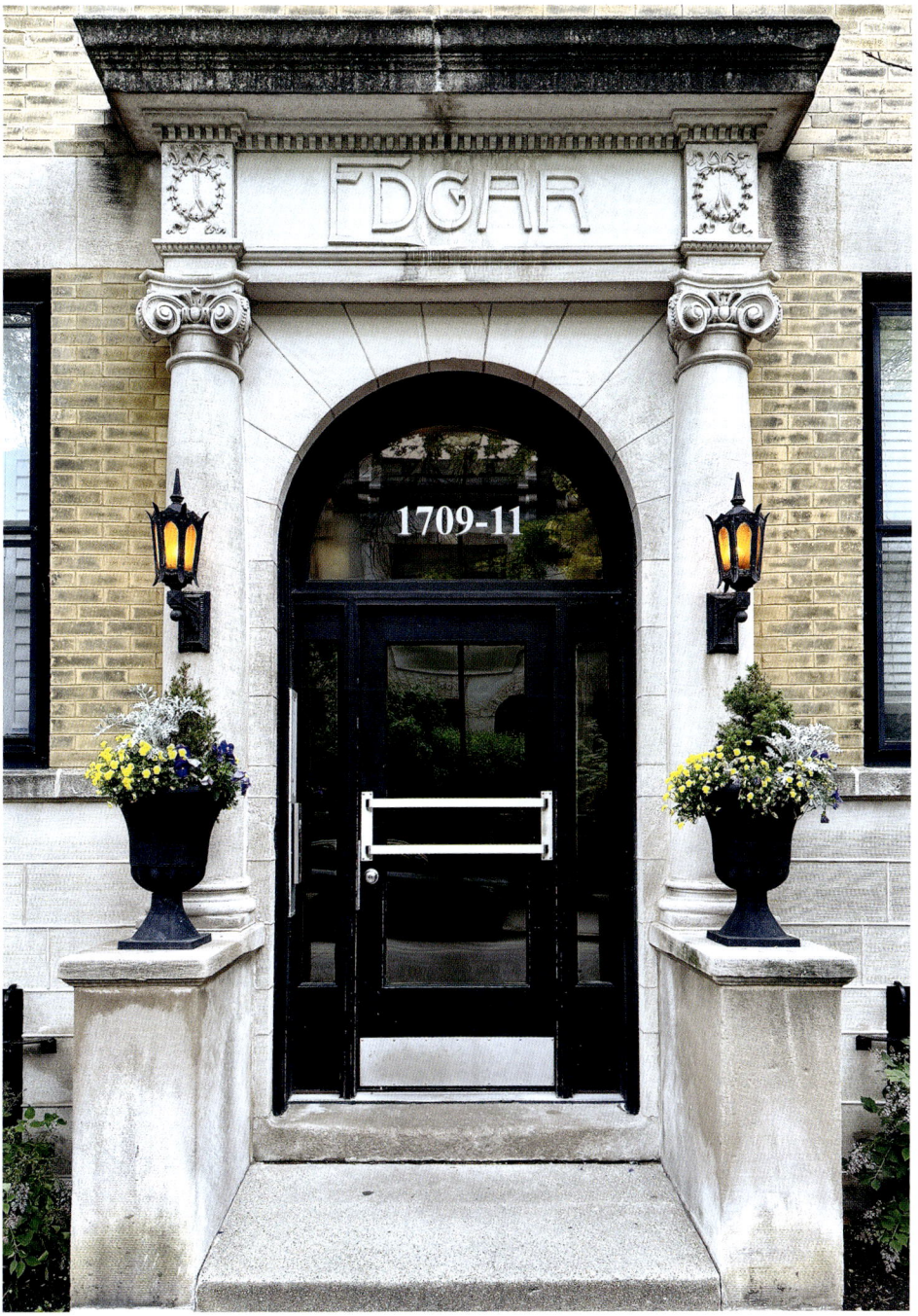

OLD TOWN

Residential

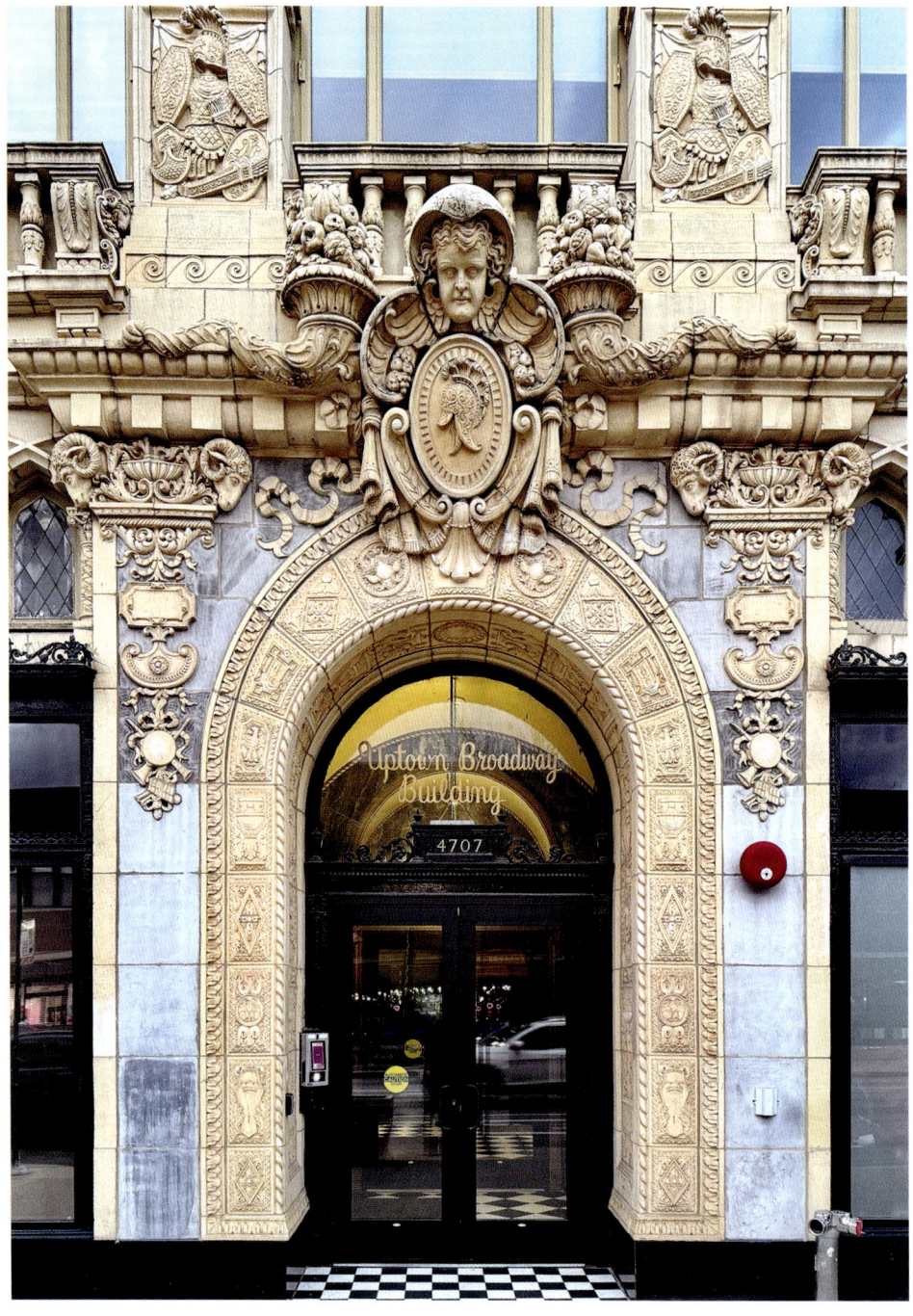

UPTOWN

Uptown Broadway Building

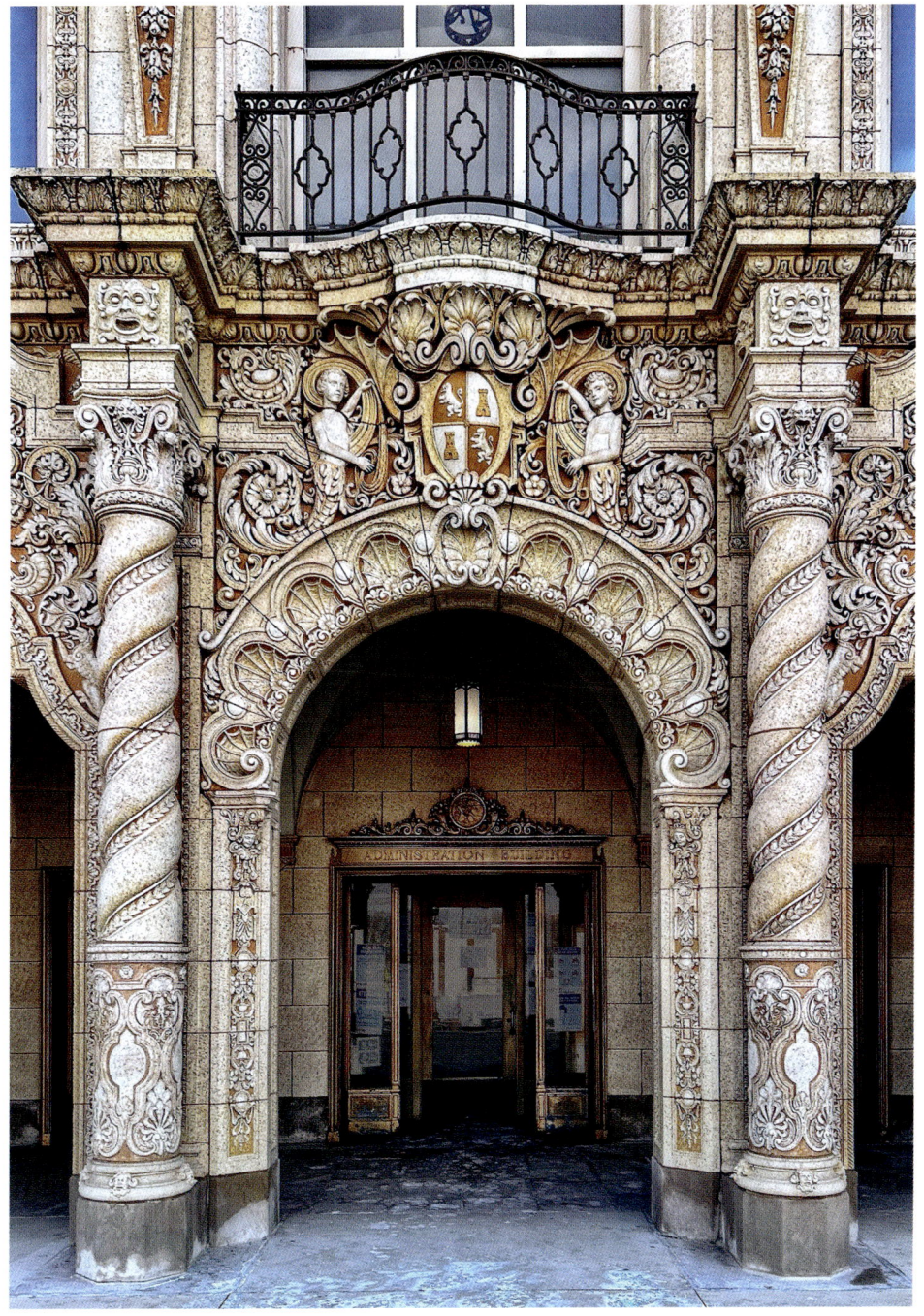

GARFIELD PARK

Garfield Park Fieldhouse

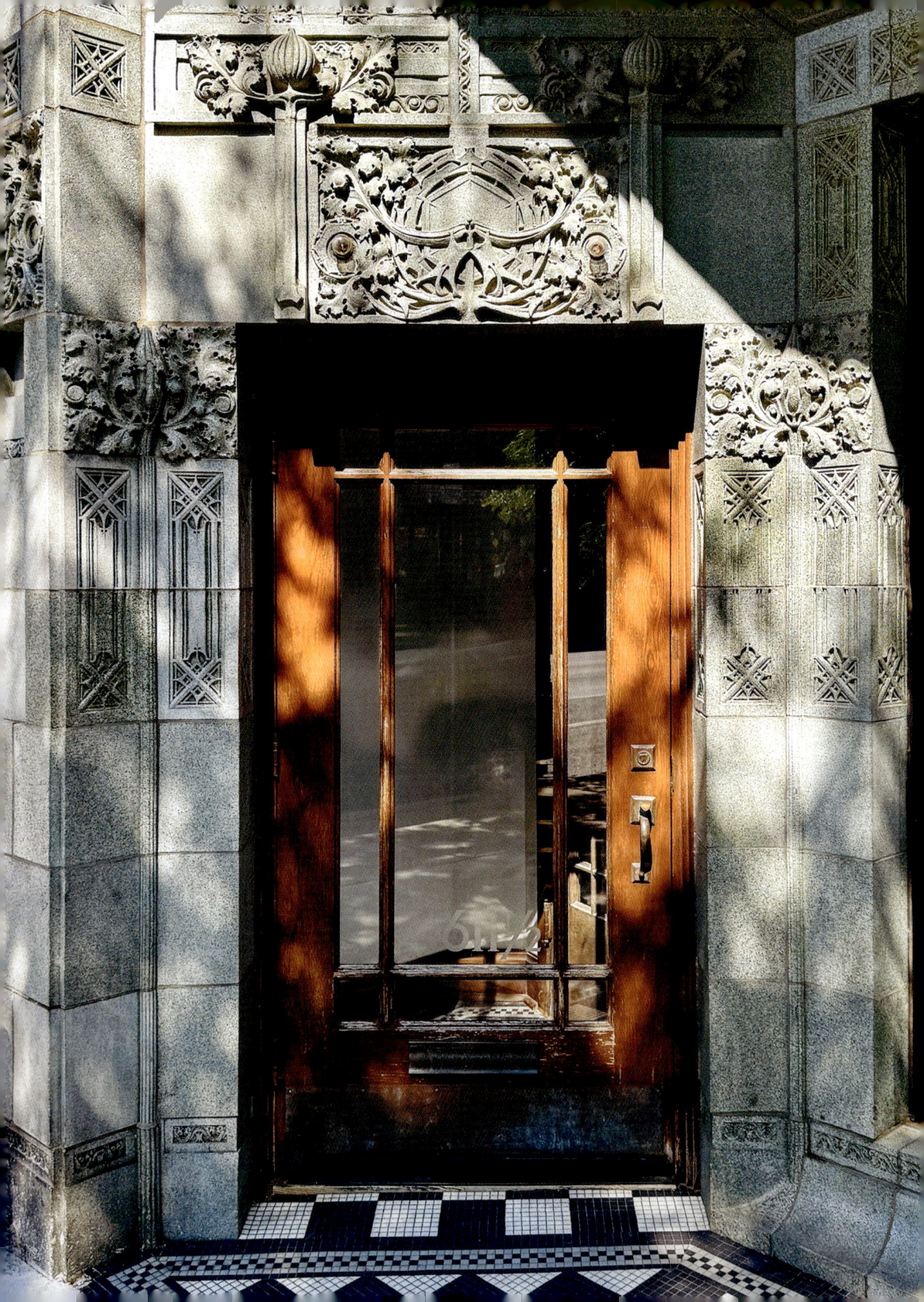

KRAUSE MUSIC STORE

Architectural Style: Sullivanesque | Year: 1922

Although he was known as "father of the skyscraper," influential architect Louis Sullivan's final work proves that you don't need height to soar. Tucked into a row of ordinary storefronts, this two-story gem at 4611 N. Lincoln Avenue sings boldly and beautifully. It's a surprising, pocket-sized expression of Sullivan's architectural philosophy.

Commissioned by music dealer William P. Krause, the building's show stopping façade was designed by Sullivan and executed by architect William C. Presto. Stylized vines curl across green-glazed terracotta, framing a grand window like a proscenium stage. Also surrounding the window are two doors, with the right opening into the store and the left (pictured here) leading to Krause's apartment above. At the top, a key-shaped cartouche emblazoned with a "K" ties the building together.

Sadly, Krause took his life during the Great Depression, and the space became a funeral home for more than sixty years. By the early 2000s, the windows were bricked in, the terracotta had dulled, and the spirit of the building was nearly lost. But in 2005, Studio V Design meticulously restored the façade, repairing the terracotta, reopening the display window, and bringing light back to the street. Today, the building houses biotech firm Briteseed.

Like an ornamental music box, Sullivan's final commercial work is small in scale but bursting with creativity and care. Known for his contributions to the development of the skyscraper, Sullivan's last act as an architect might not be his most grandiose, but it still hits all the right notes.

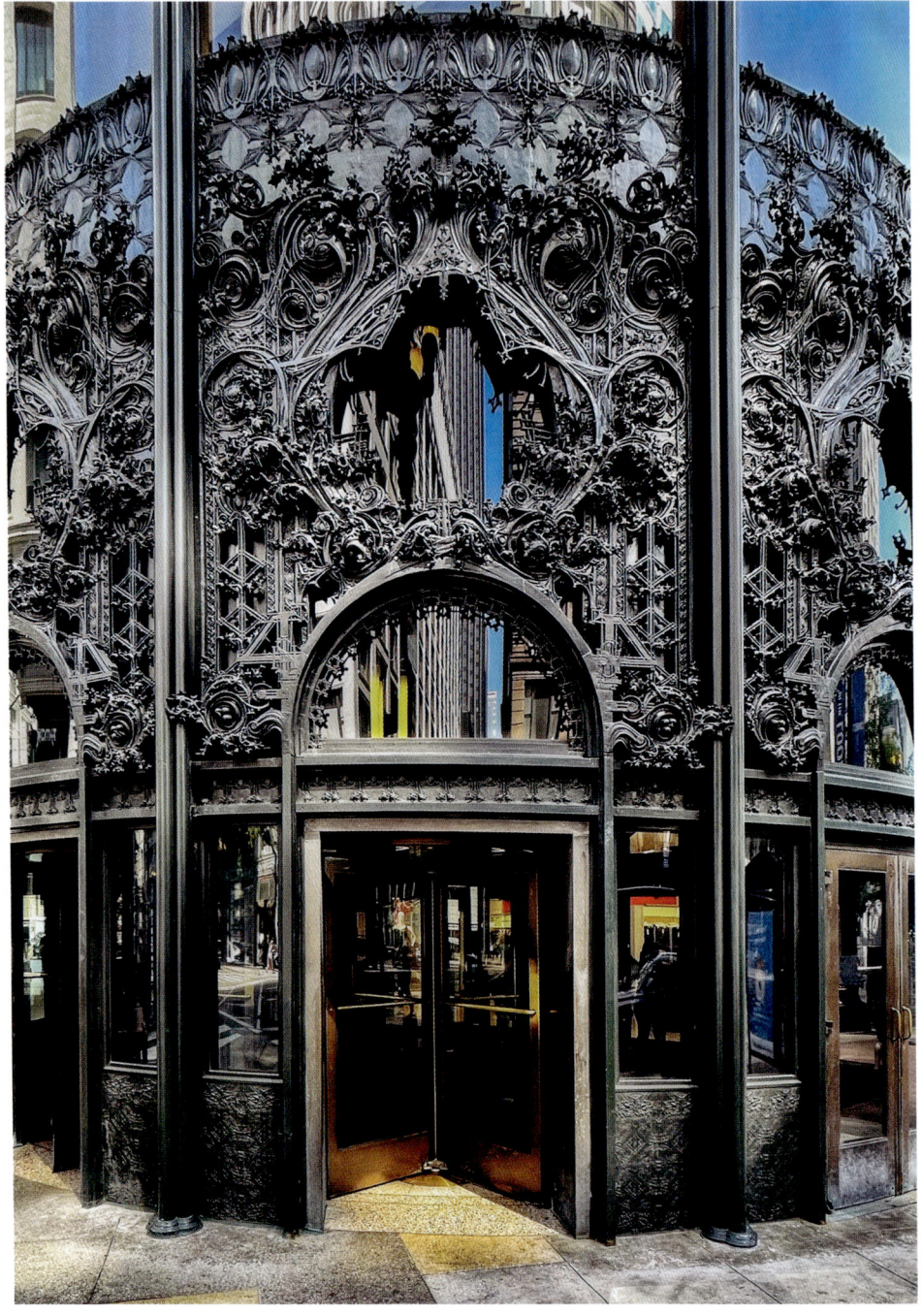

THE LOOP

Sullivan Center

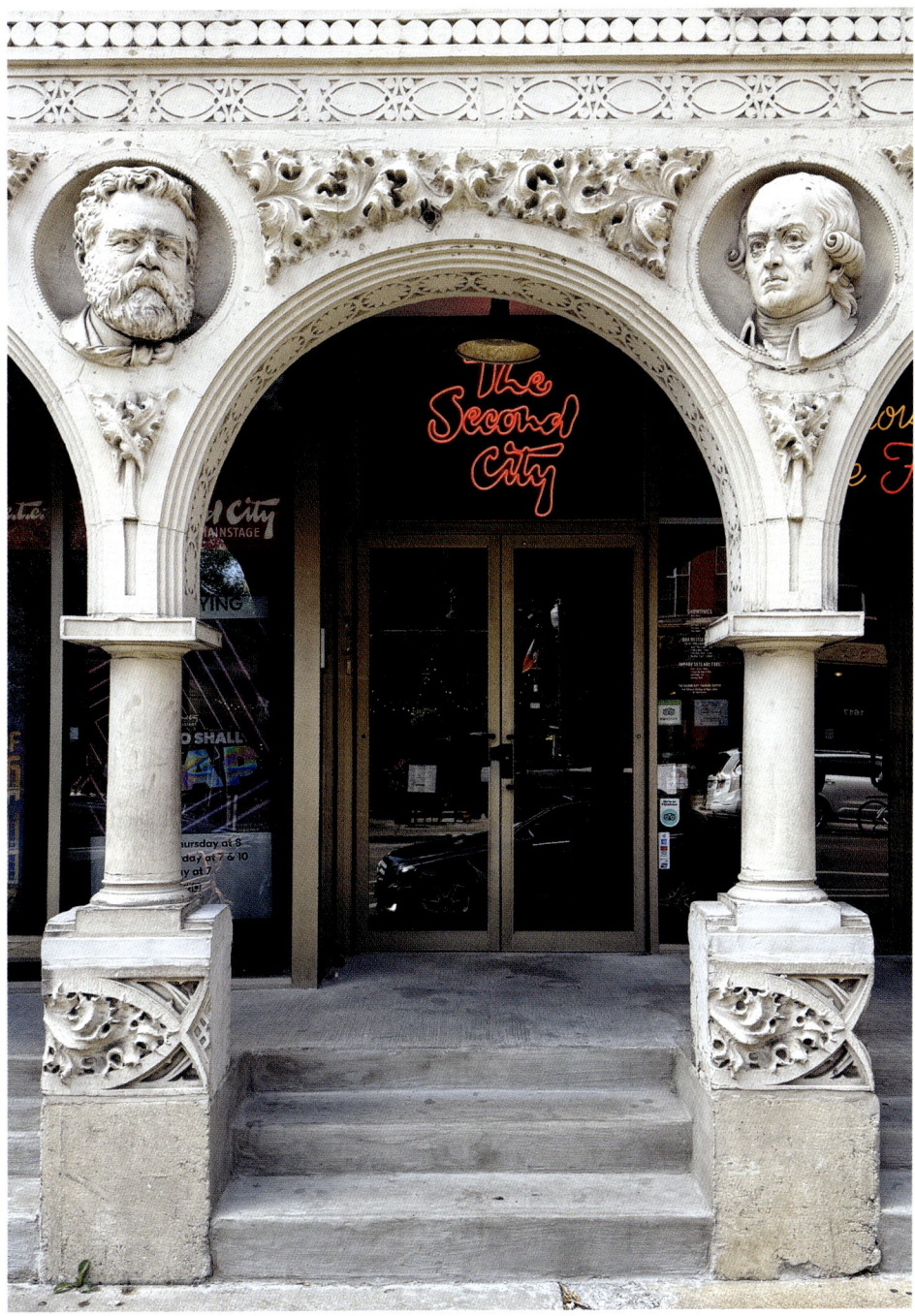

OLD TOWN

The Second City

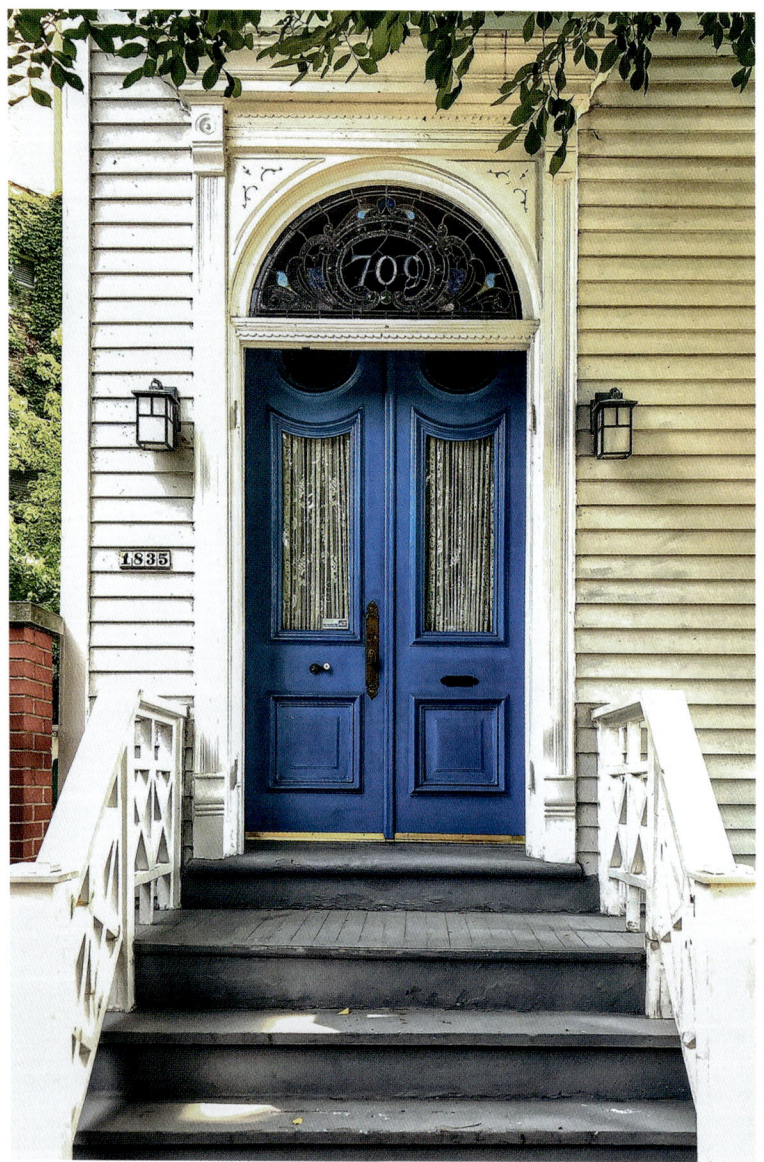

OLD TOWN

Residential

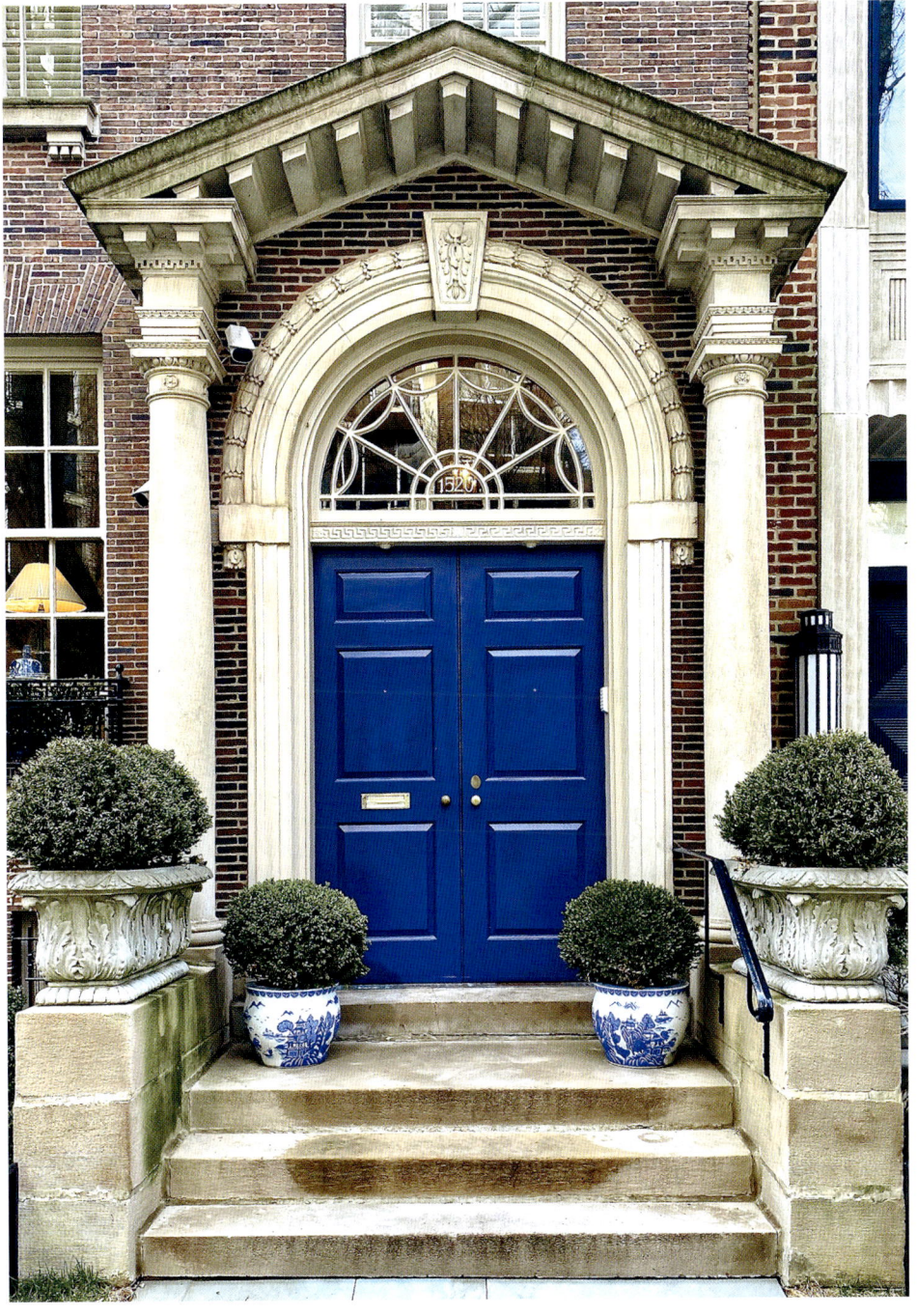

GOLD COAST

Residential

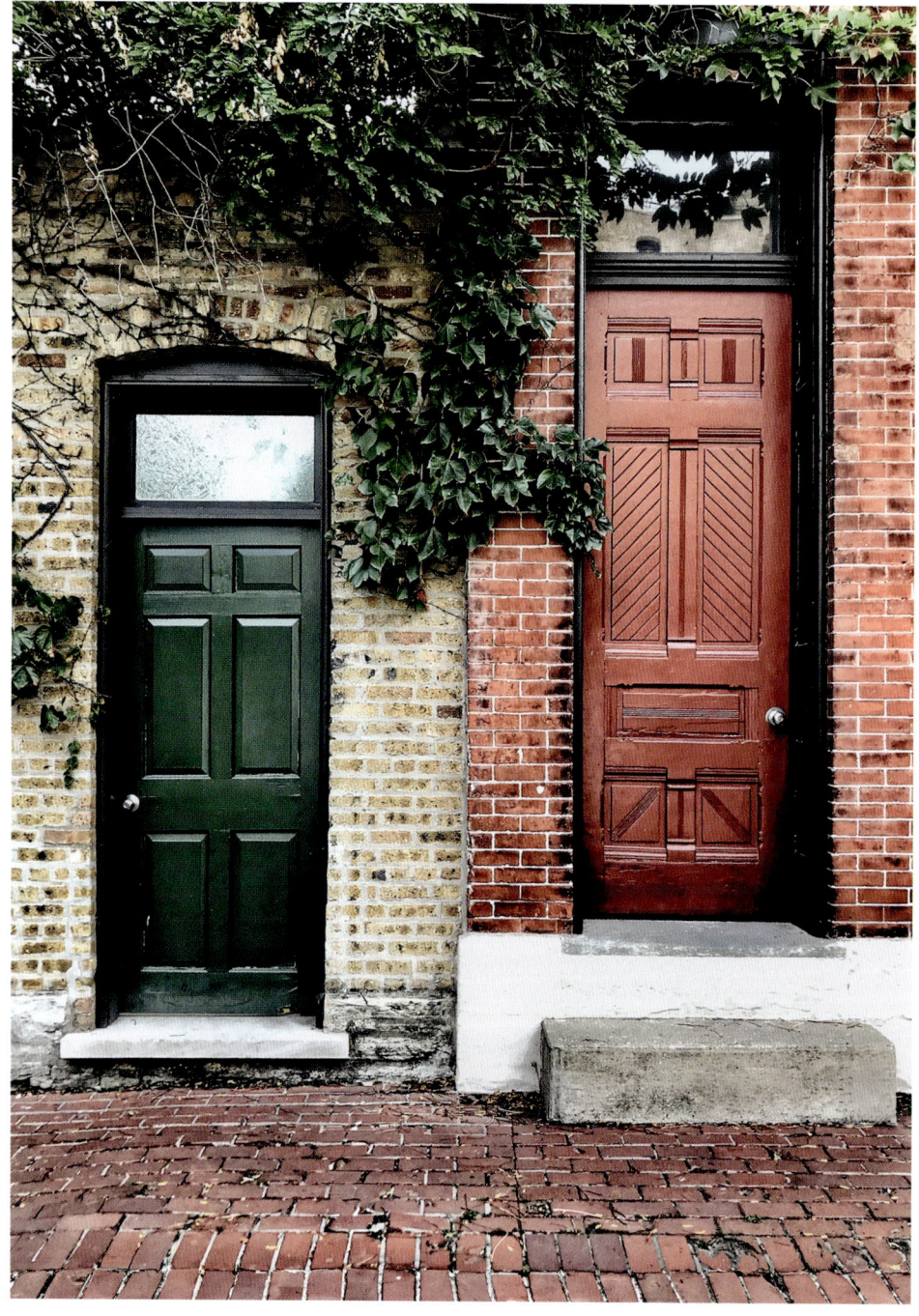

OLD TOWN

Residential

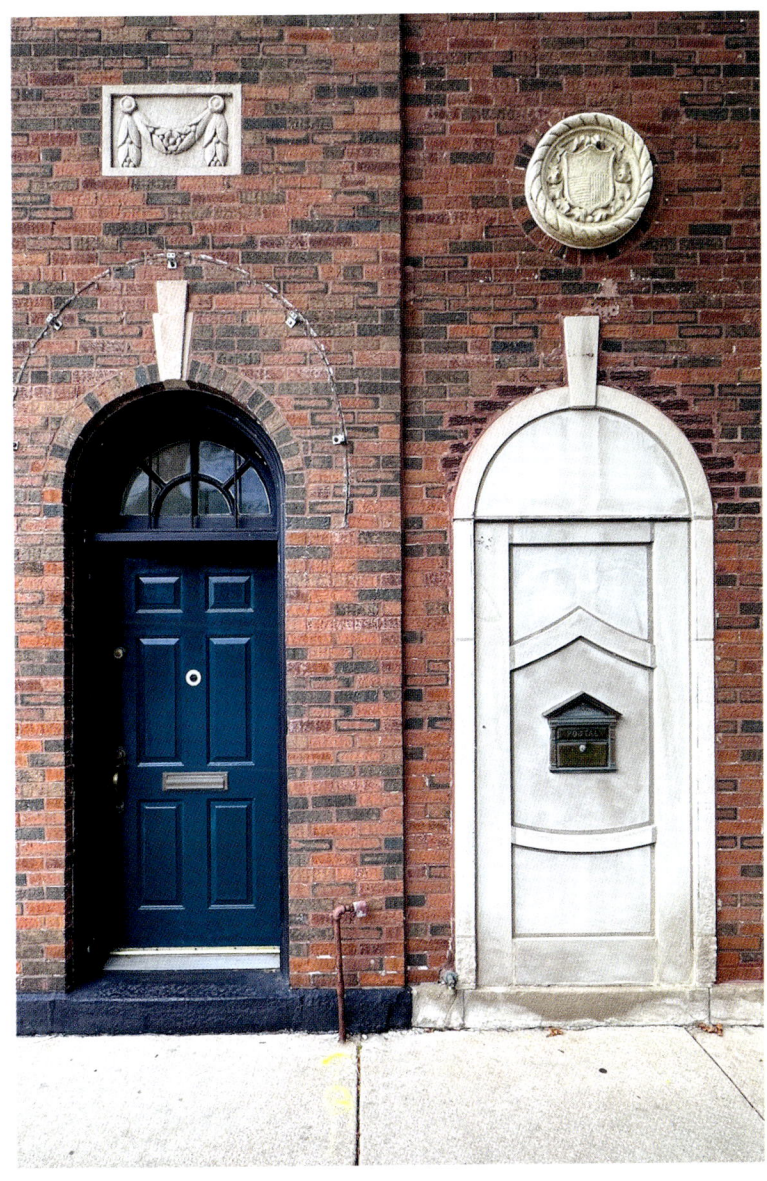

NEAR NORTH

Residential

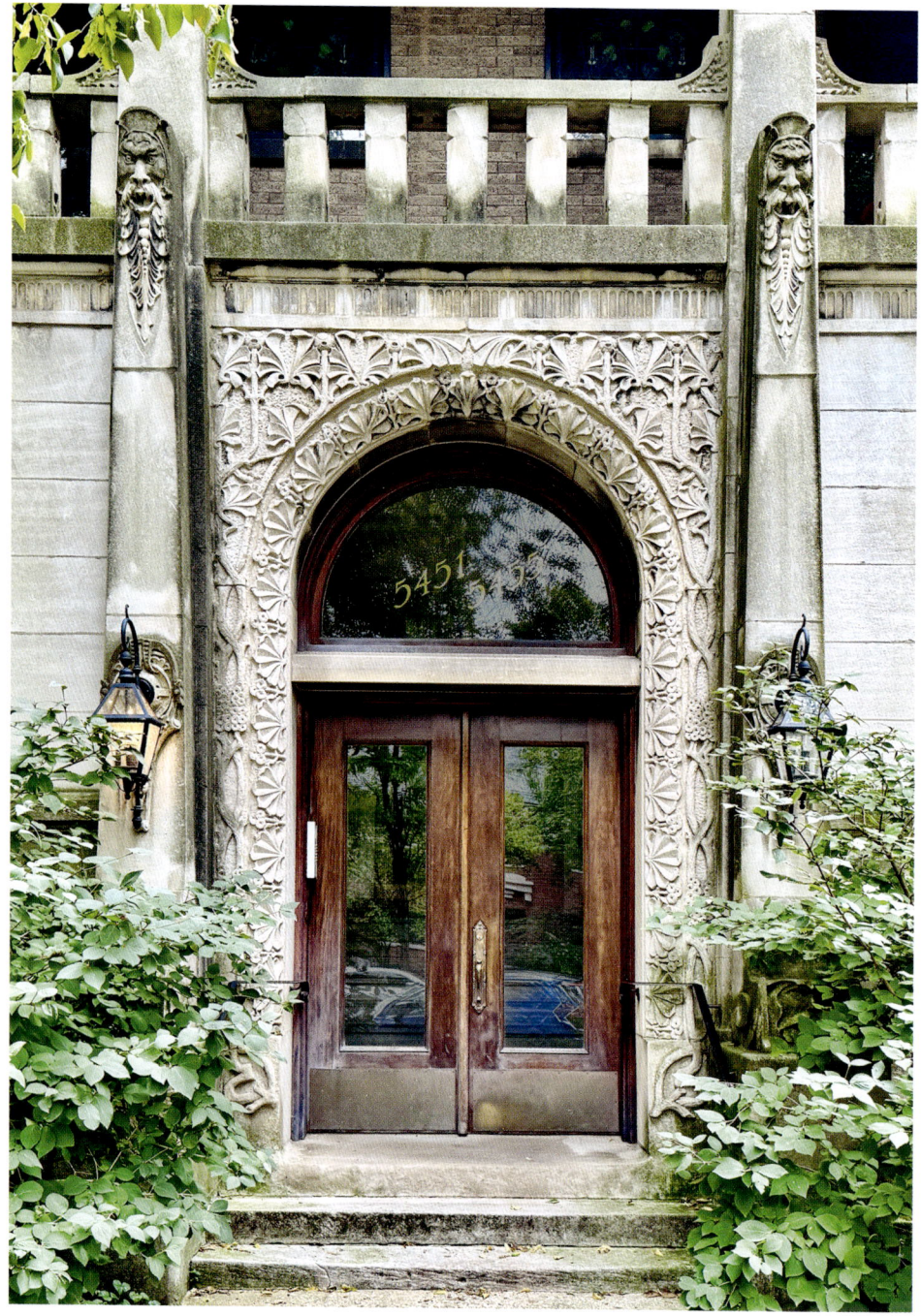

HYDE PARK

Residential

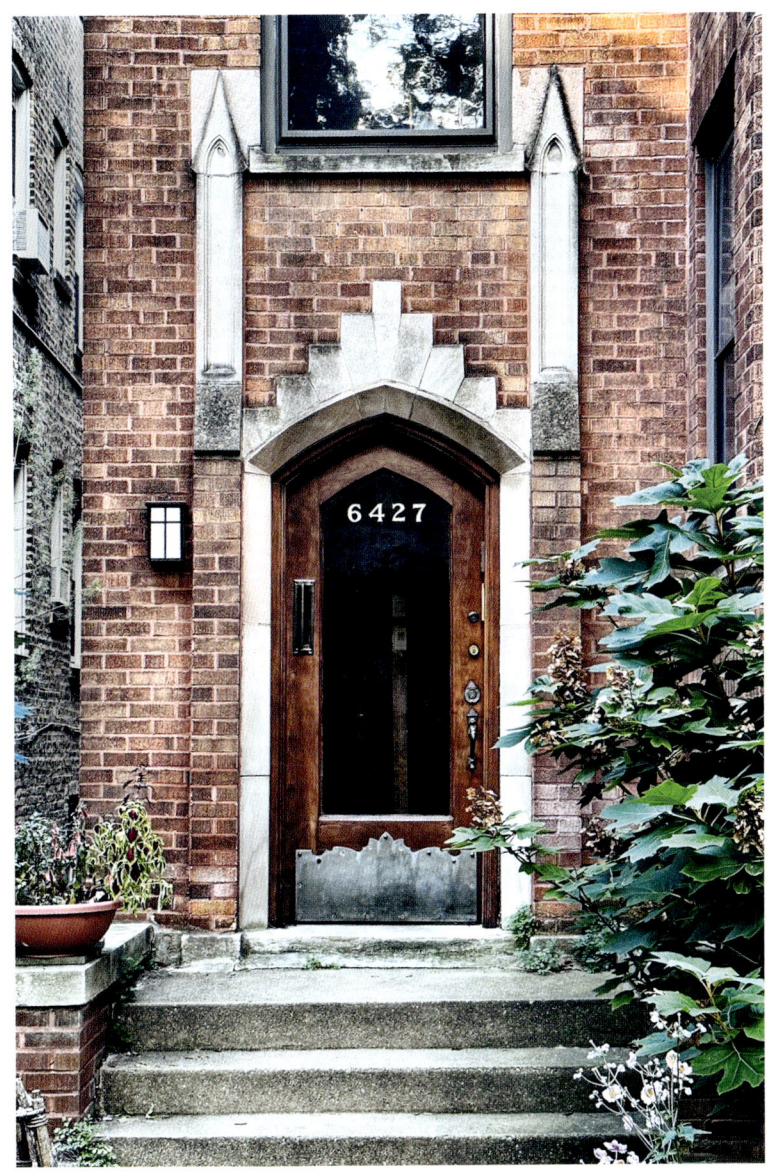

ROGERS PARK

Residential

THE MUSEUM OF SCIENCE & INDUSTRY

Architectural Style: Beaux Arts | Year: 1893

Originally built as the Palace of Fine Arts for the 1893 World's Columbian Exposition, the belle of the White City ball still stands more than a century later, with a renewed purpose.

While all of the Chicago World's Fair's dreamy neo-classical structures were temporary, the Palace of Fine Arts was also fireproof in order to safely house its priceless artworks. Instead of just painted plaster mix over wood, the original building had a brick and steel frame. Despite outlasting its neighbors, the grand façade was falling apart by the 1920s.

So Chicago did what it does best: reinvent. Sears executive Julius Rosenwald, inspired by his children's excitement at an interactive museum exhibit in Munich, decided to bring that experience to his hometown of Chicago. Beginning in 1926 and with Rosenwald's financial backing, the building's exterior was reconstructed in limestone and reopened in 1933 as the Museum of Science and Industry.

A true example of Beaux Arts style, the museum is organized in a perfectly symmetrical cross and decorated with classical adornments inspired by ancient Greek and Roman structures. And you can't miss the bronze-paneled doors. 14 bas-relief squares represent different fields of science, including mathematics, physics, medicine, and architecture. Its large metal doors invite visitors to step into a modern world of discovery and progress.

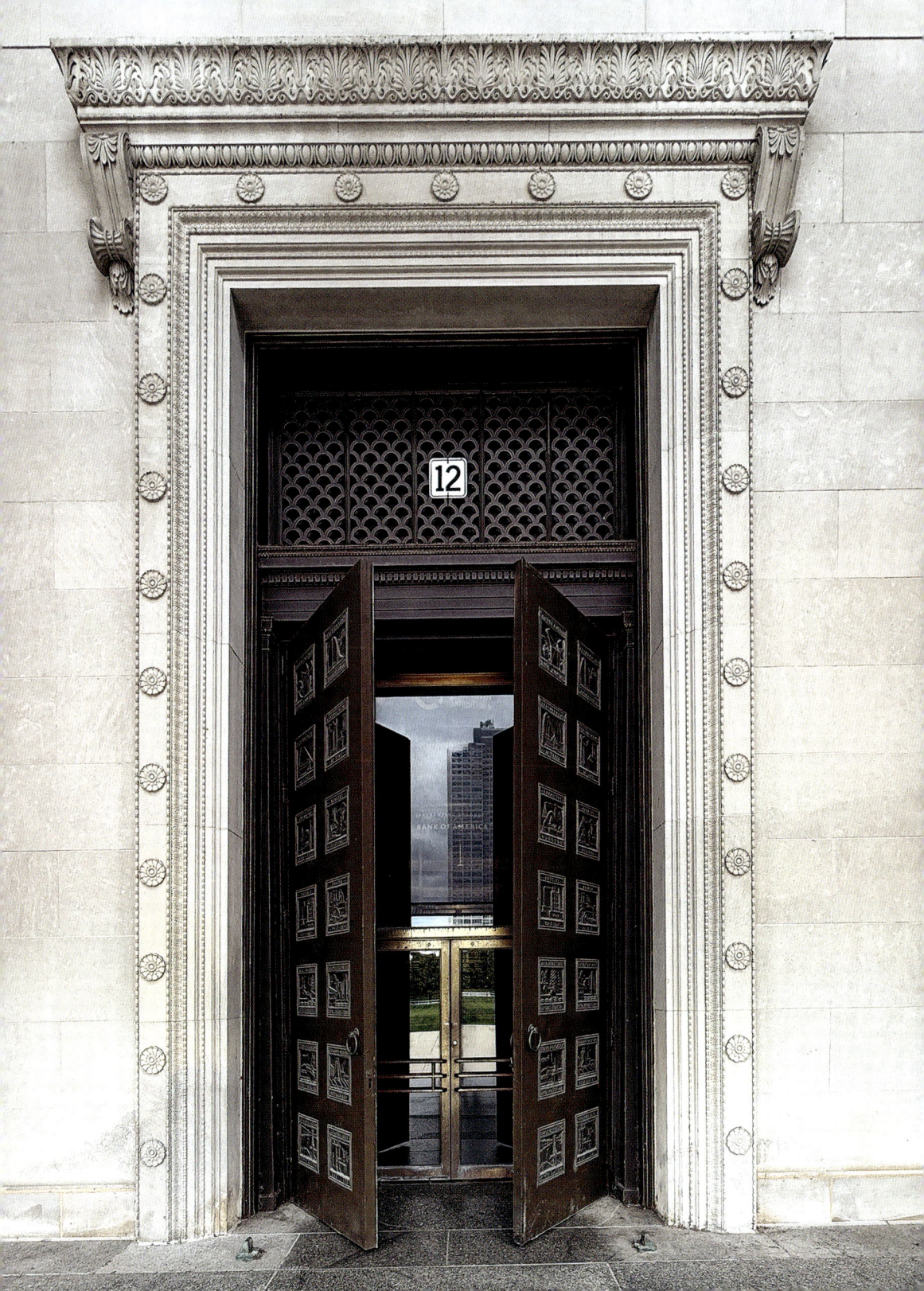

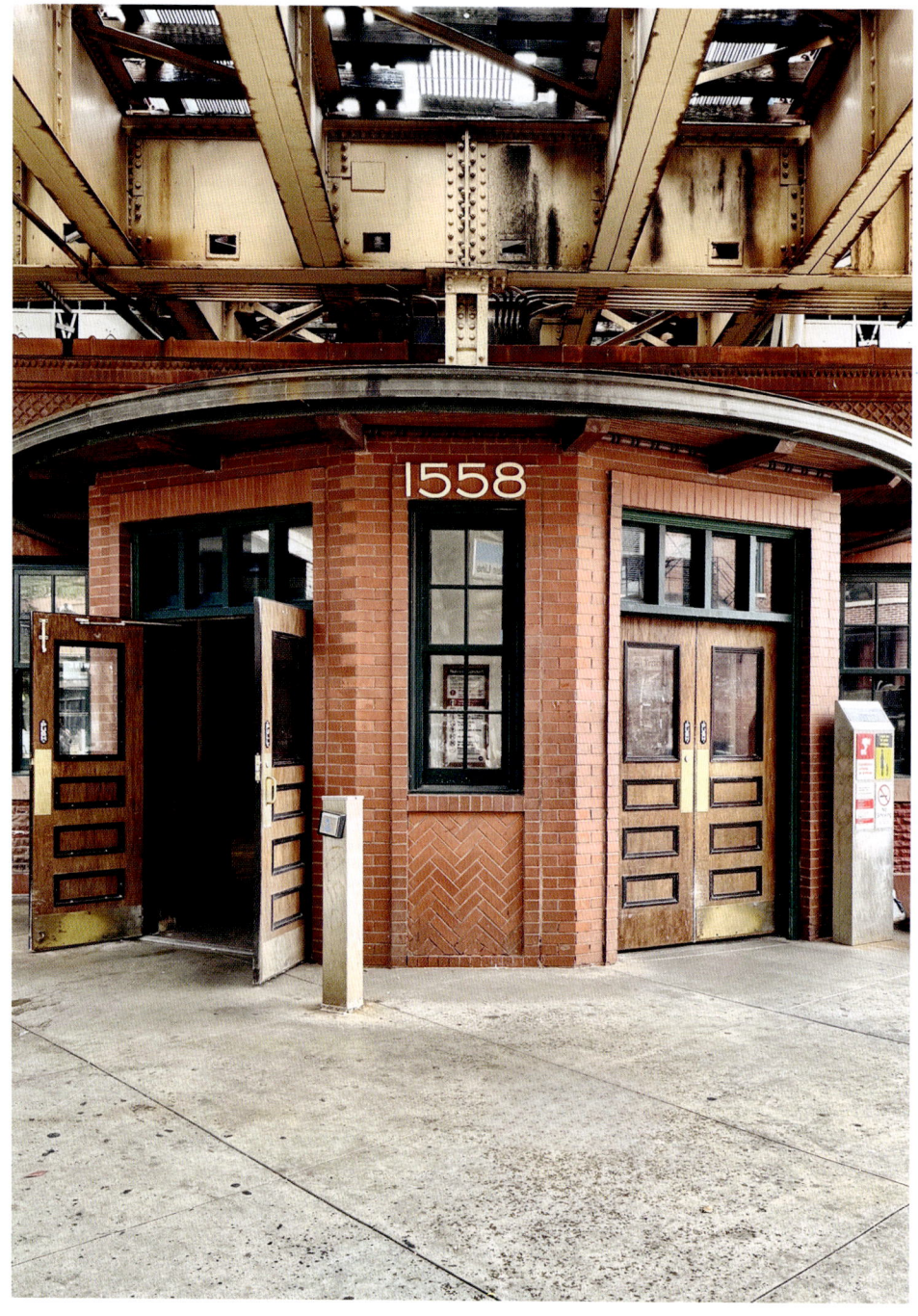

WICKER PARK

Damen Blue Line L Station

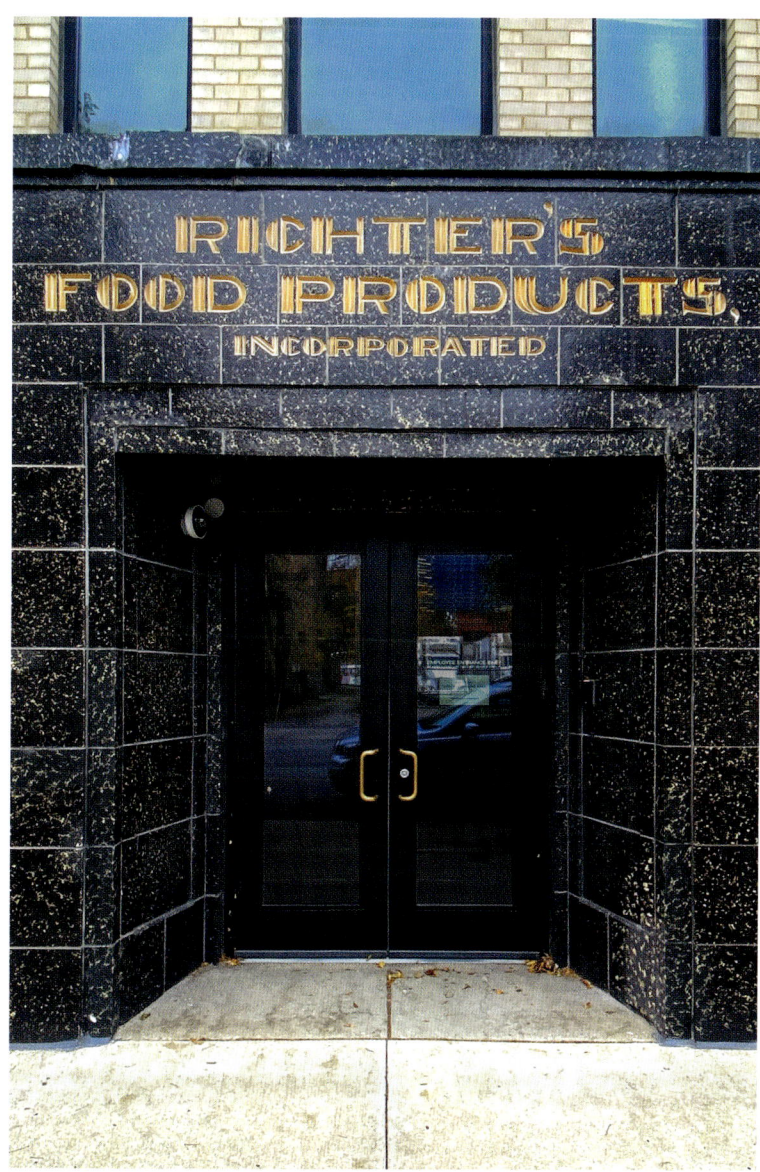

WEST LOOP

Former Richter's Food Products

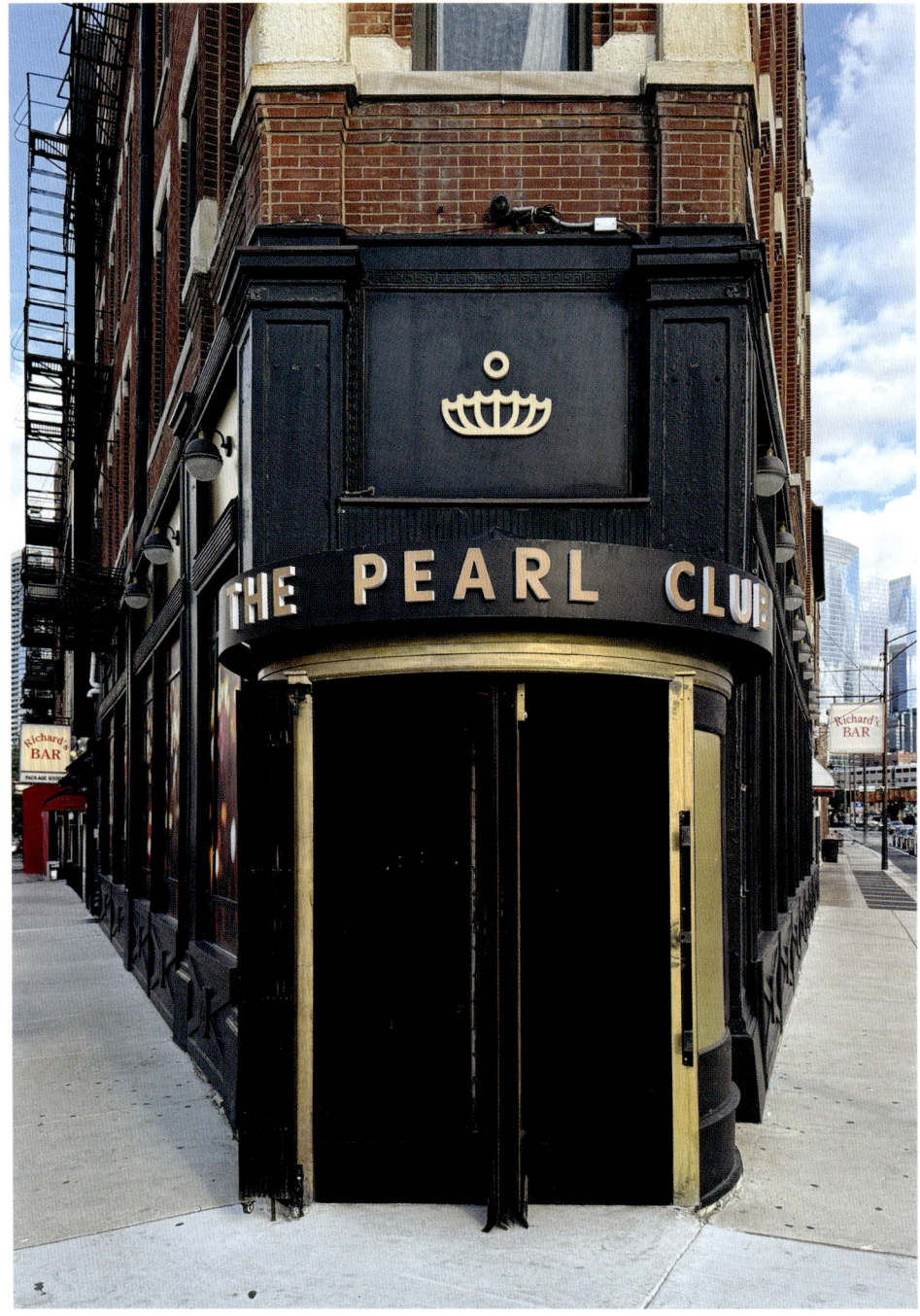

WEST TOWN

Cocktail Bar

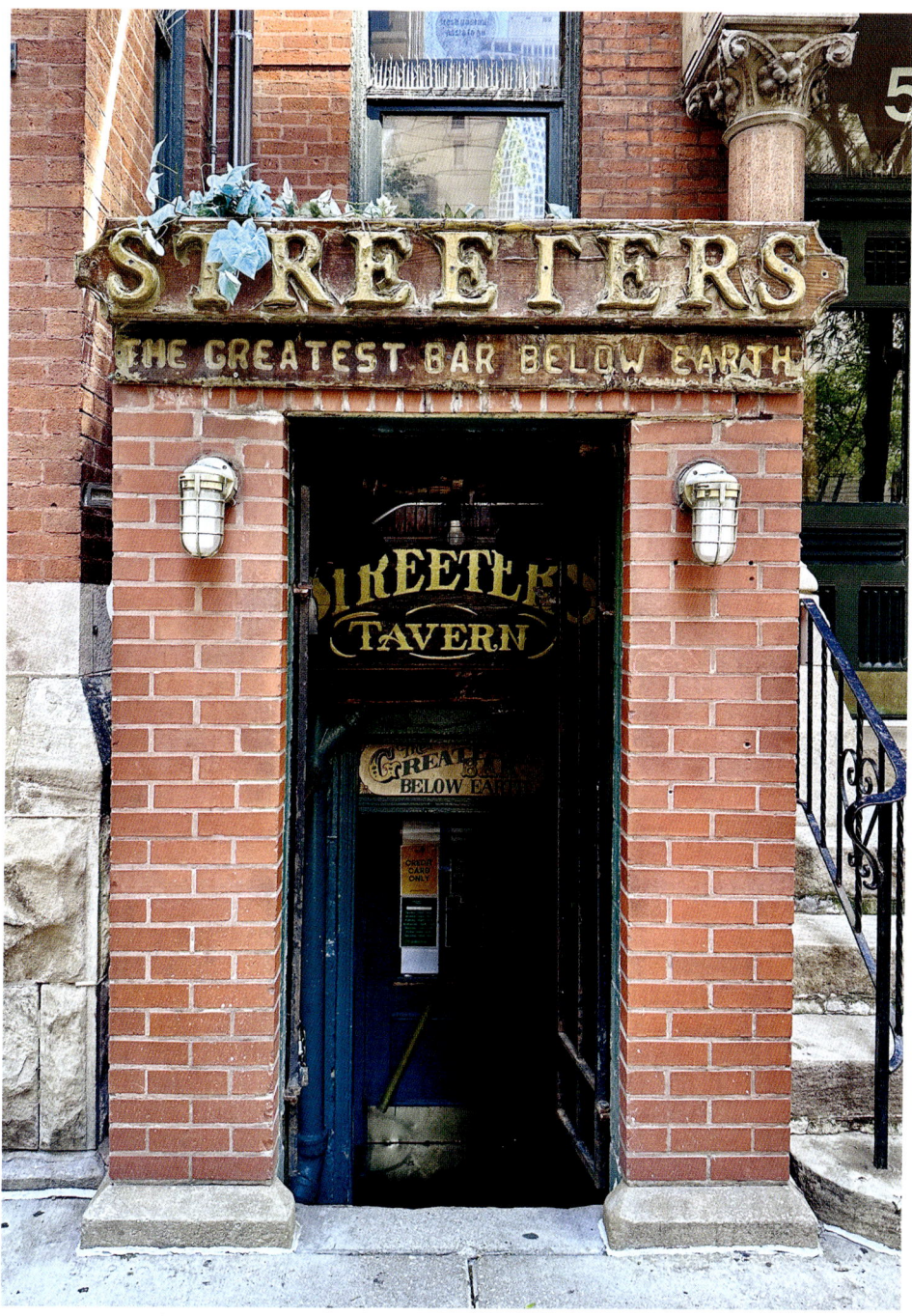

NEAR NORTH

Bar

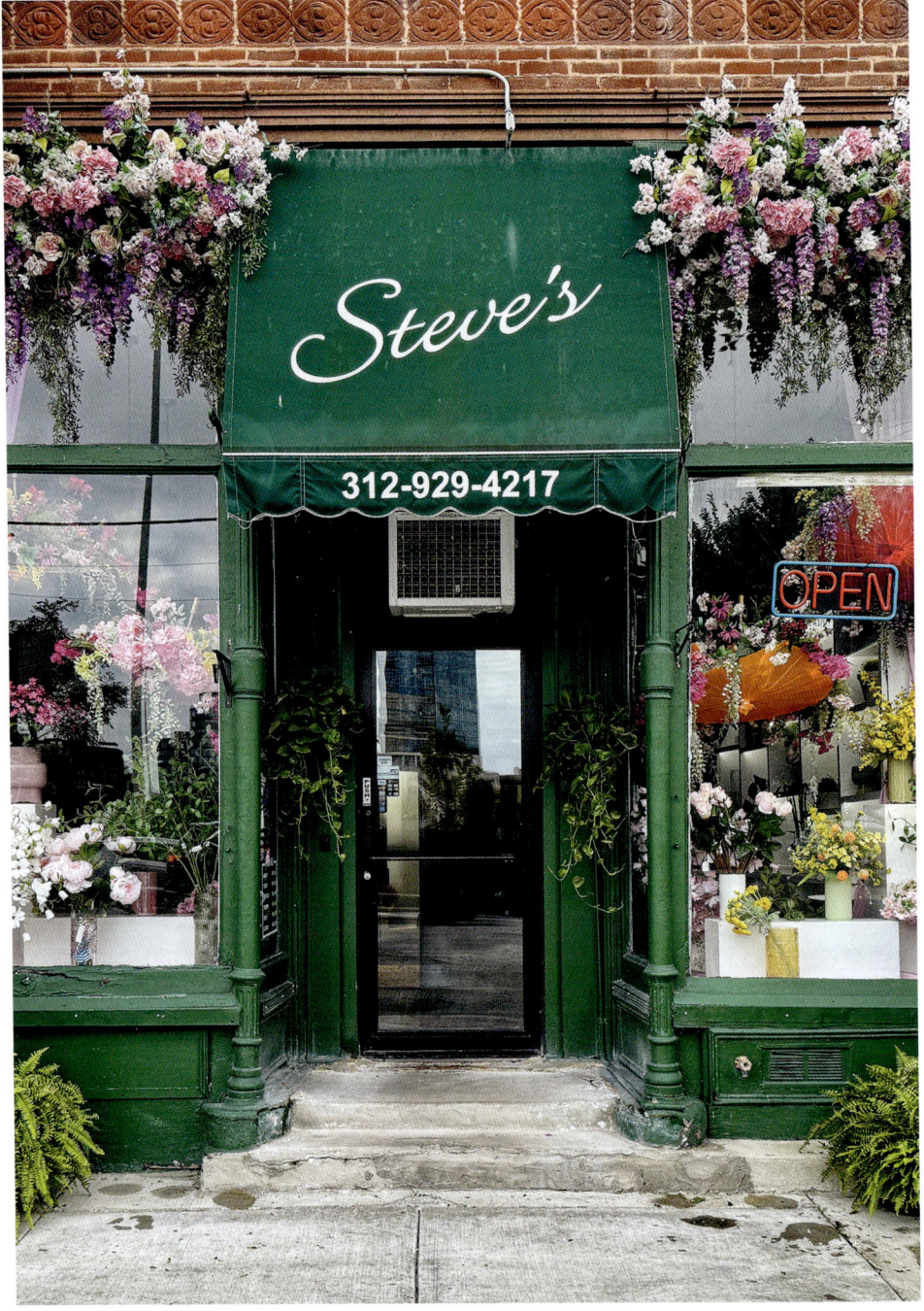

WEST TOWN

Flower Shop

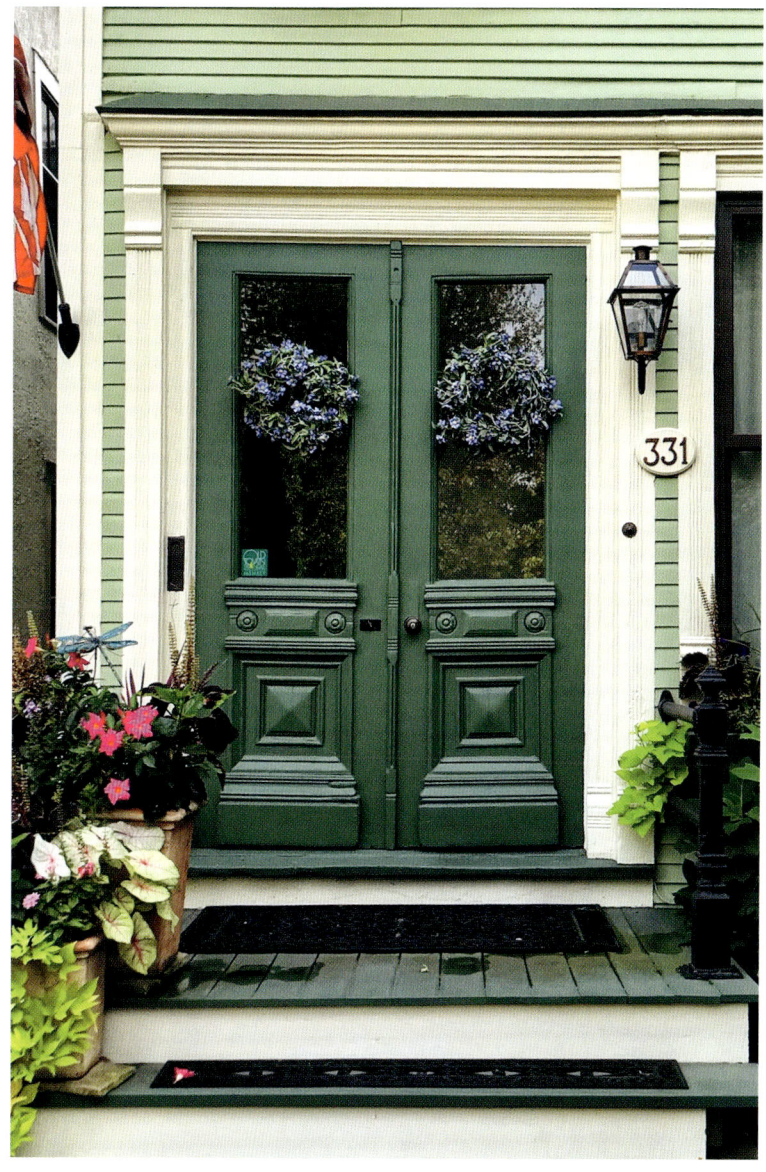

OLD TOWN

Residential

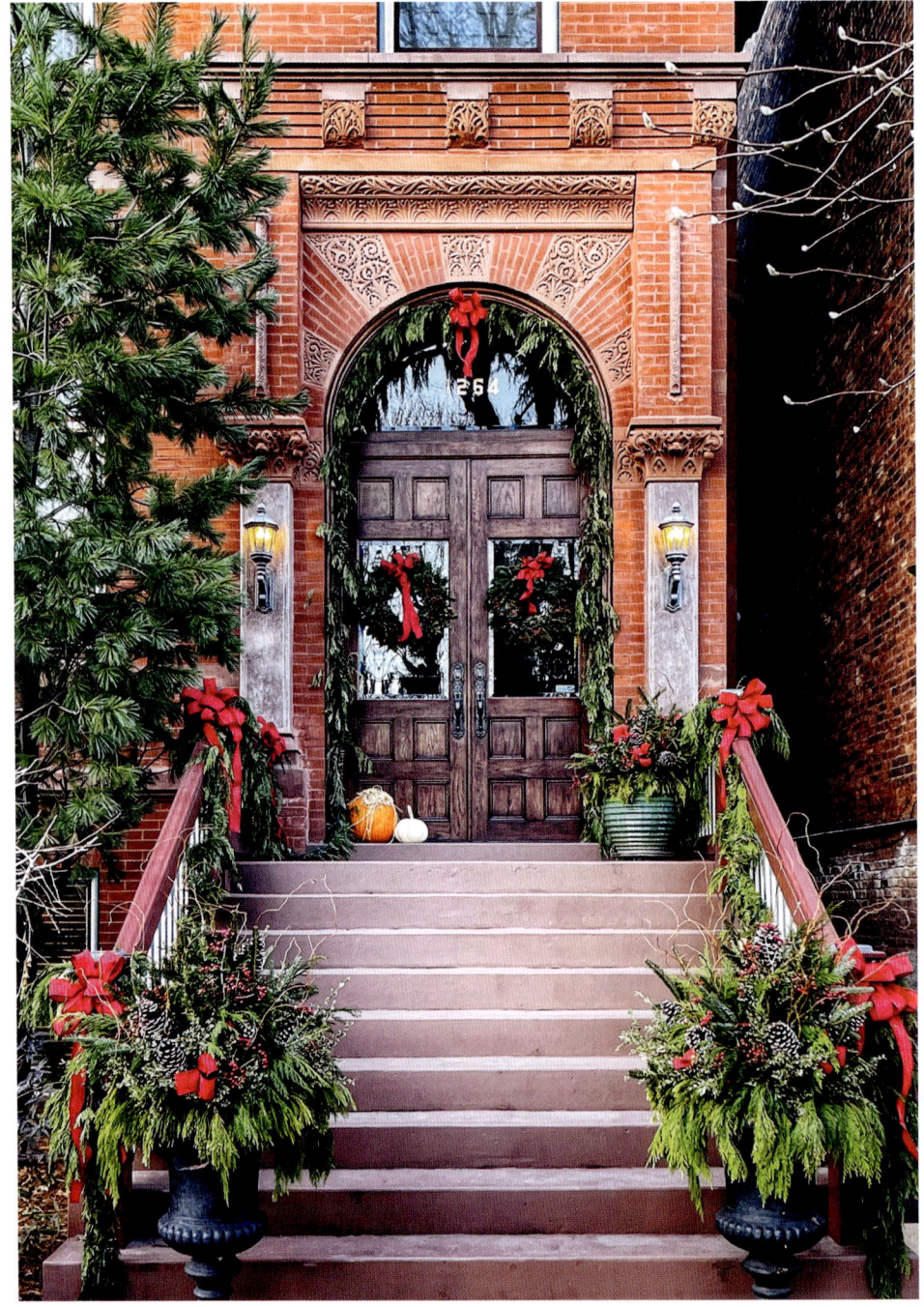

LITTLE ITALY

Residential

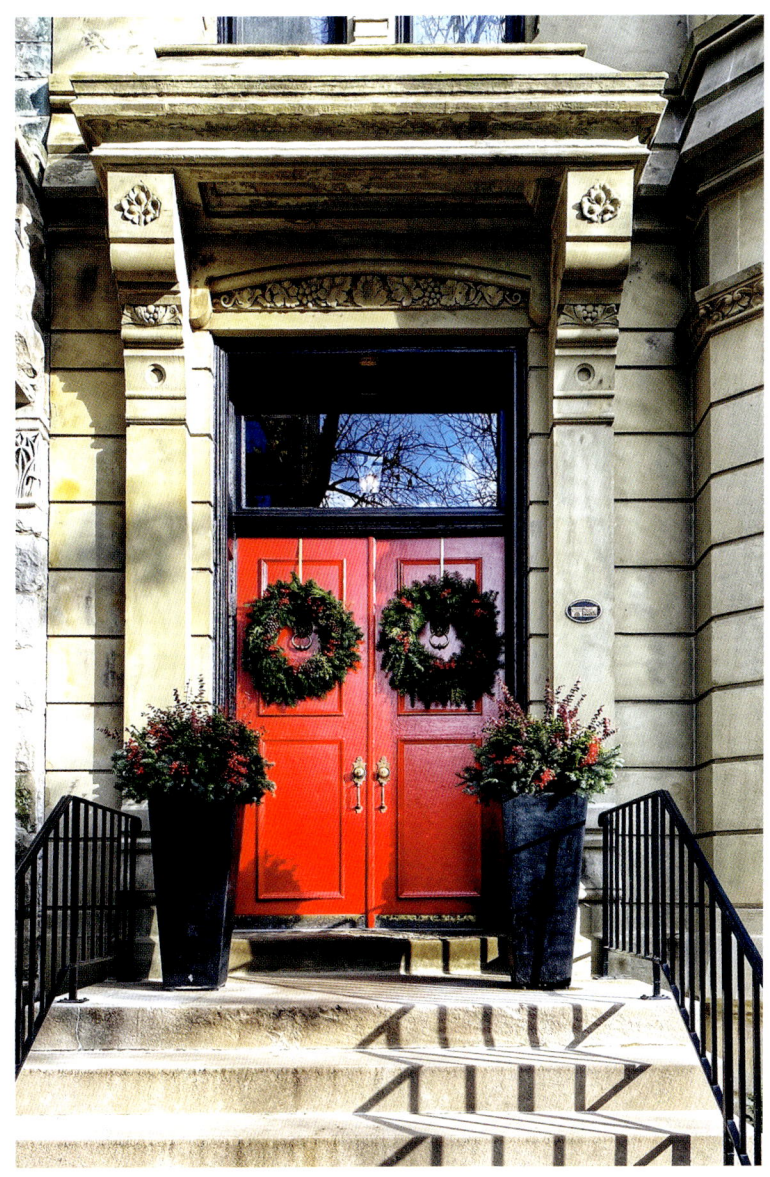

GOLD COAST

Residential

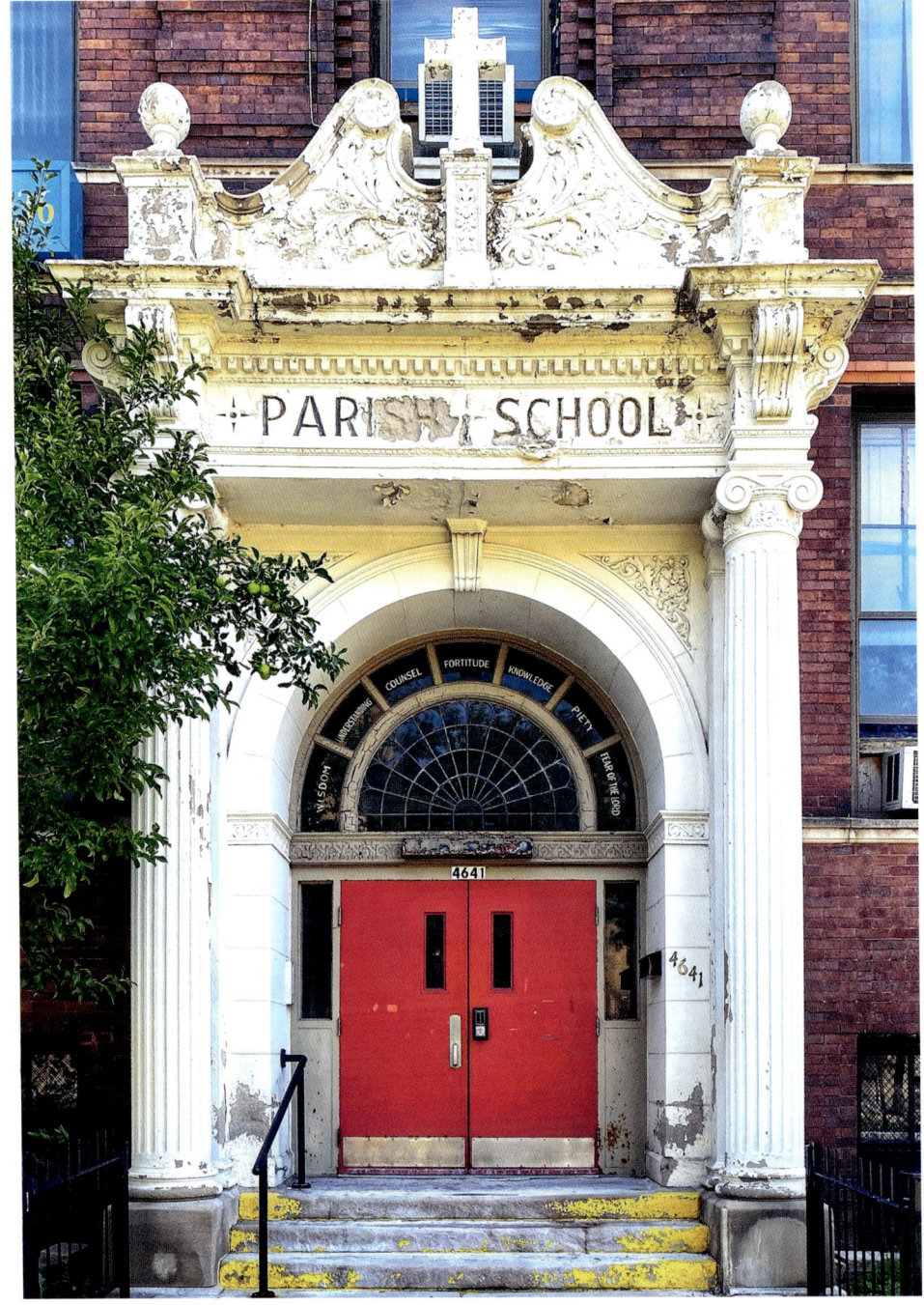

RAVENSWOOD

Former Our Lady of Lourdes School

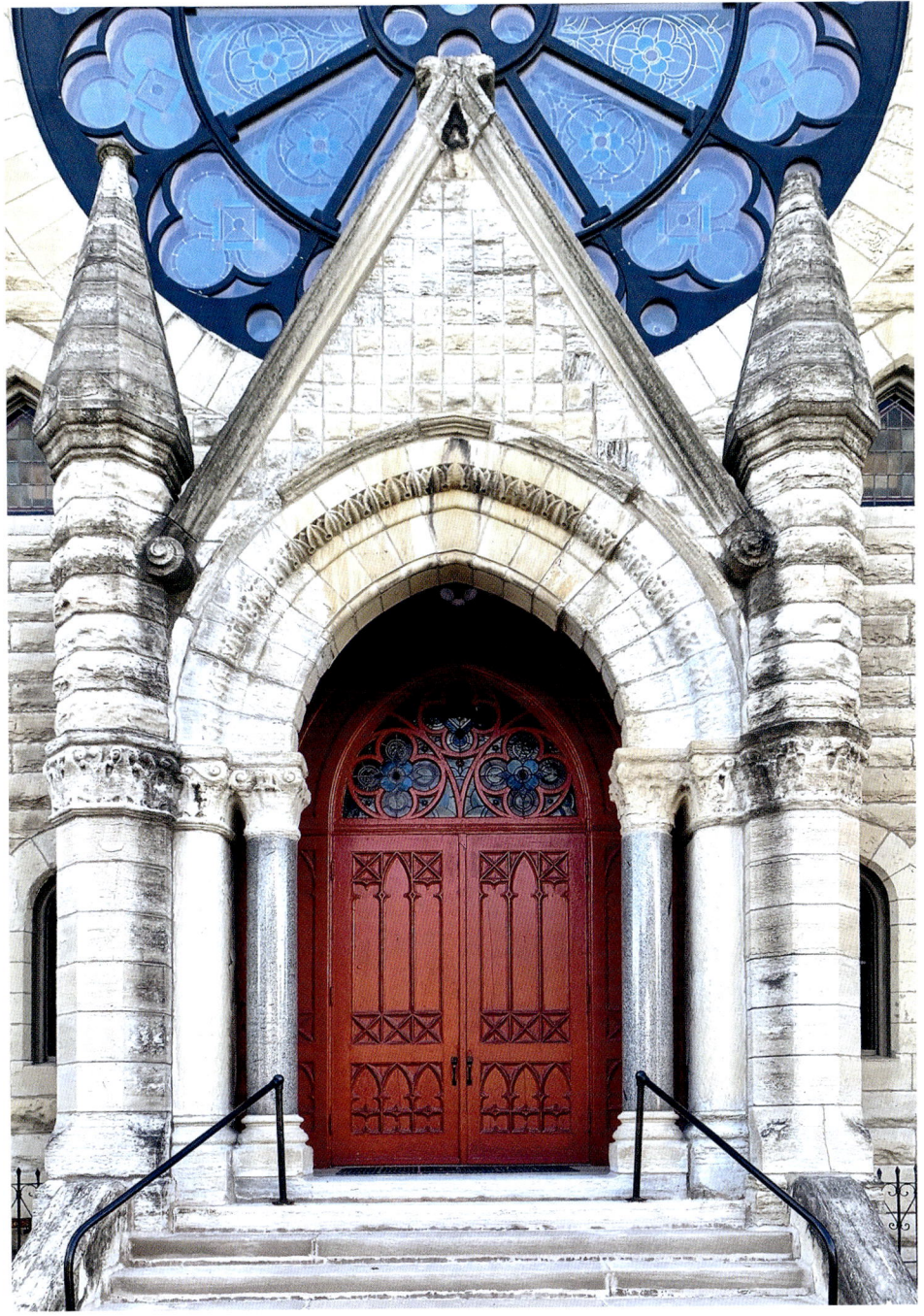

LITTLE ITALY

First Immanuel Lutheran Church of Chicago

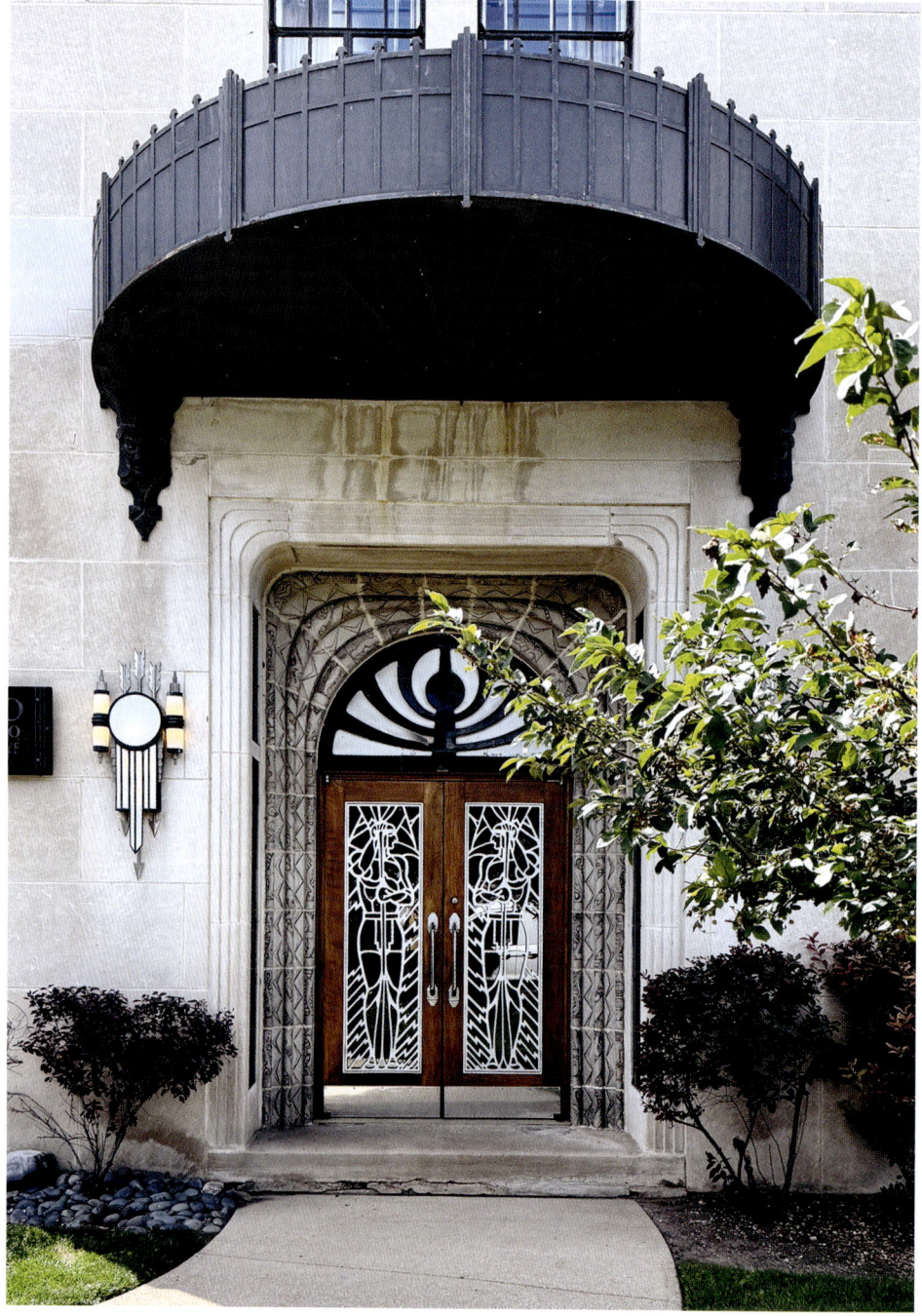

KENWOOD

Residential

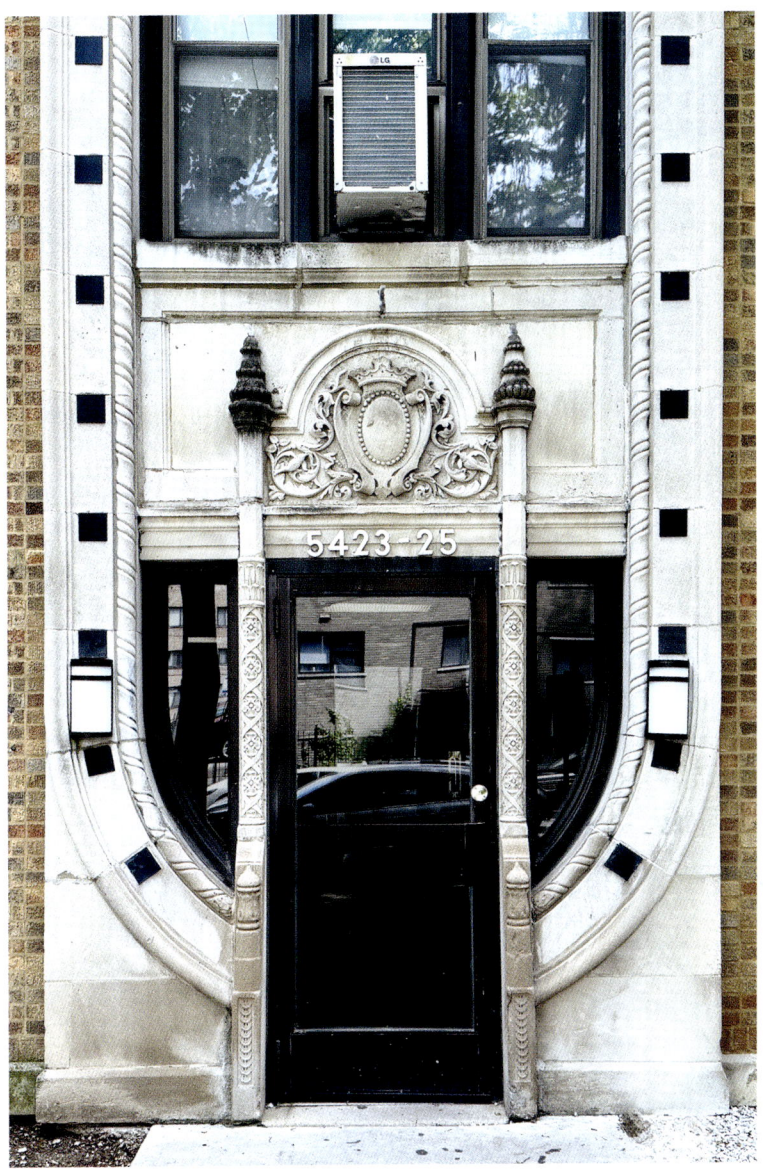

EDGEWATER

Residential

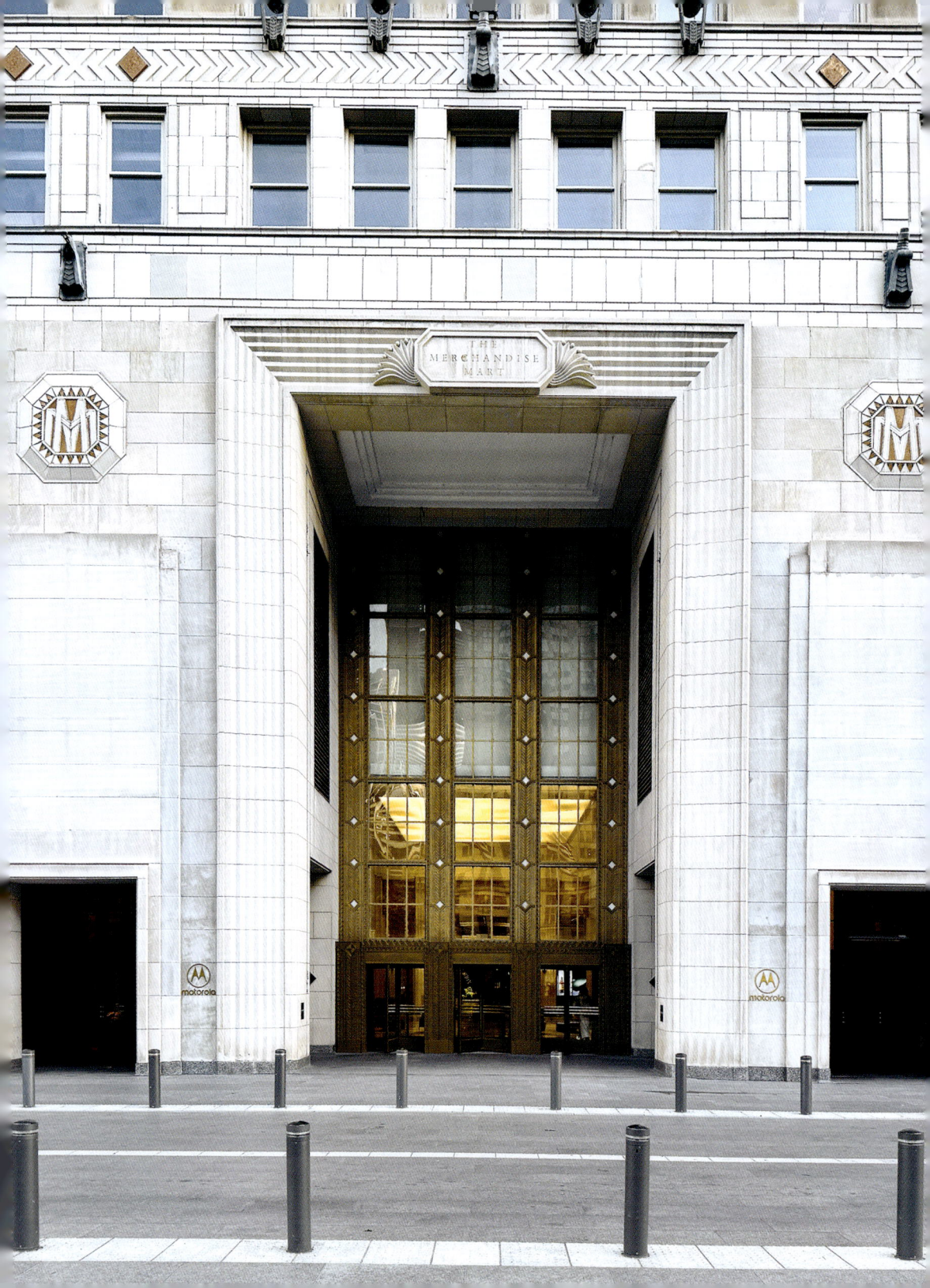

THE MERCHANDISE MART

Architectural Style: Art Deco | Year: 1930

Occupying more than two city blocks along the Chicago River, the Merchandise Mart was the world's largest building at the time of its completion in 1930. With more than four million square feet of floor space, the building was originally developed by Marshall Field & Co. as a marketplace for retailers to purchase their stock.

Designed by architect Alfred P. Shaw to be a "city within a city," this Art Deco mammoth reflected the optimism of the 1920s. The building's steel-framed exterior is clad in limestone, terracotta, and bronze, and its art deco stylings reflect many of the style's popular motifs. A logo featuring interlocked initials of the Merchandise Mart can be seen throughout the building, as well as above the building's doorways.

Inside the Mart's lobby, 17 murals painted by Jules Guérin illustrate commerce throughout the world, including the countries of origin for items sold in the building. The lobby is defined by eight square marble piers with interior storefronts in embossed bronze trim. The terrazzo floor is a pattern of squares and stripes bordered by overscaled chevrons inlaid with the same initial logo seen throughout the building.

In 1953, when his family owned the building, Joseph Kennedy commissioned eight large-scale bronze busts to commemorate outstanding American merchants, including Marshall Field and Aaron Montgomery Ward. These busts rest on white pedestals lining the riverfront and face north towards the Mart's gold front door.

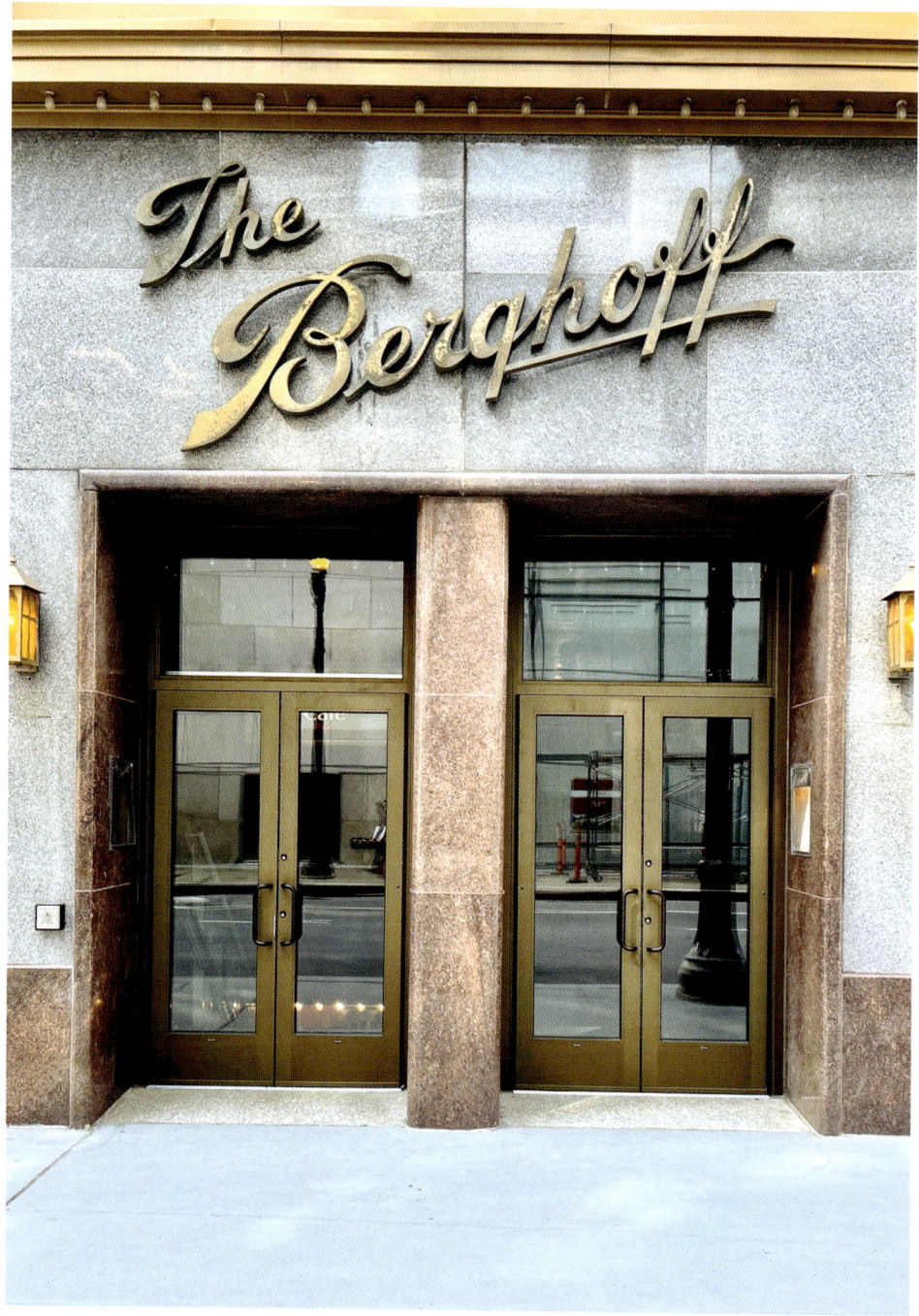

THE LOOP

The Berghoff Restaurant

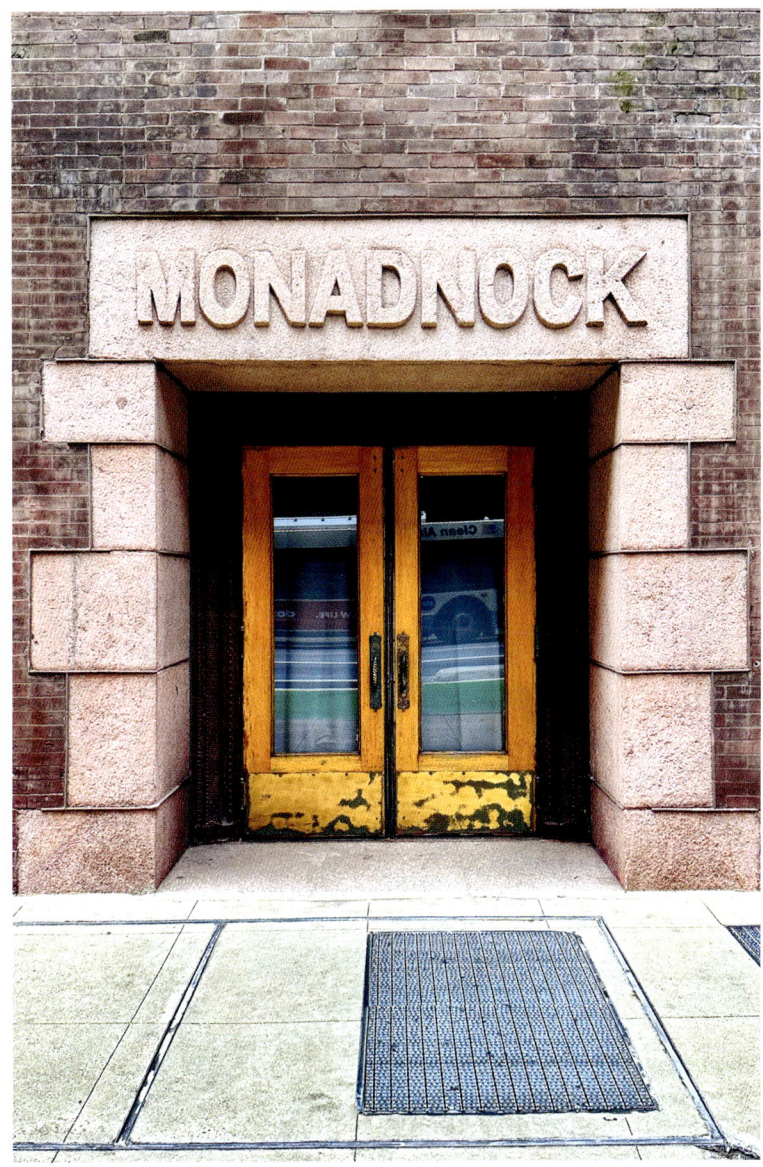

THE LOOP

The Monadnock Building

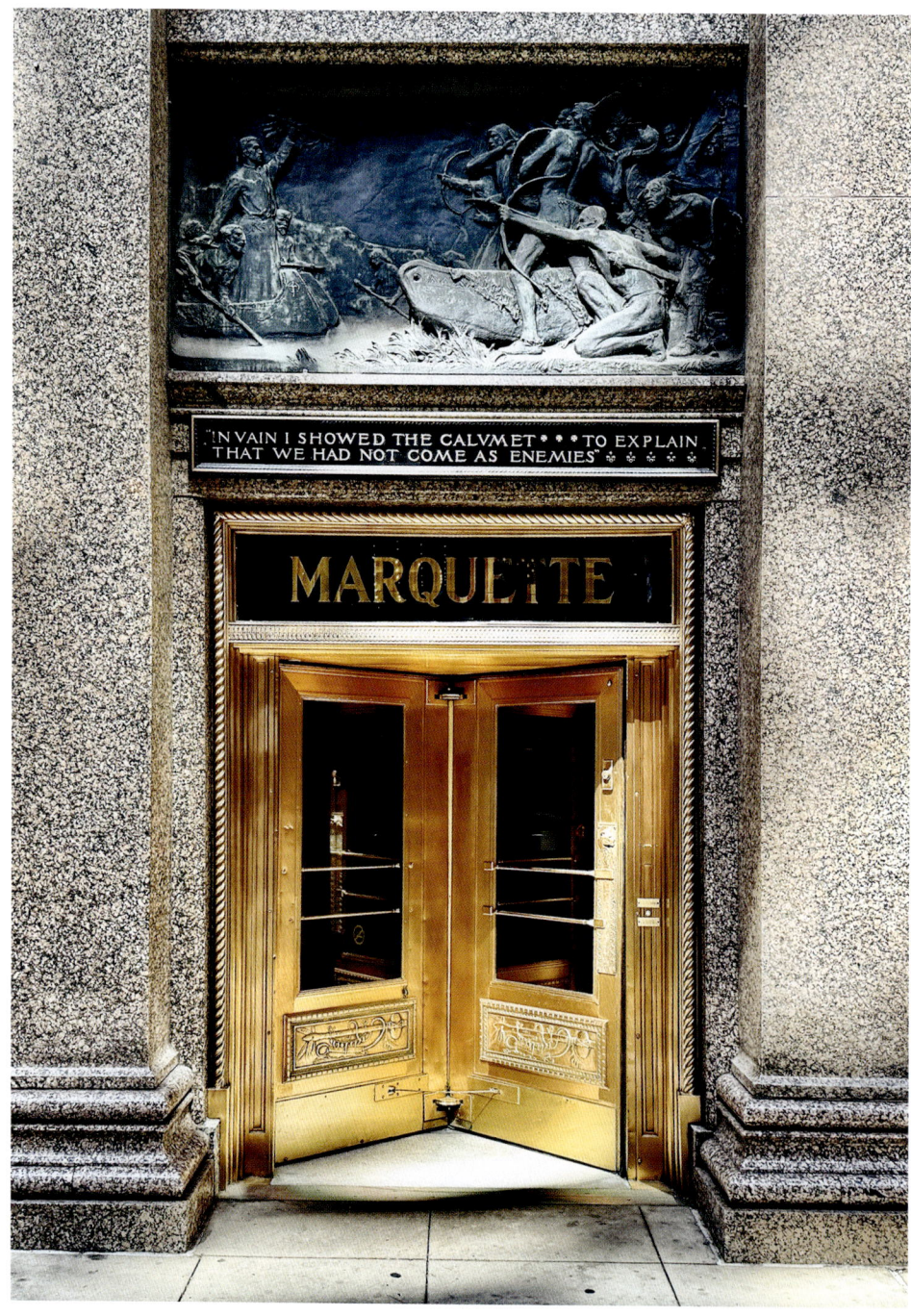

THE LOOP

Marquette Building

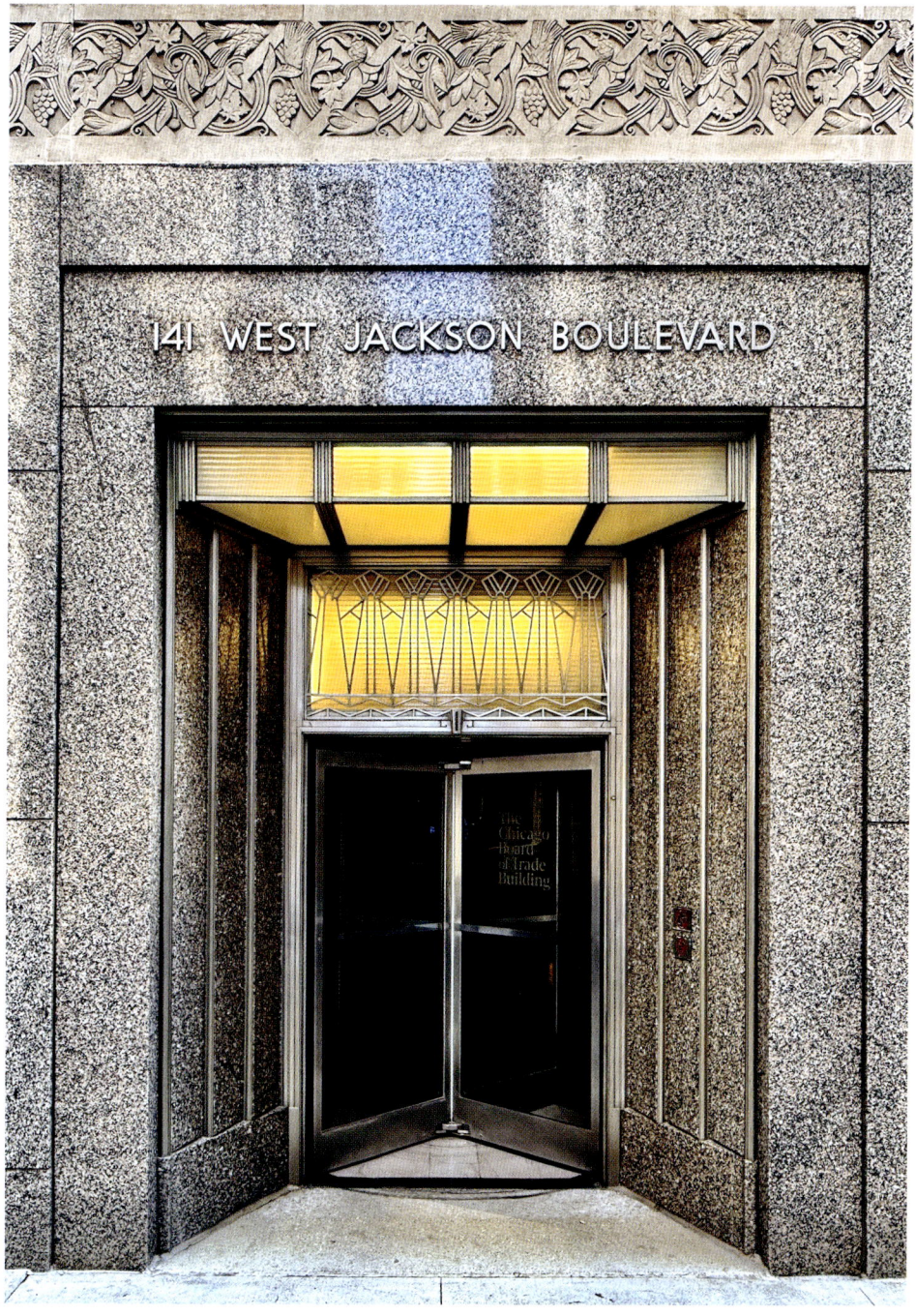

THE LOOP

Chicago Board of Trade Building

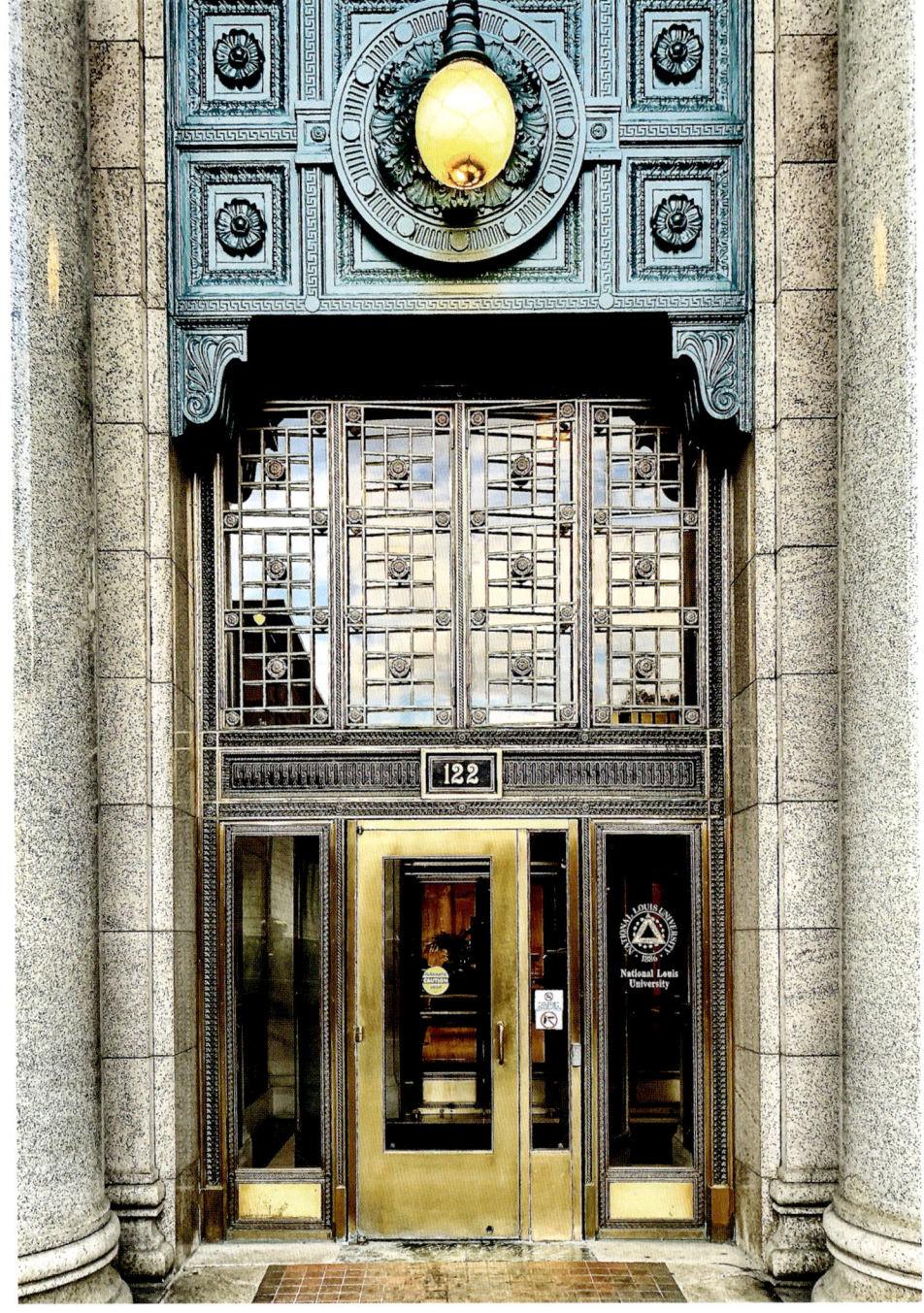

THE LOOP

Peoples Gas Building

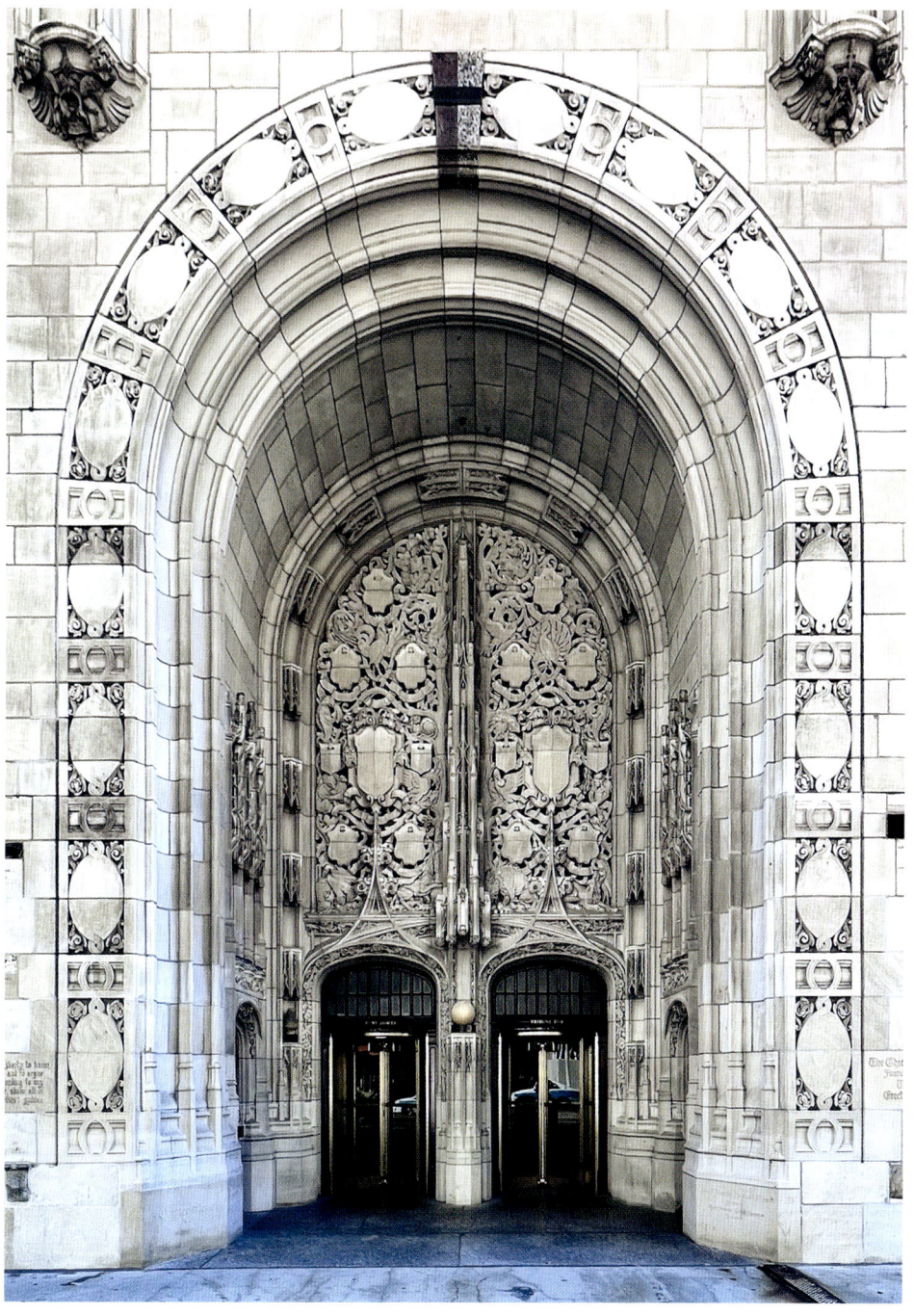

STREETERVILLE

Tribune Tower

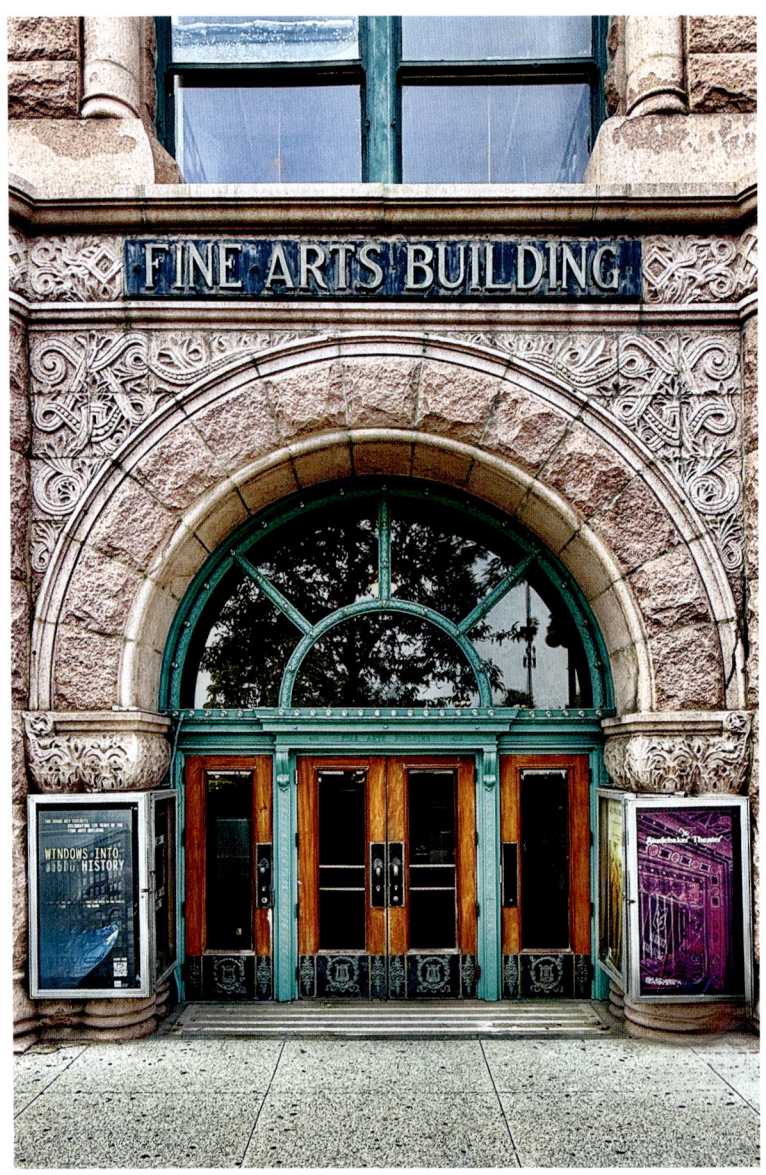

THE LOOP

Fine Arts Building

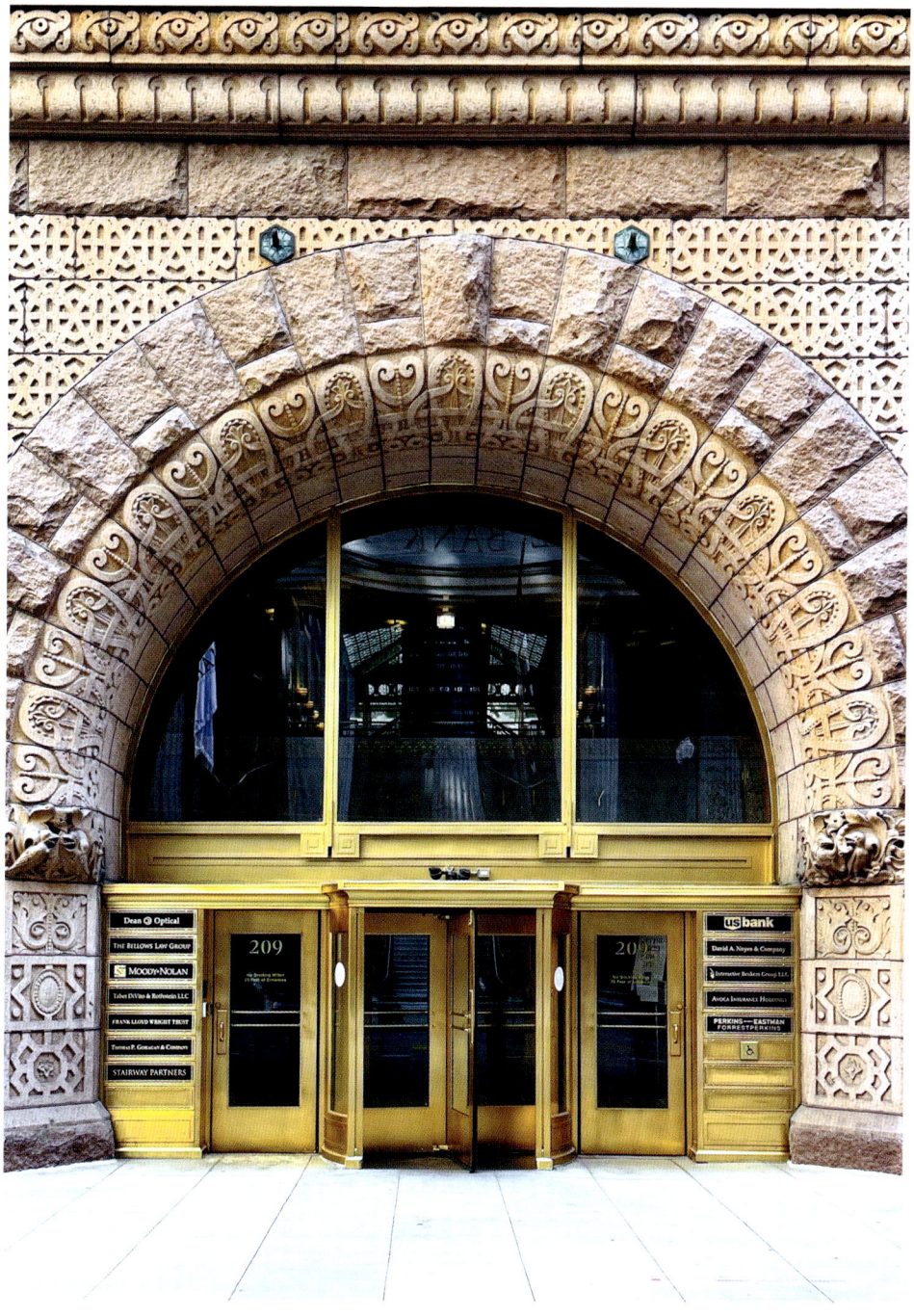

THE LOOP

The Rookery

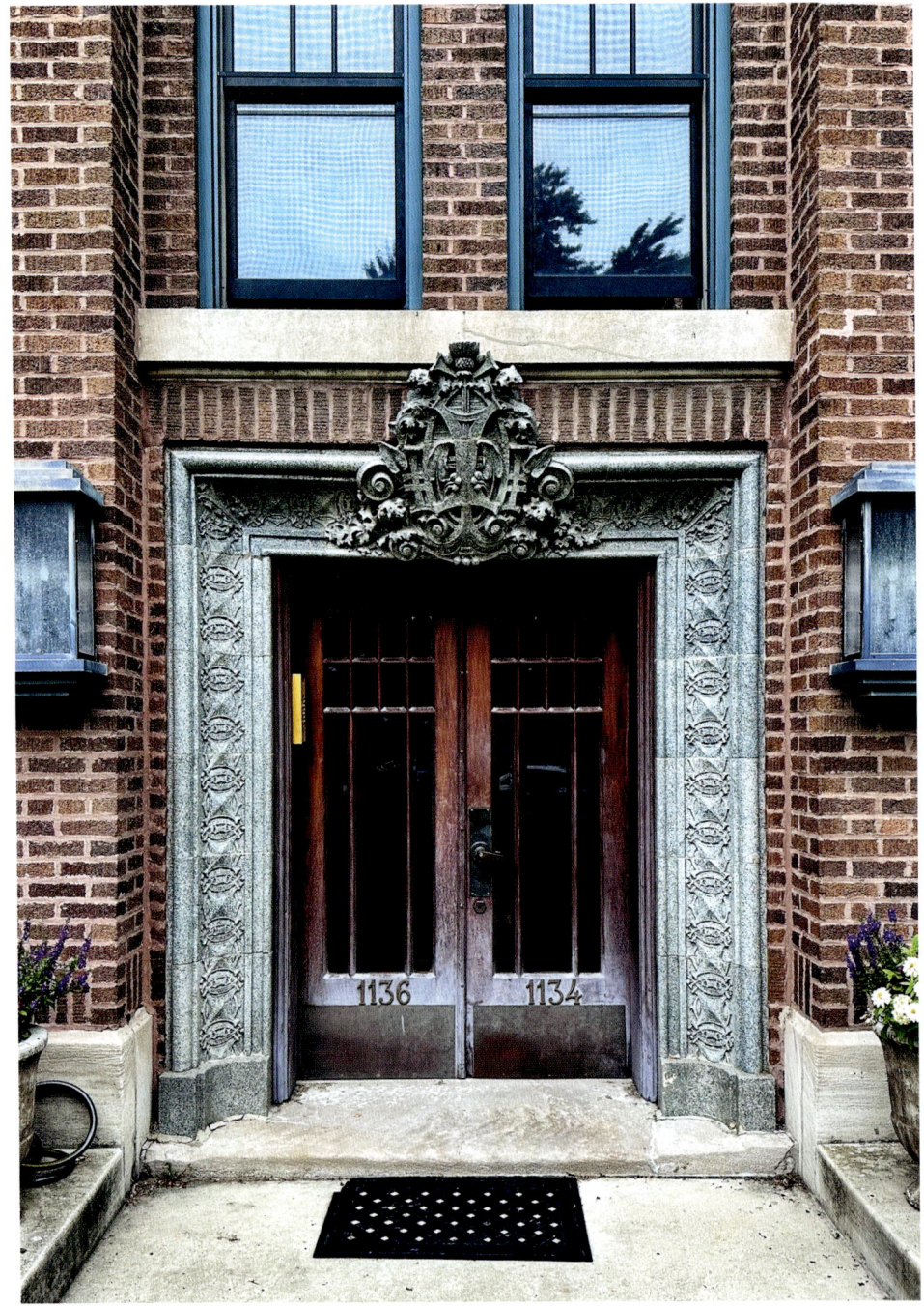

ROGERS PARK

Residential

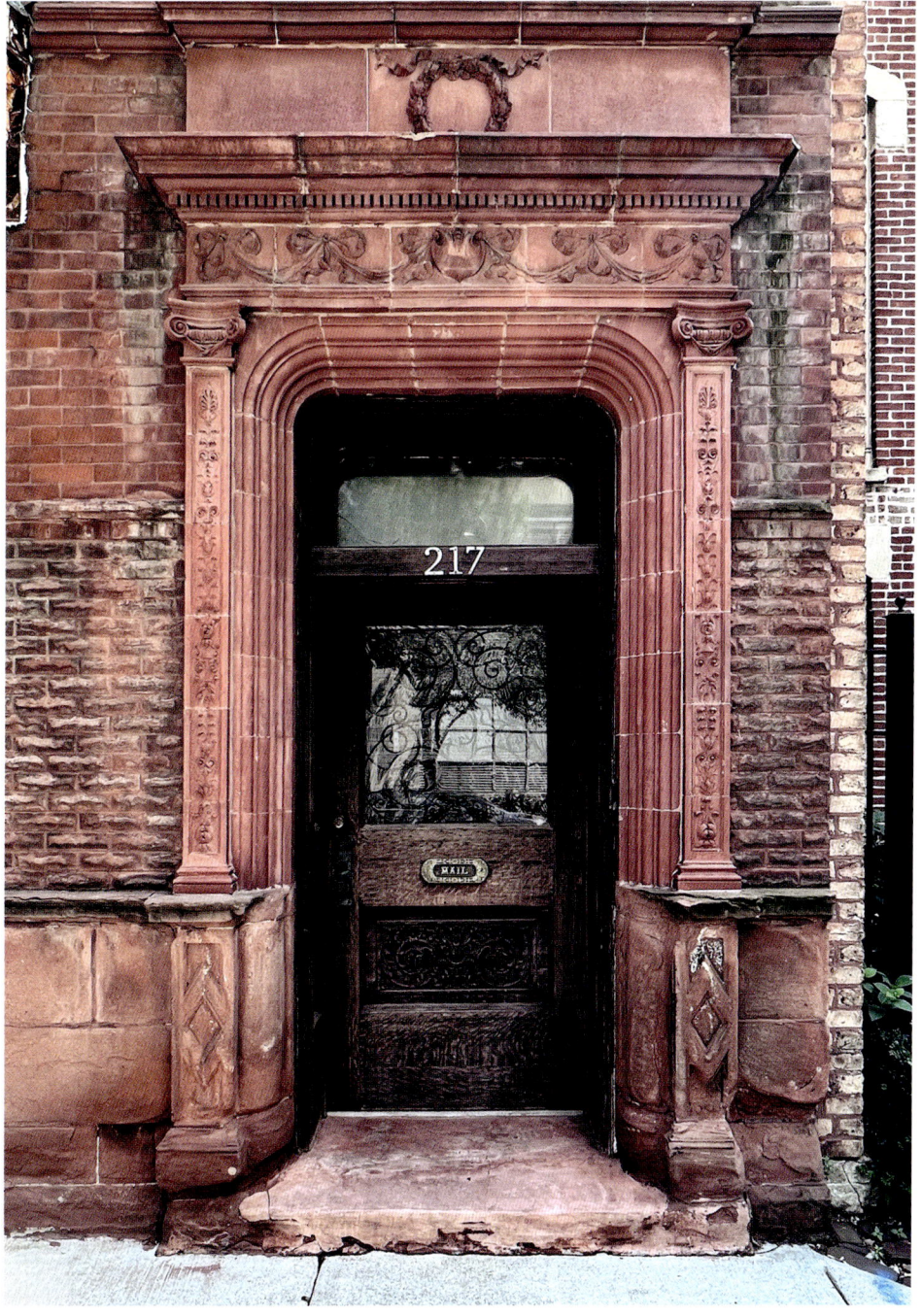

SOUTH LOOP

Residential

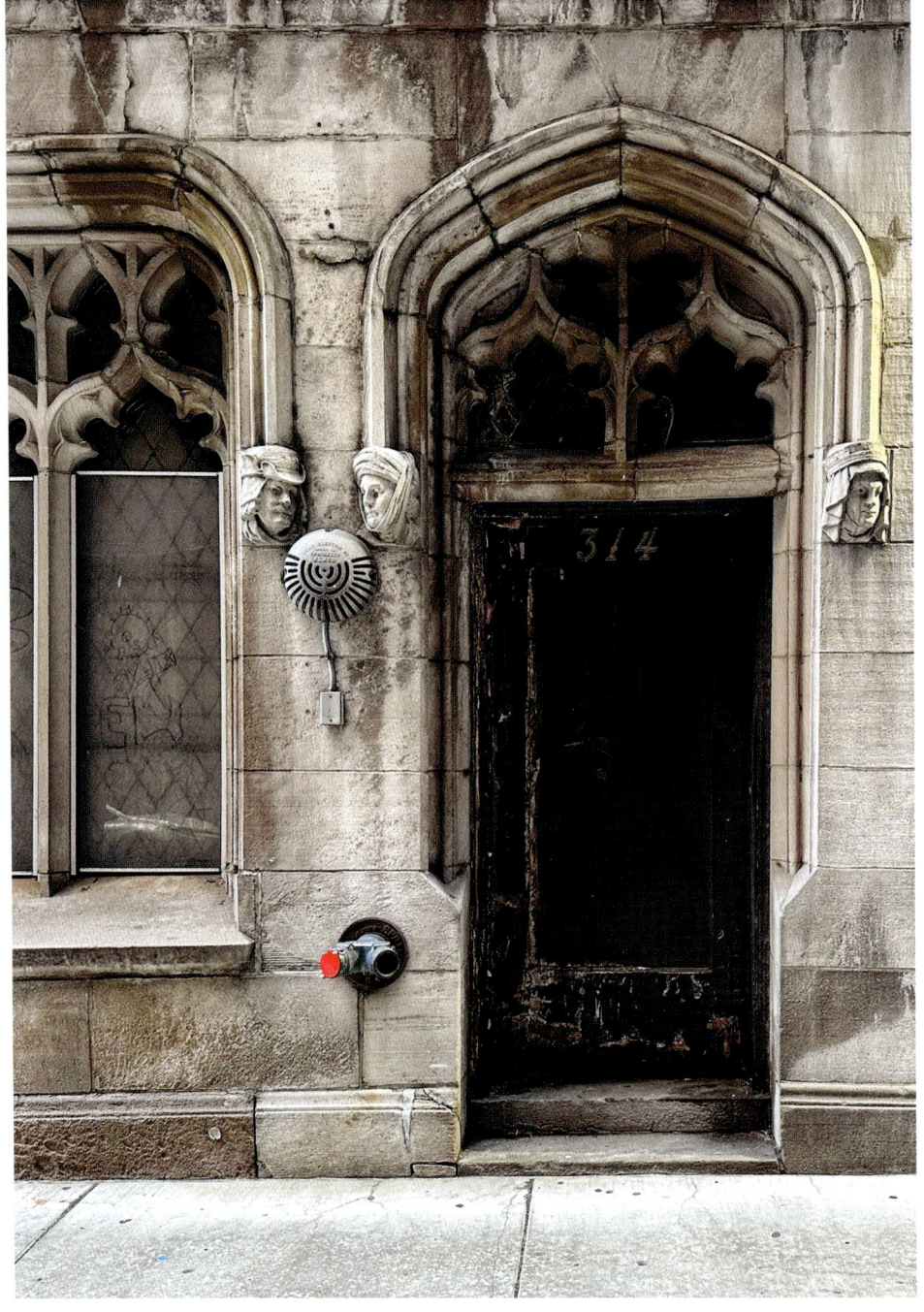

THE LOOP

Chicago Engineers Building

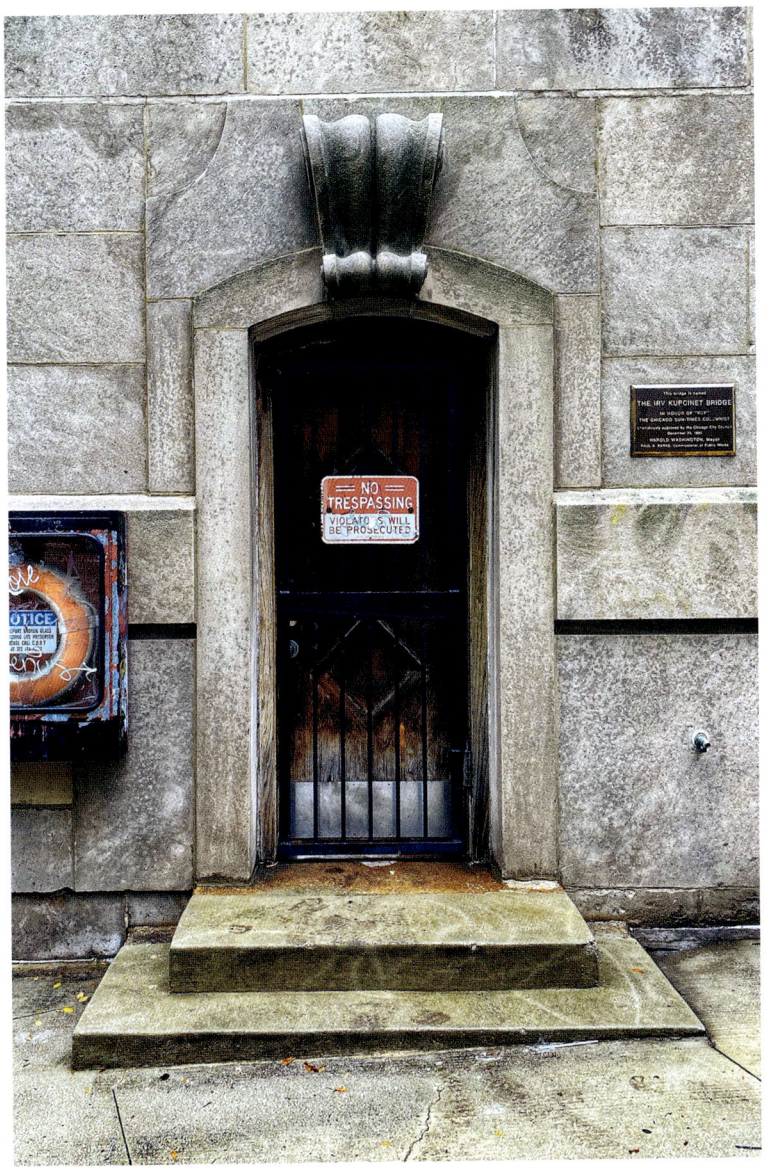

RIVER NORTH

Wabash Avenue Bridge Tower

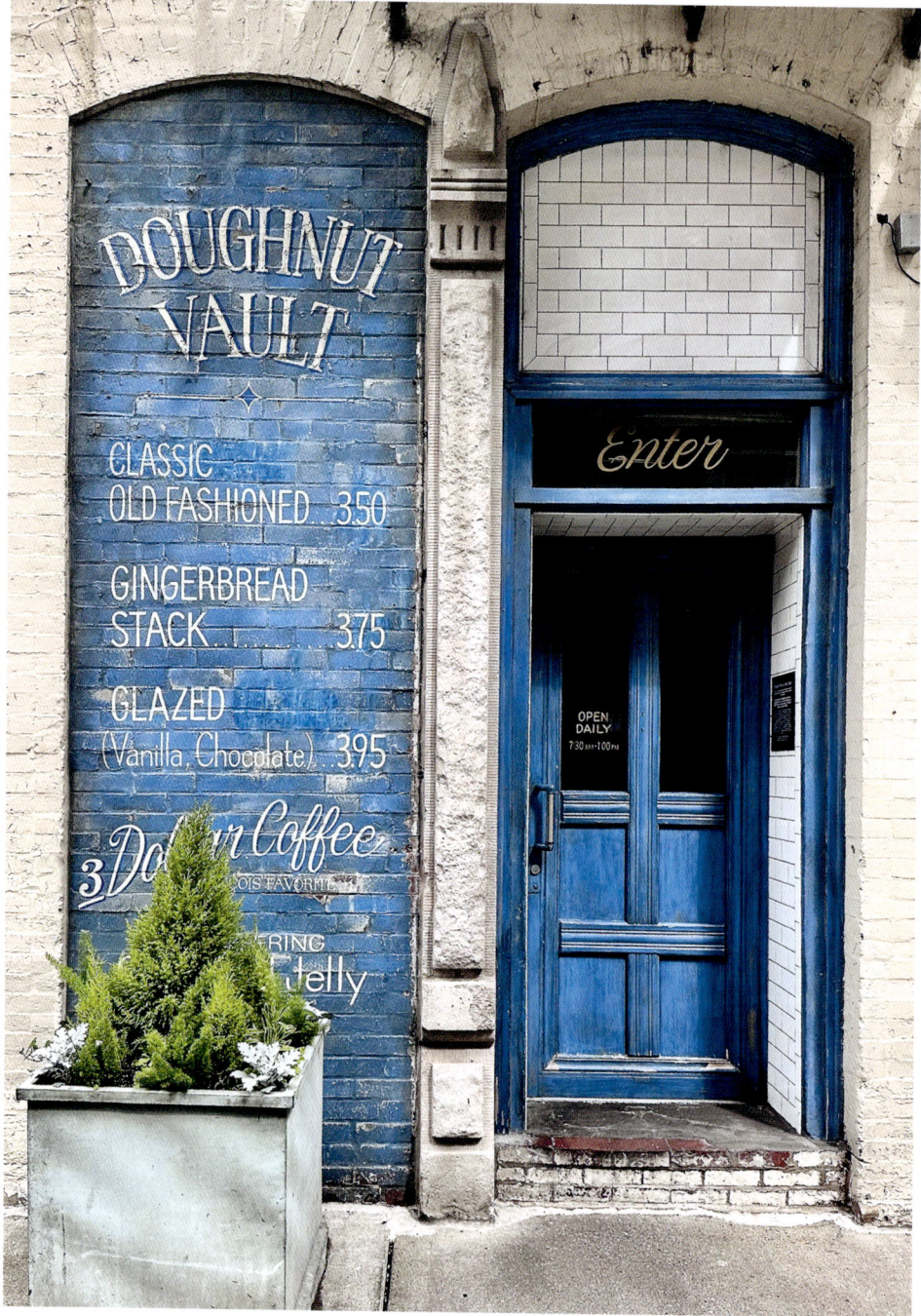

RIVER NORTH

Bakery

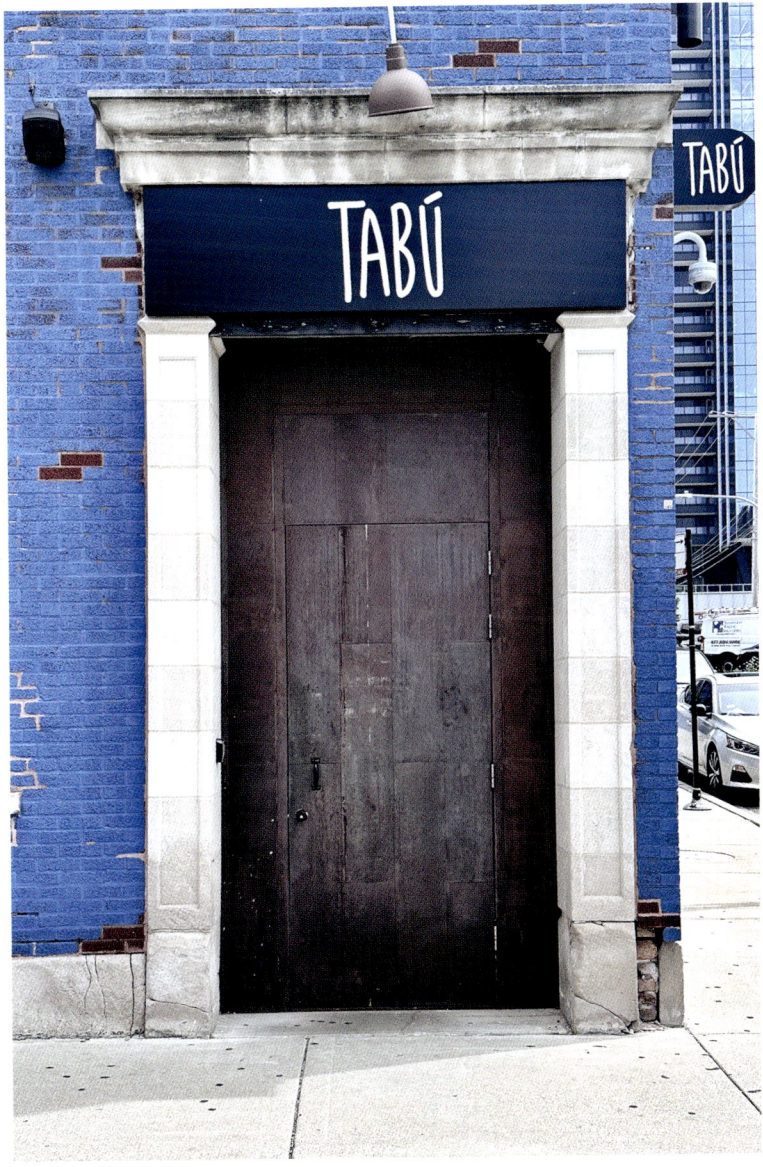

WEST TOWN

Restaurant

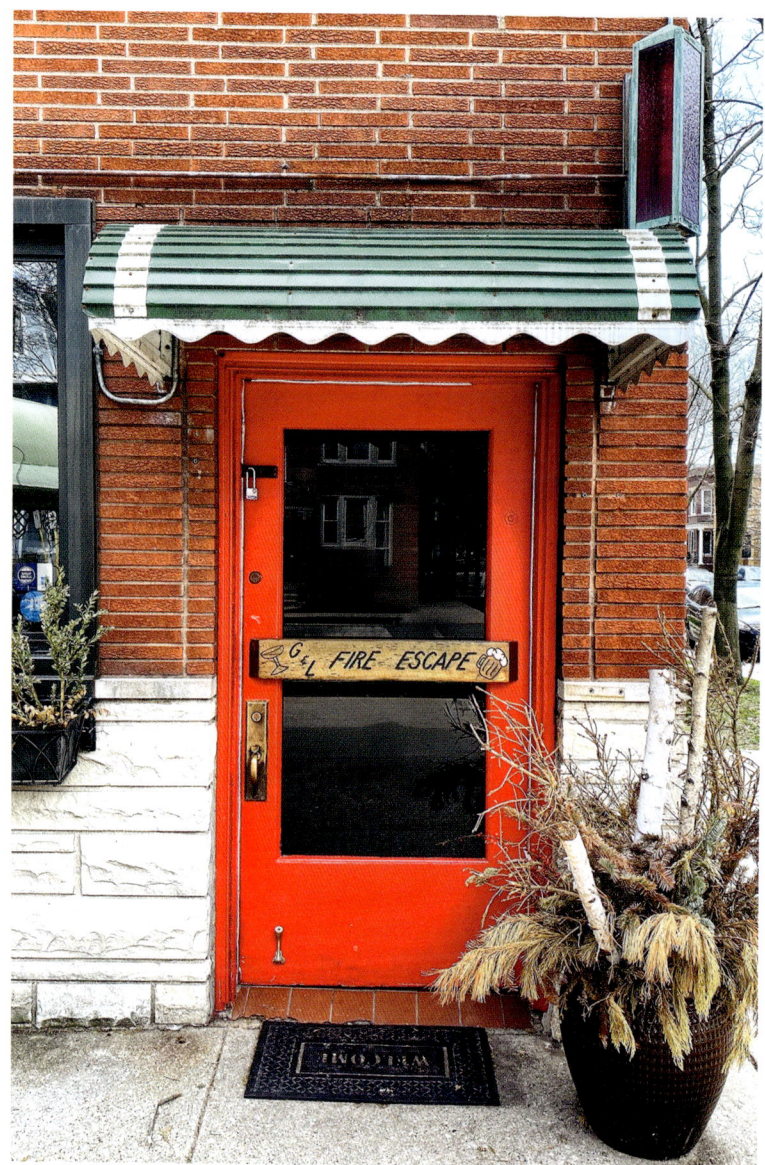

NORTH CENTER

Tavern

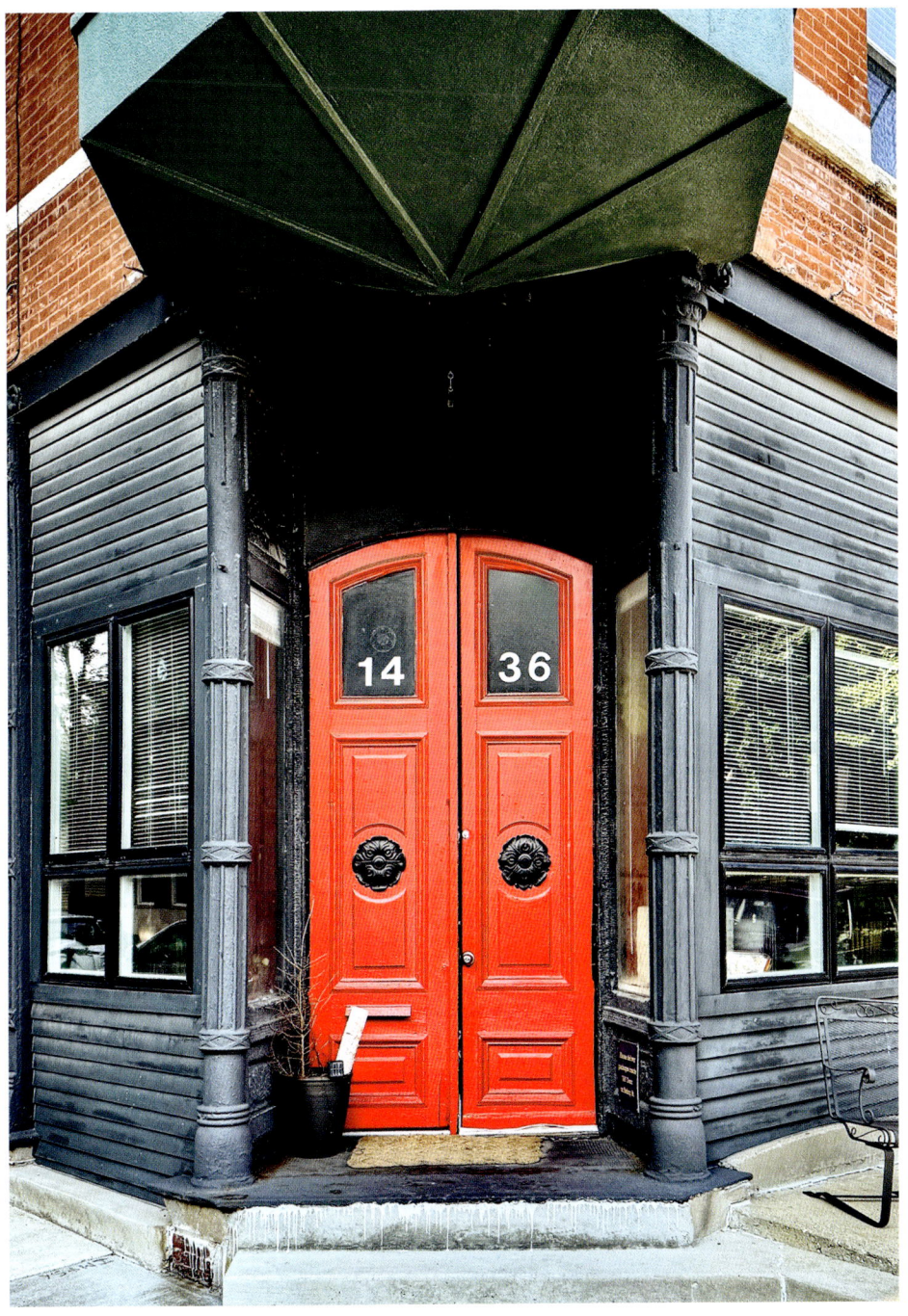

NOBLE SQUARE

Residential

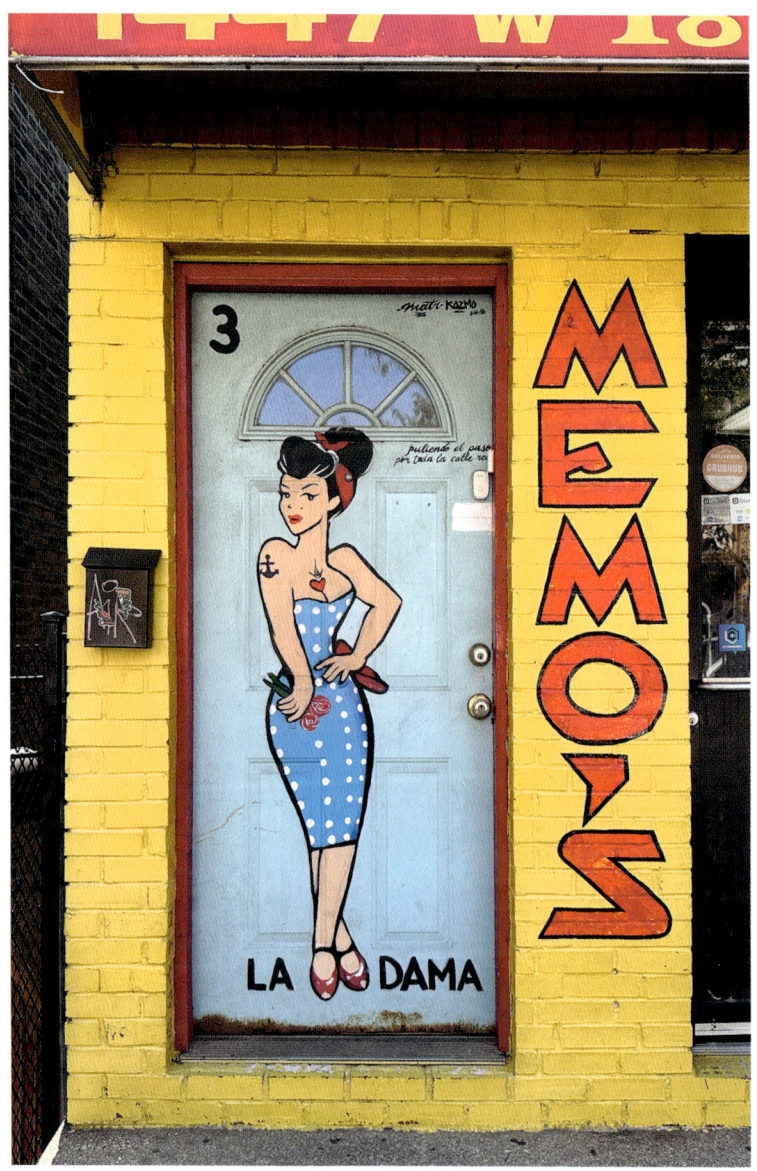

PILSEN

Restaurant

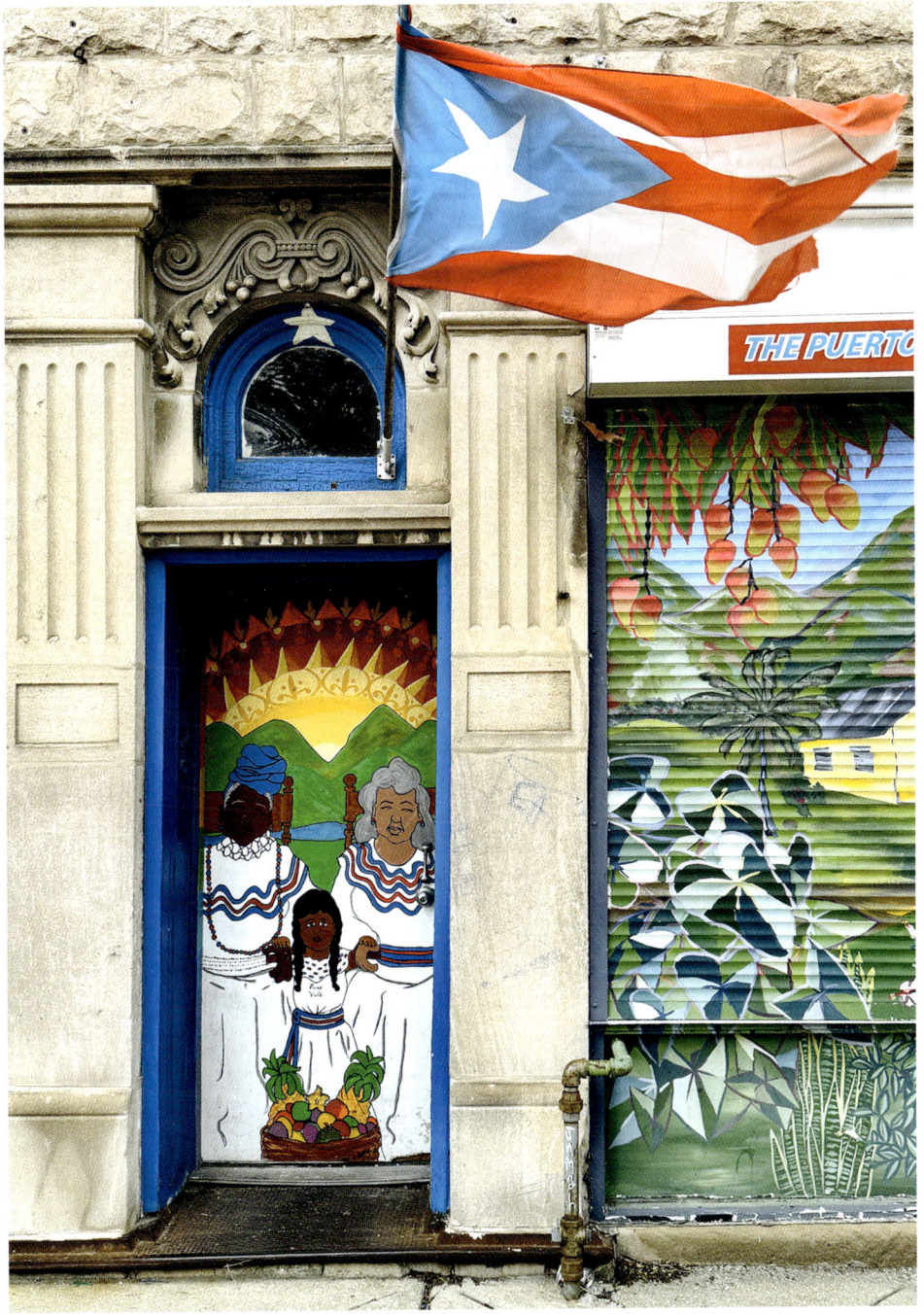

HUMBOLDT PARK

Puerto Rican Cultural Center

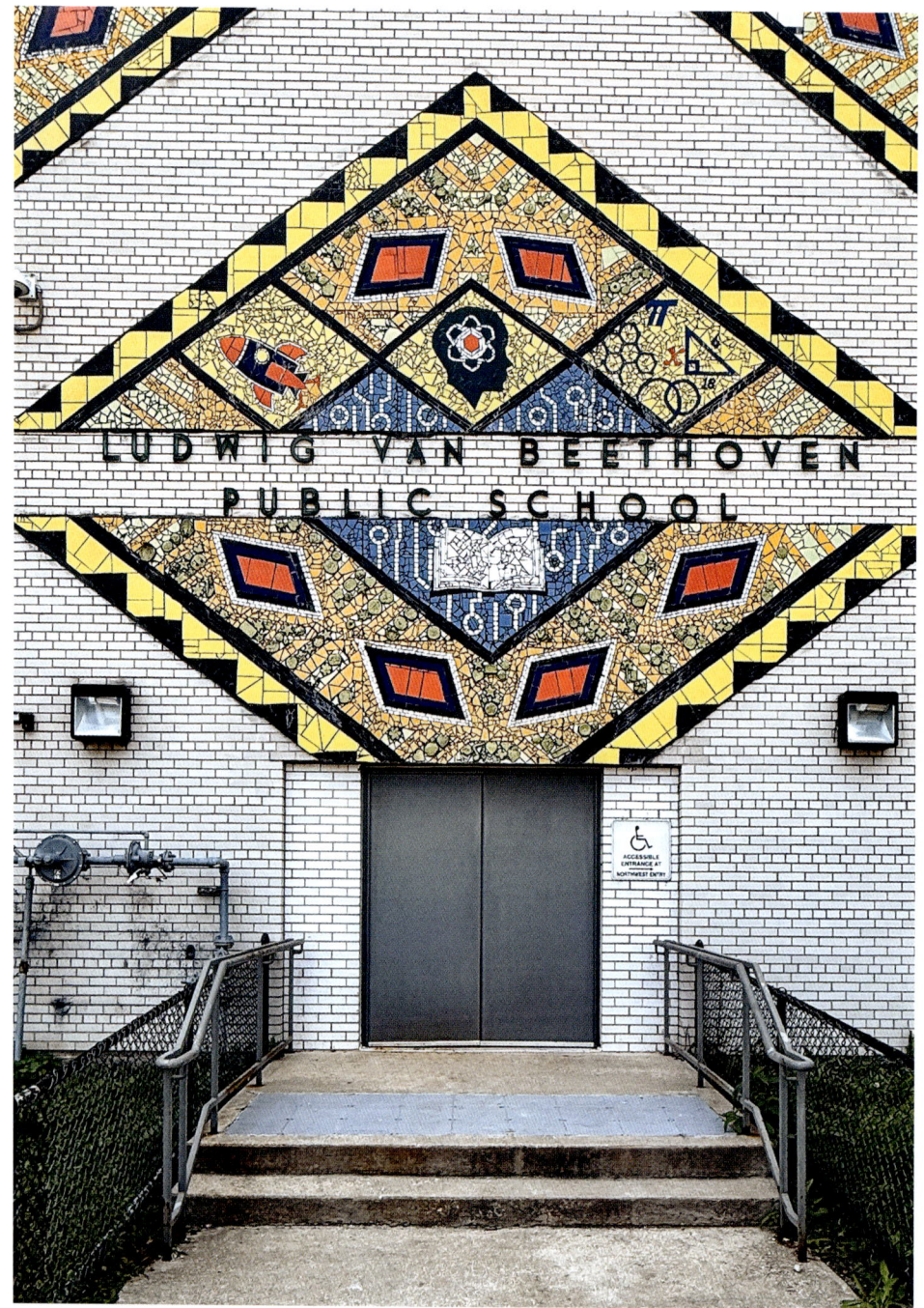

BRONZEVILLE

Ludwig Van Beethoven Elementary School

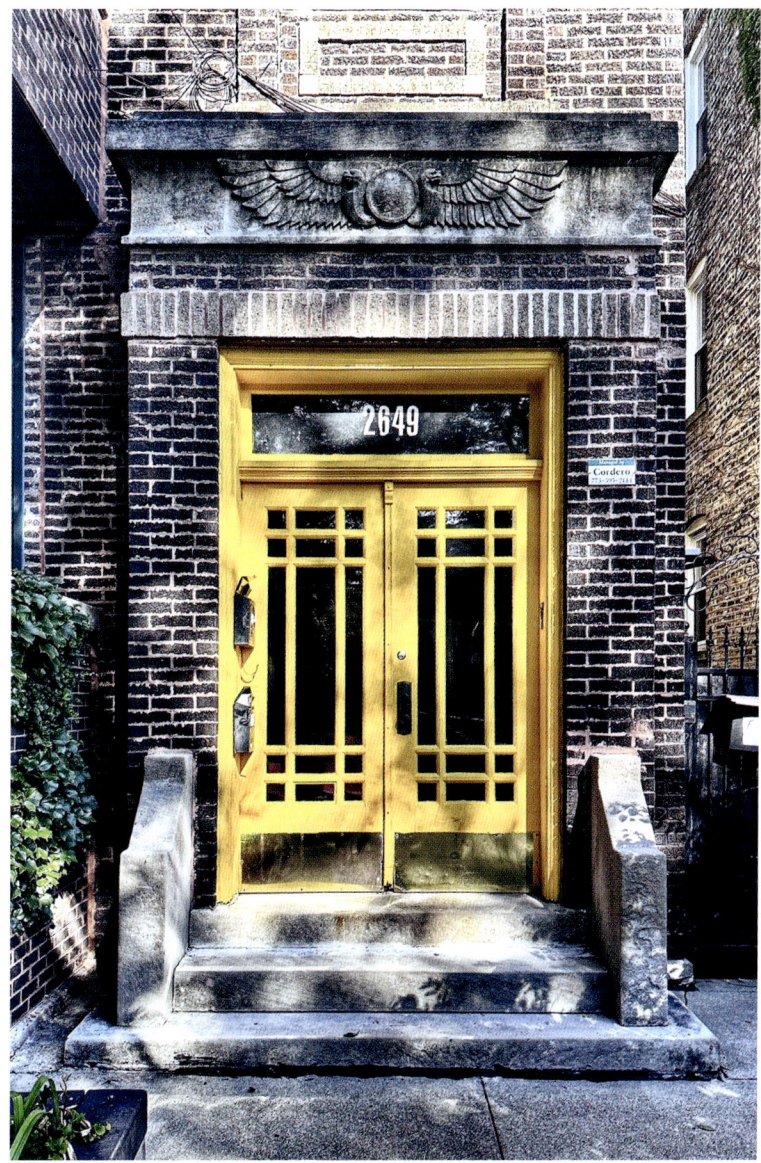

LOGAN SQUARE

Residential

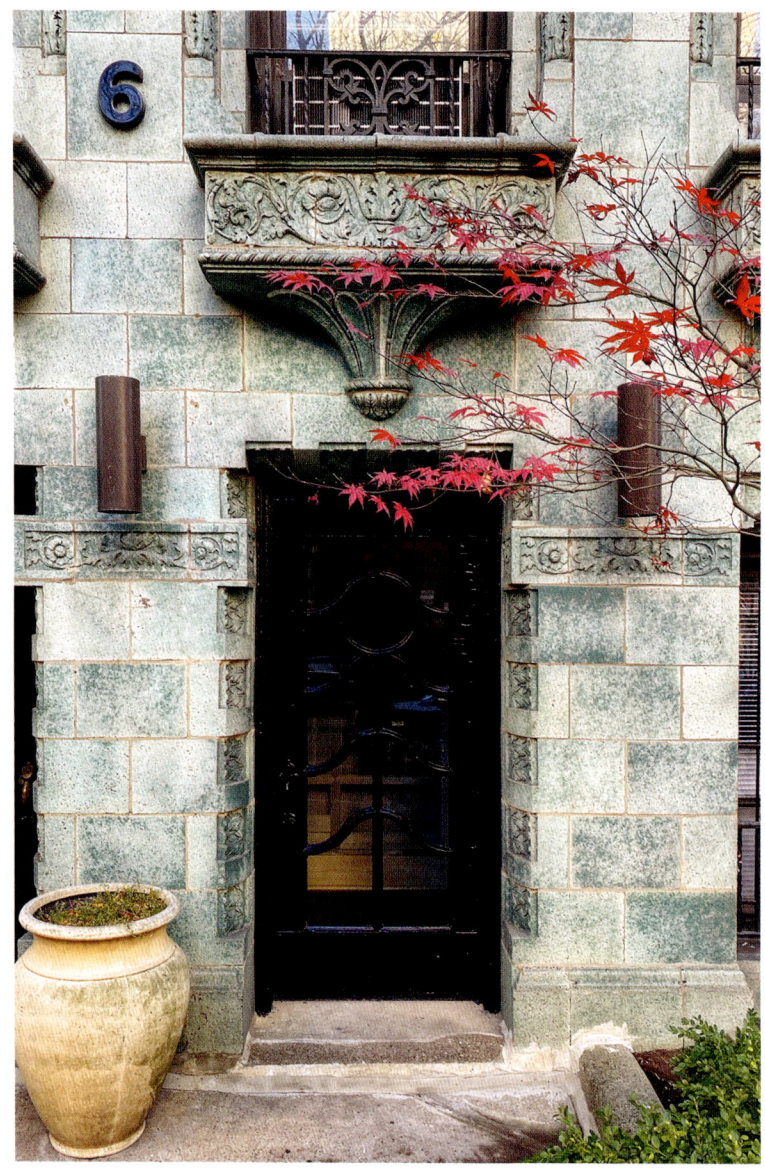

LINCOLN PARK

Residential

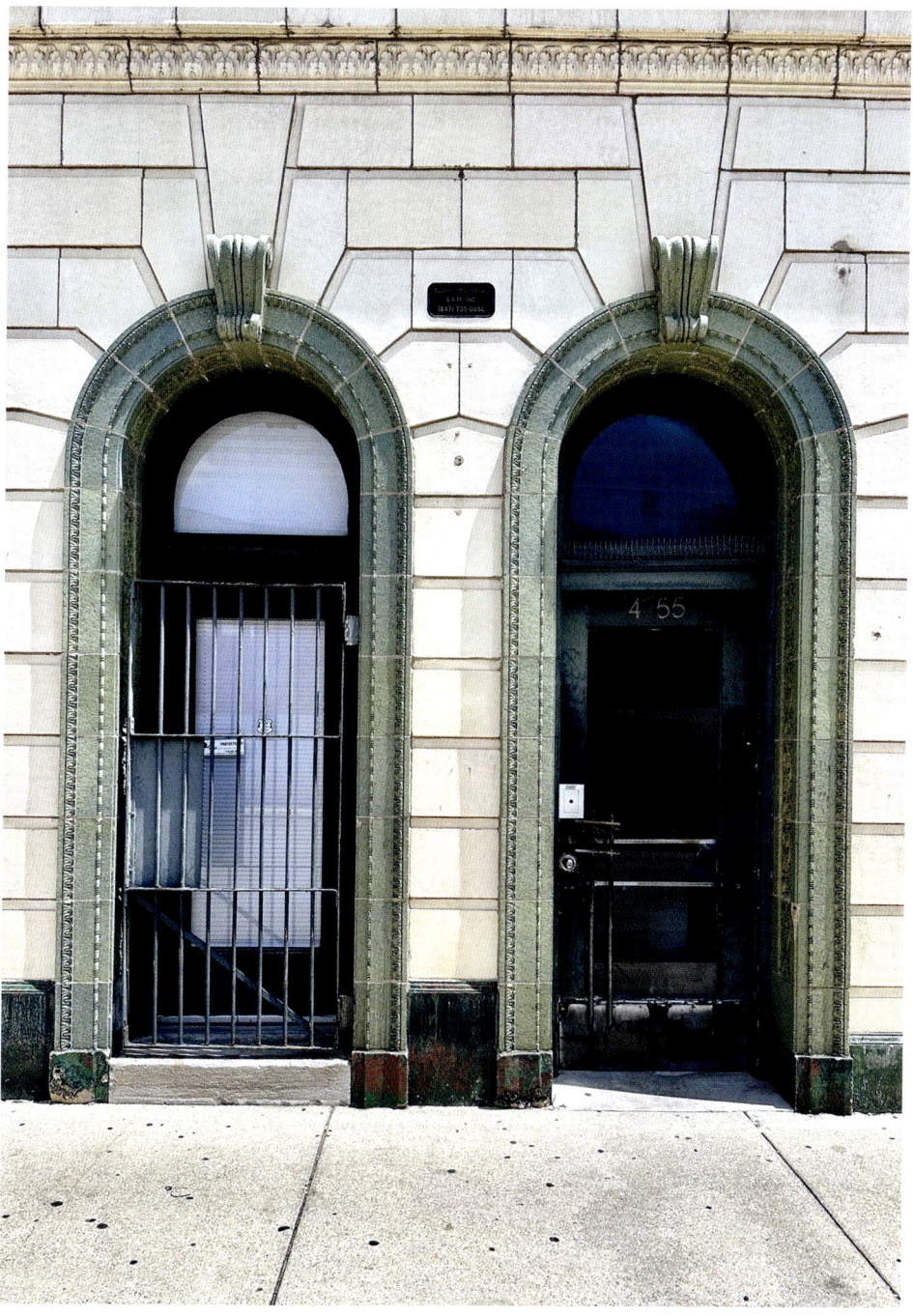

ALBANY PARK

Residential

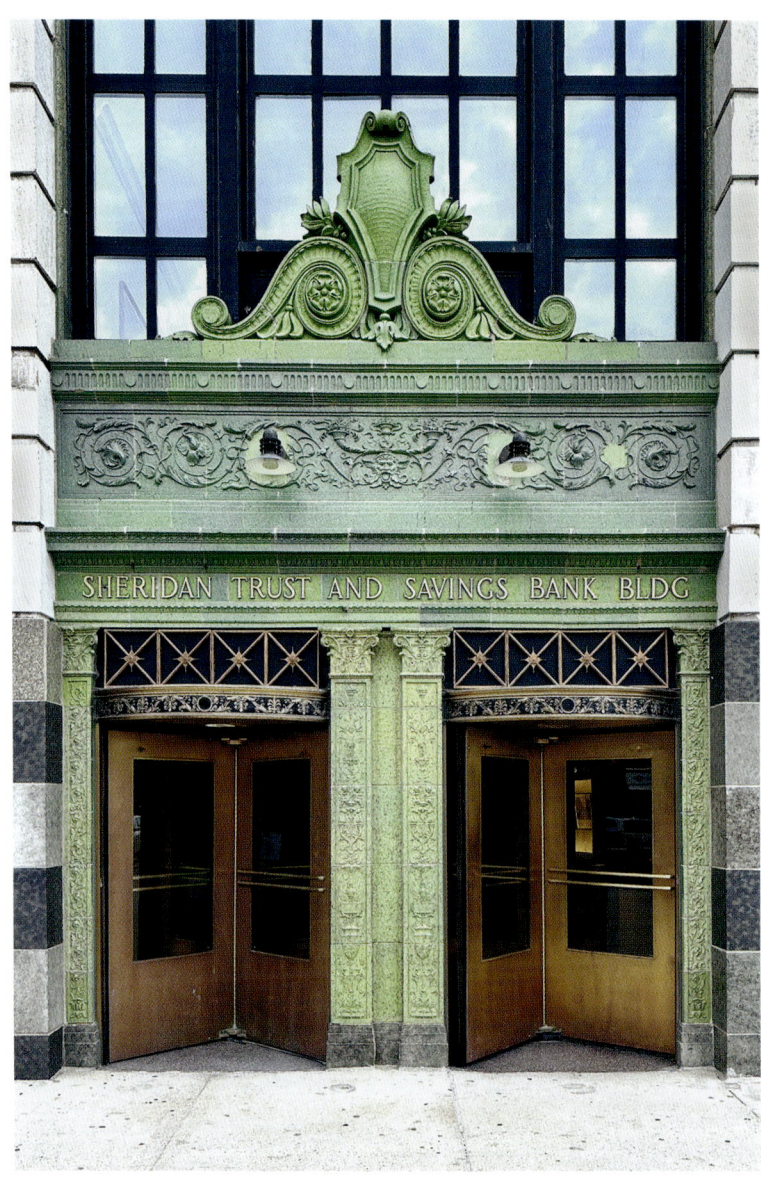

UPTOWN

Sheridan Trust and Savings Bank Building

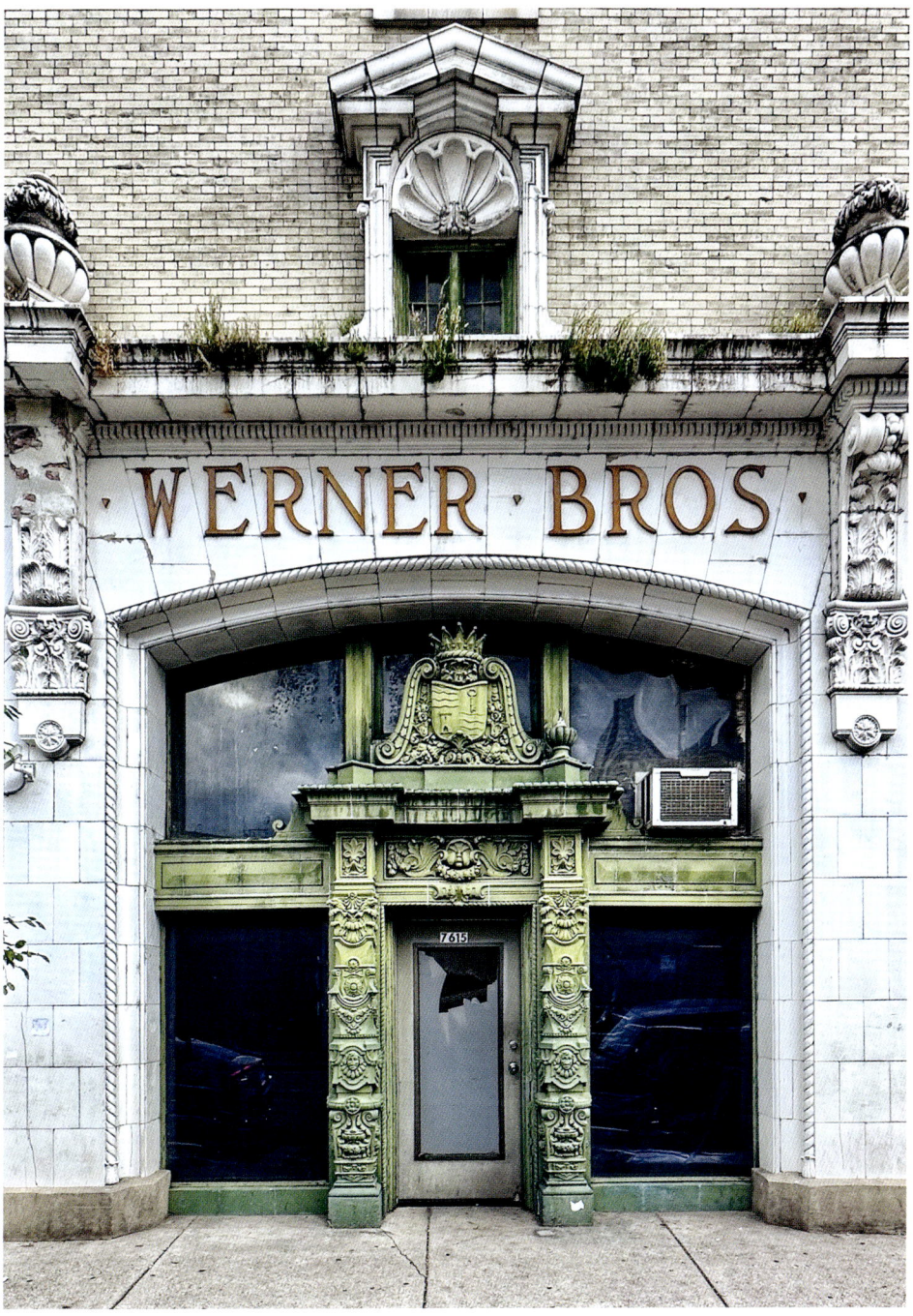

ROGERS PARK

Werner Brothers Storage Building

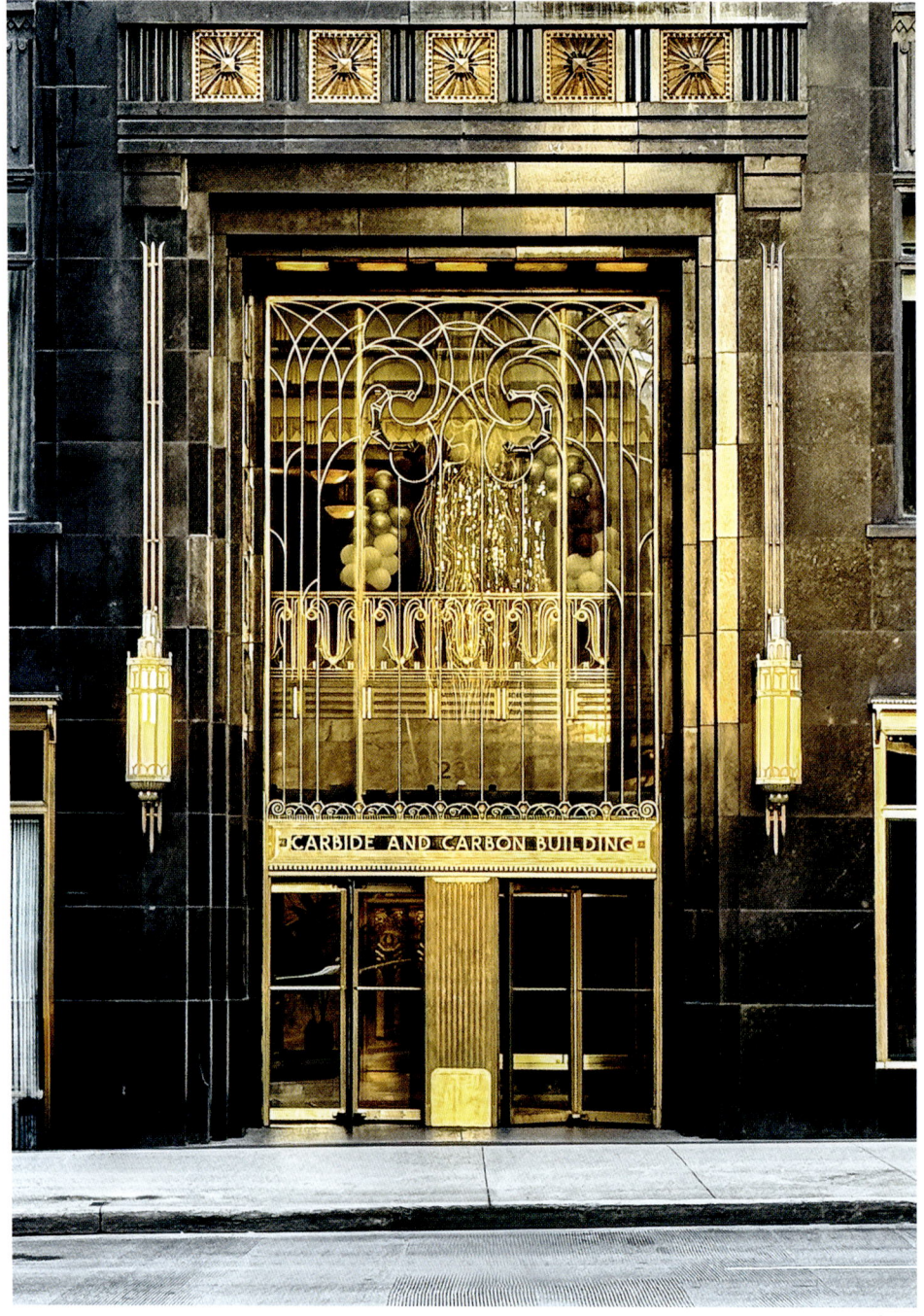

THE LOOP

Carbide and Carbon Building

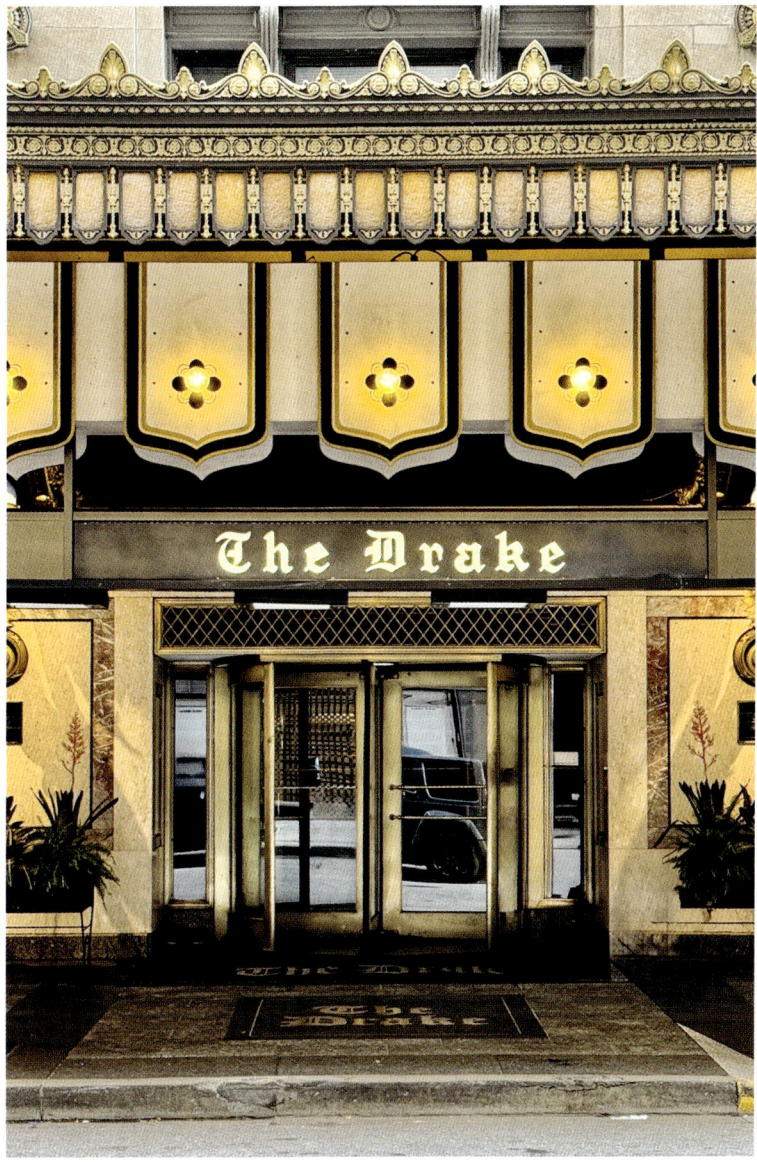

GOLD COAST

The Drake Hotel

C.D. PEACOCK JEWELRY STORE

Architectural Style: Classical Revival | Year: 1927

A vestige of another time, the iconic doors of the original C.D. Peacock jewelry store stand in a building with just as much history as the peacocks themselves.

Tiffany and Co.'s Louis Comfort Tiffany designed the bronze doors for the C.D. Peacock jewelry store, which opened on the first floor of The Palmer House hotel in 1927. The door's panels consist of solid bronze and depict two peacocks in profile, a motif that carries through many Tiffany creations throughout the hotel, inspired directly by the jeweler. Originally founded as The House of Peacock in 1837, the since renamed retailer is known as Chicago's oldest jewelry store. Although its flagship no longer sits at The Palmer House, its iconic doors still remain.

The Palmer House itself has elaborate beginnings as well. The building was originally built in 1870 as a wedding present from Potter Palmer to his wife, Bertha. Only a year after its initial completion, the building was destroyed in 1871 by the Great Chicago Fire, but was soon rebuilt in 1873. Later in 1925, the hotel was demolished and then expanded by Chicago architecture firm Holabird & Roche to accommodate a booming downtown economy, becoming the structure we recognize today.

Bertha Palmer, a leading Chicago socialite of her time, was also known as a generous benefactor of the arts. Her affinity for fine art and luxury continued to influence the design and decor of the hotel. A prime example of the stylish grandeur Bertha loved and inspired, it is easy to see why these doors continue to captivate passersby.

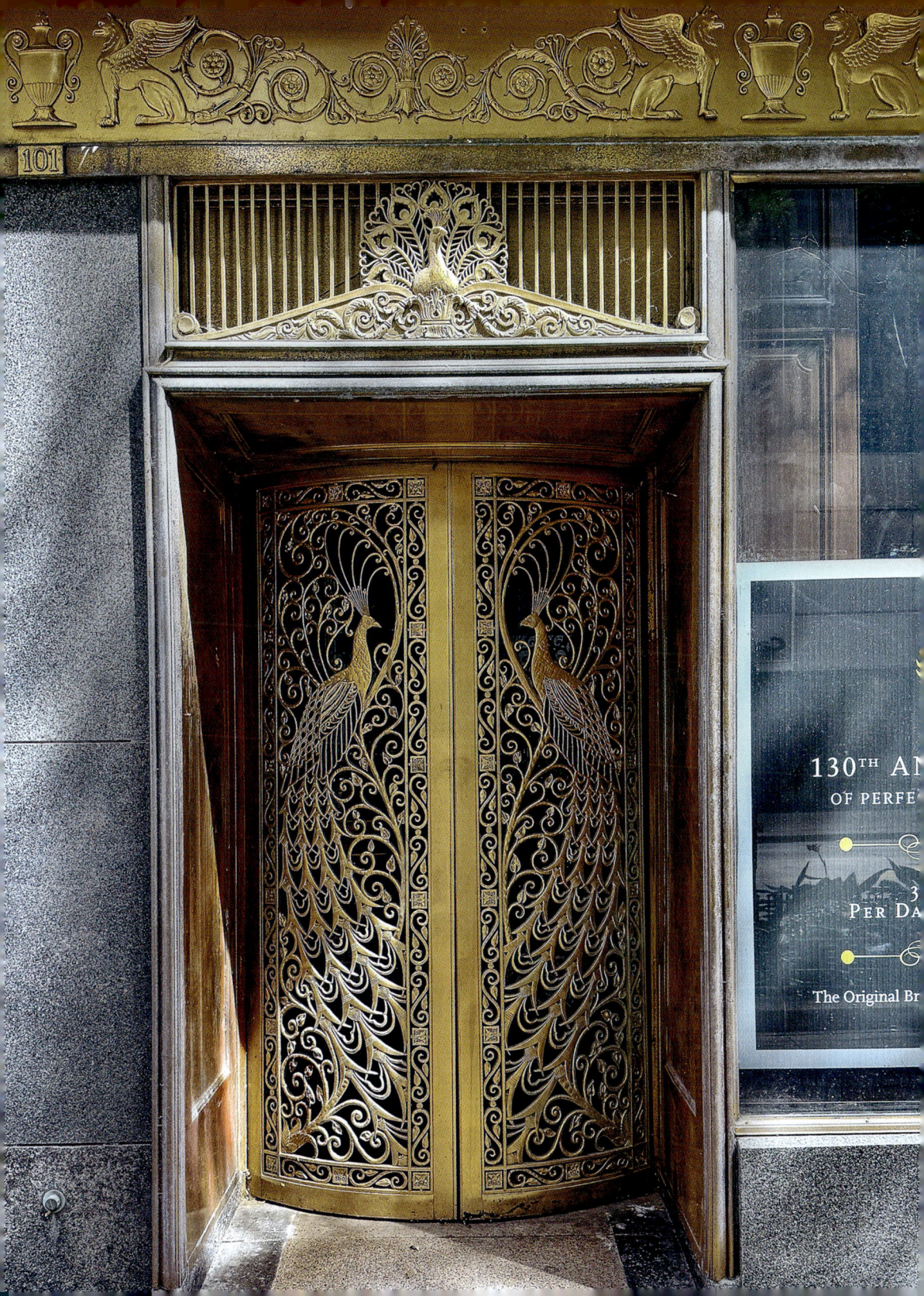

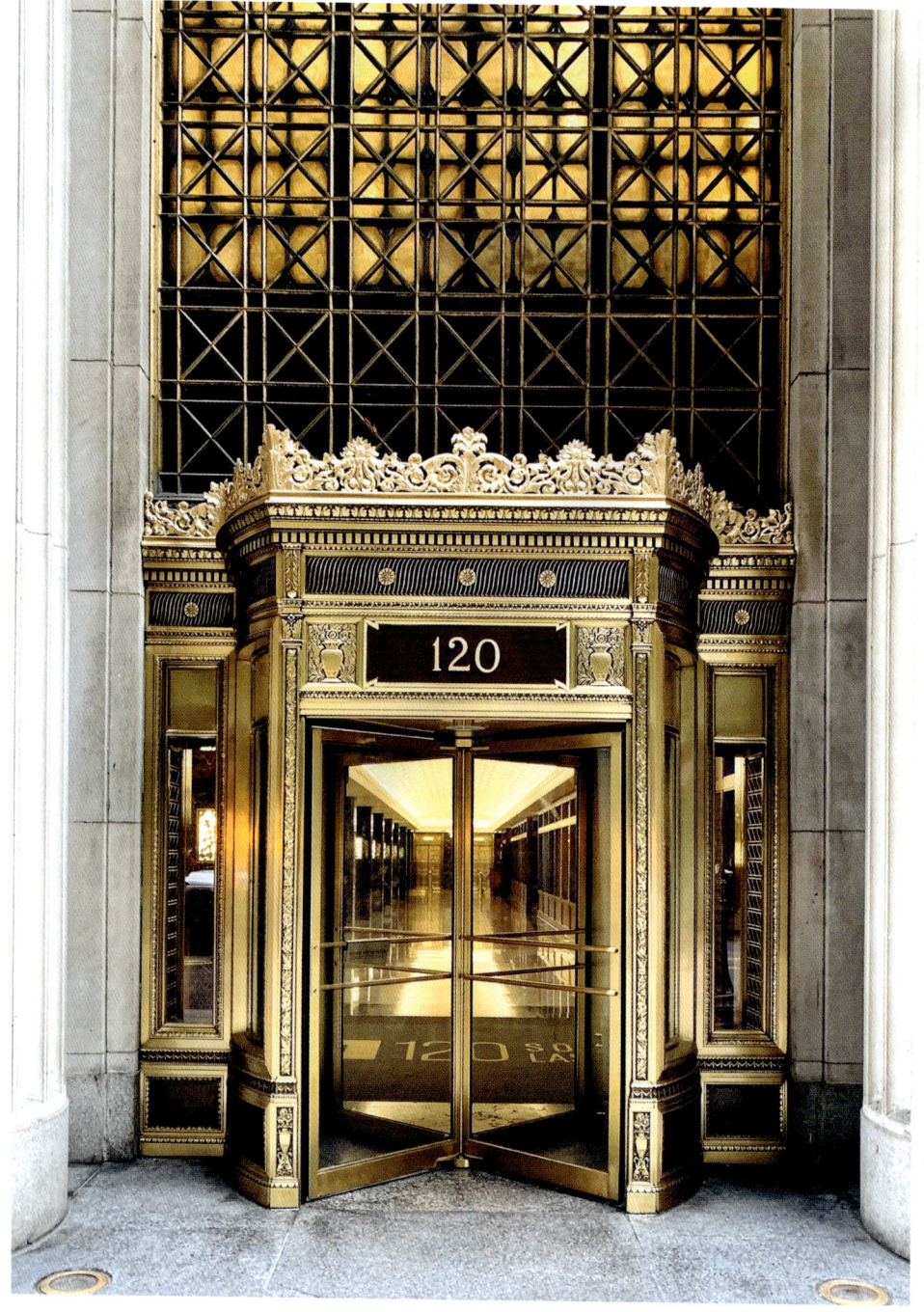

THE LOOP

120 North LaSalle

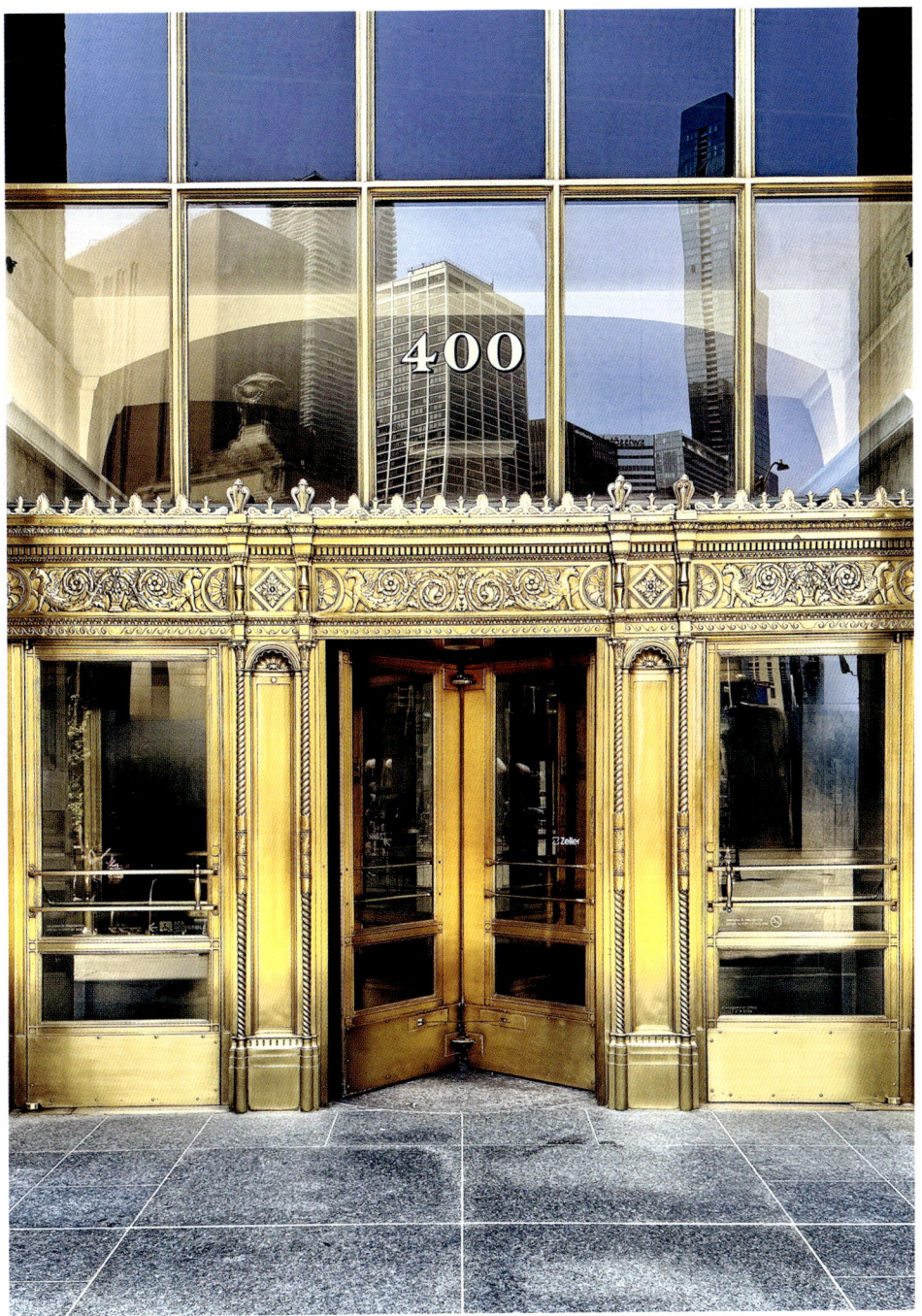

NEAR NORTH

The Wrigley Building

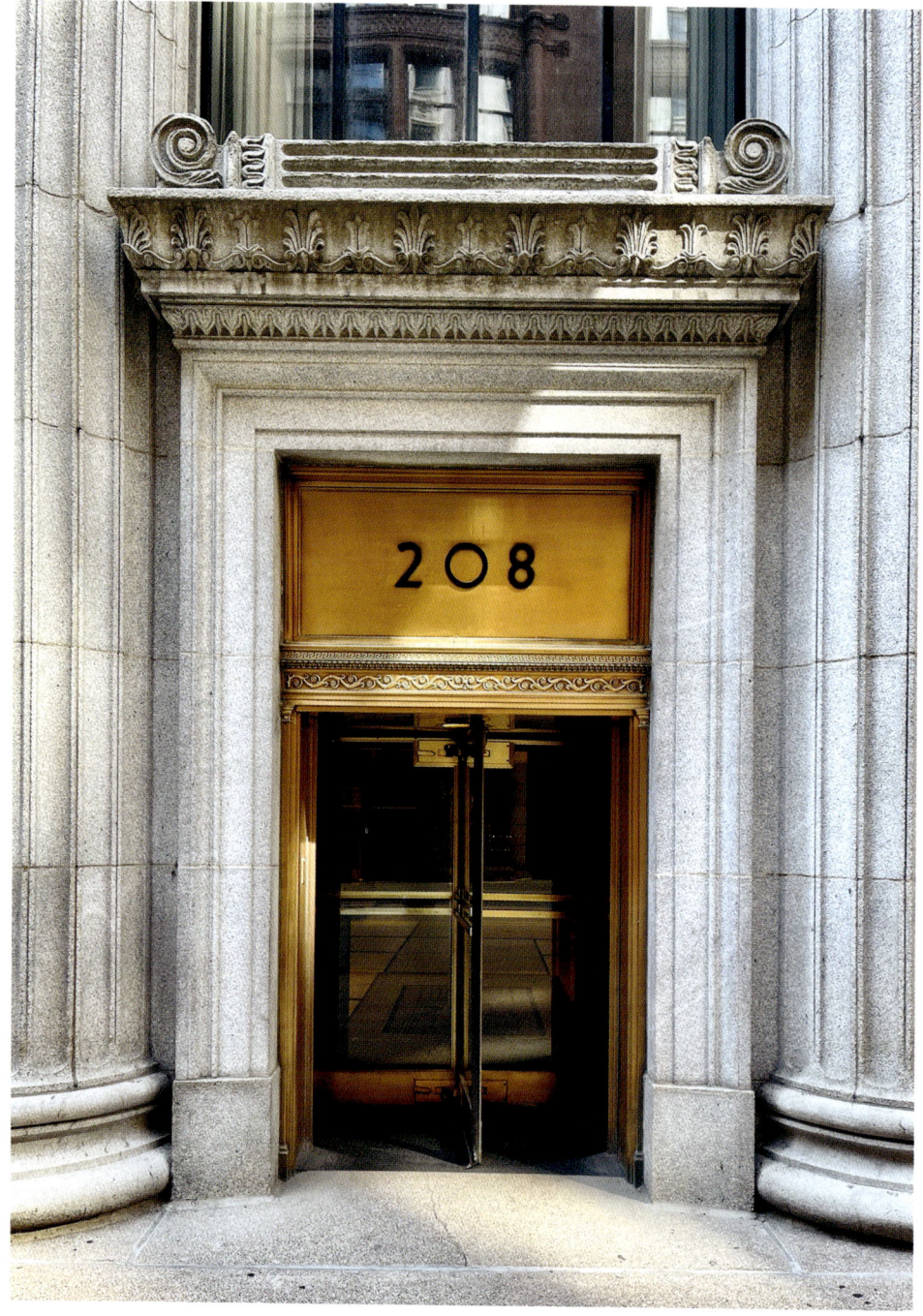

THE LOOP

City National Bank and Trust Company Building

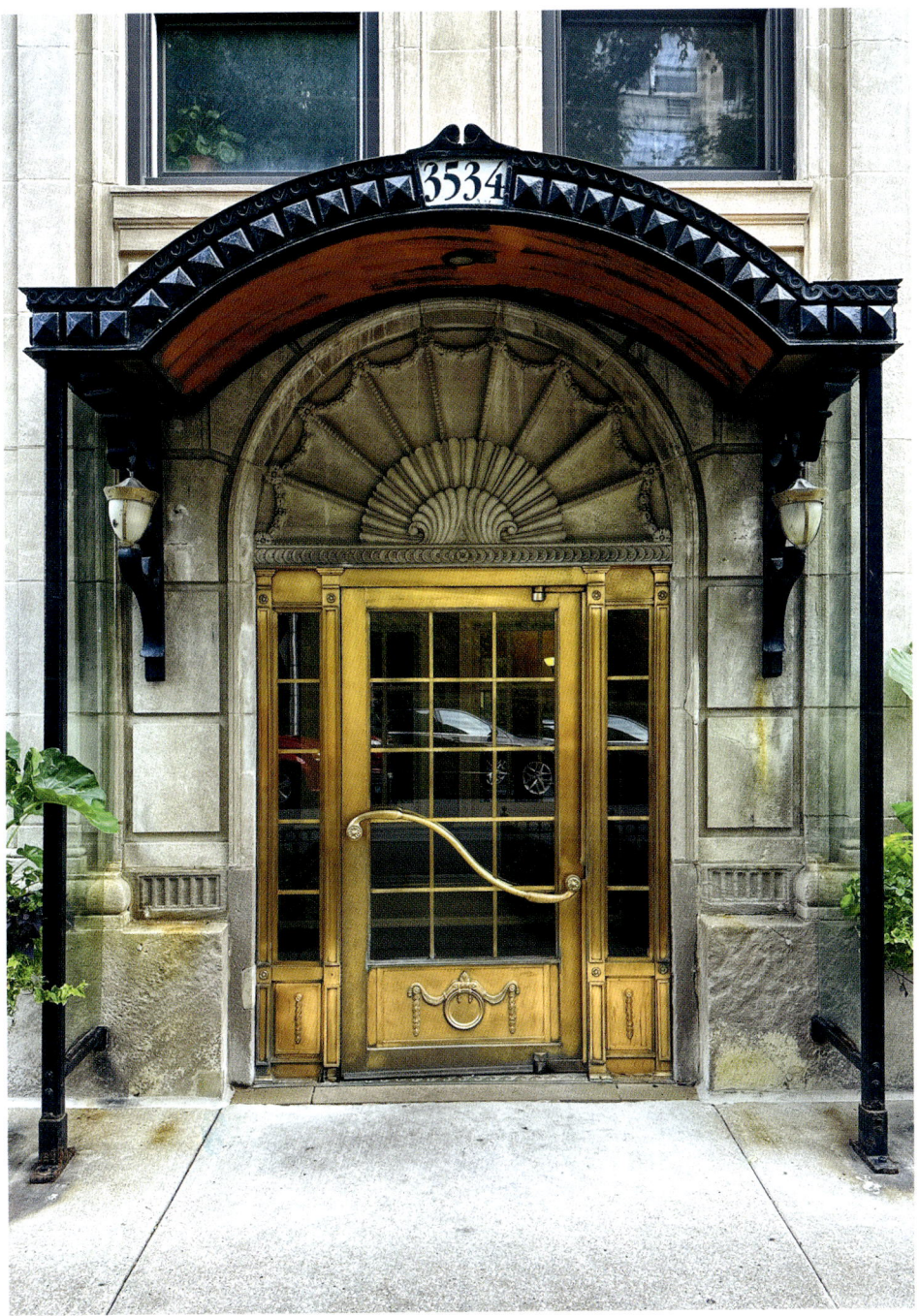

LAKEVIEW

Residential

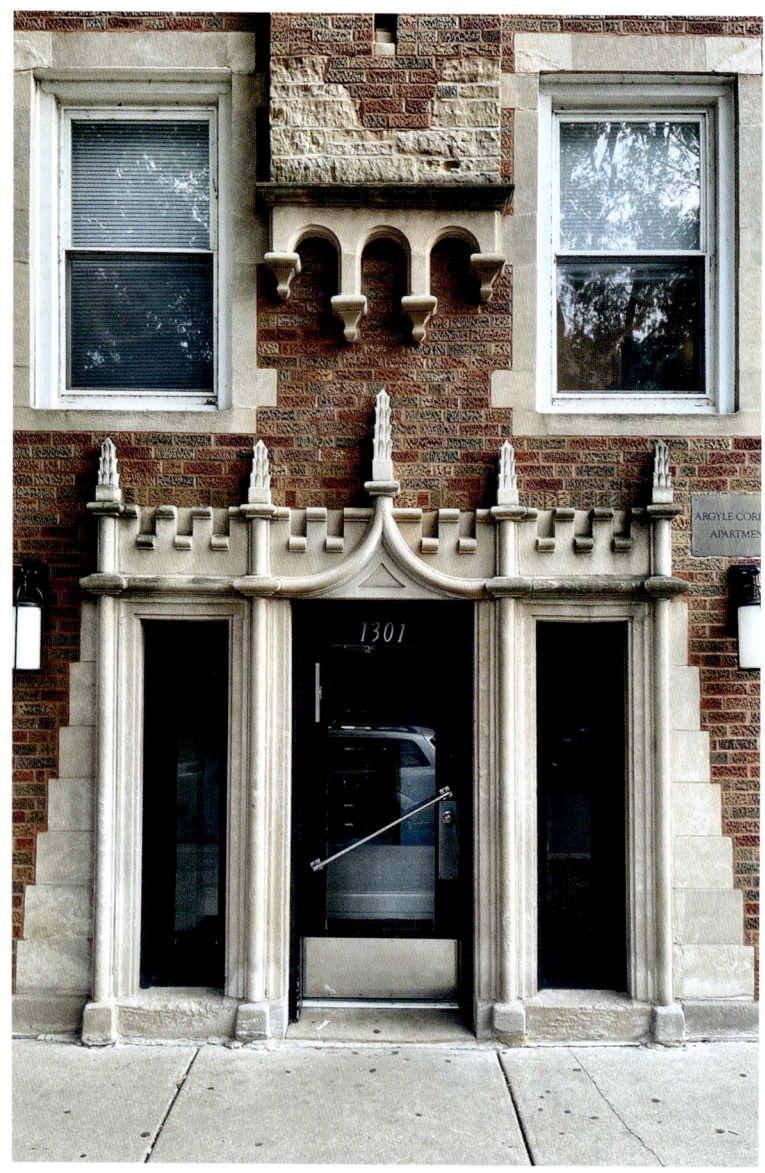

UPTOWN

Residential

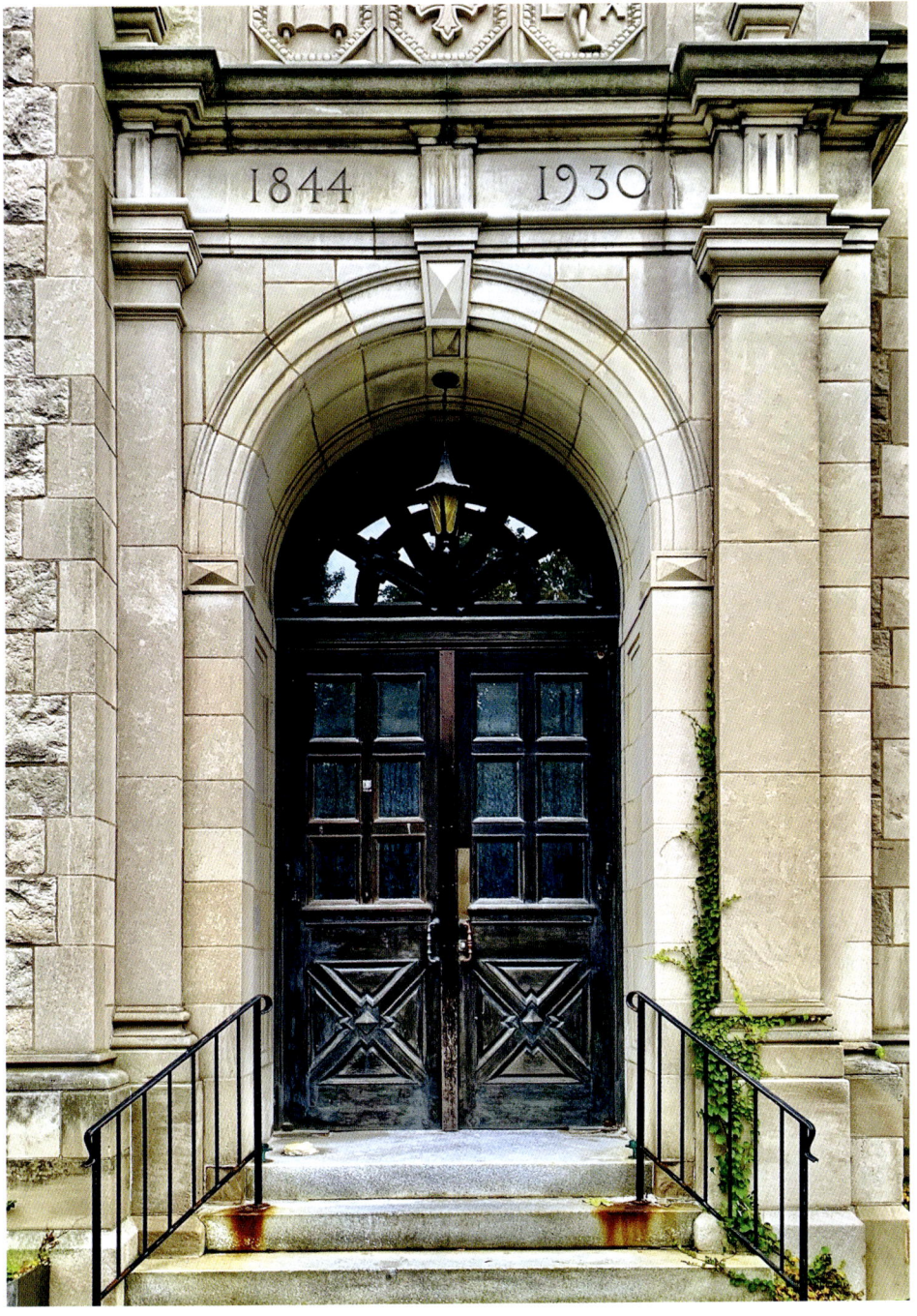

HYDE PARK

University of Chicago

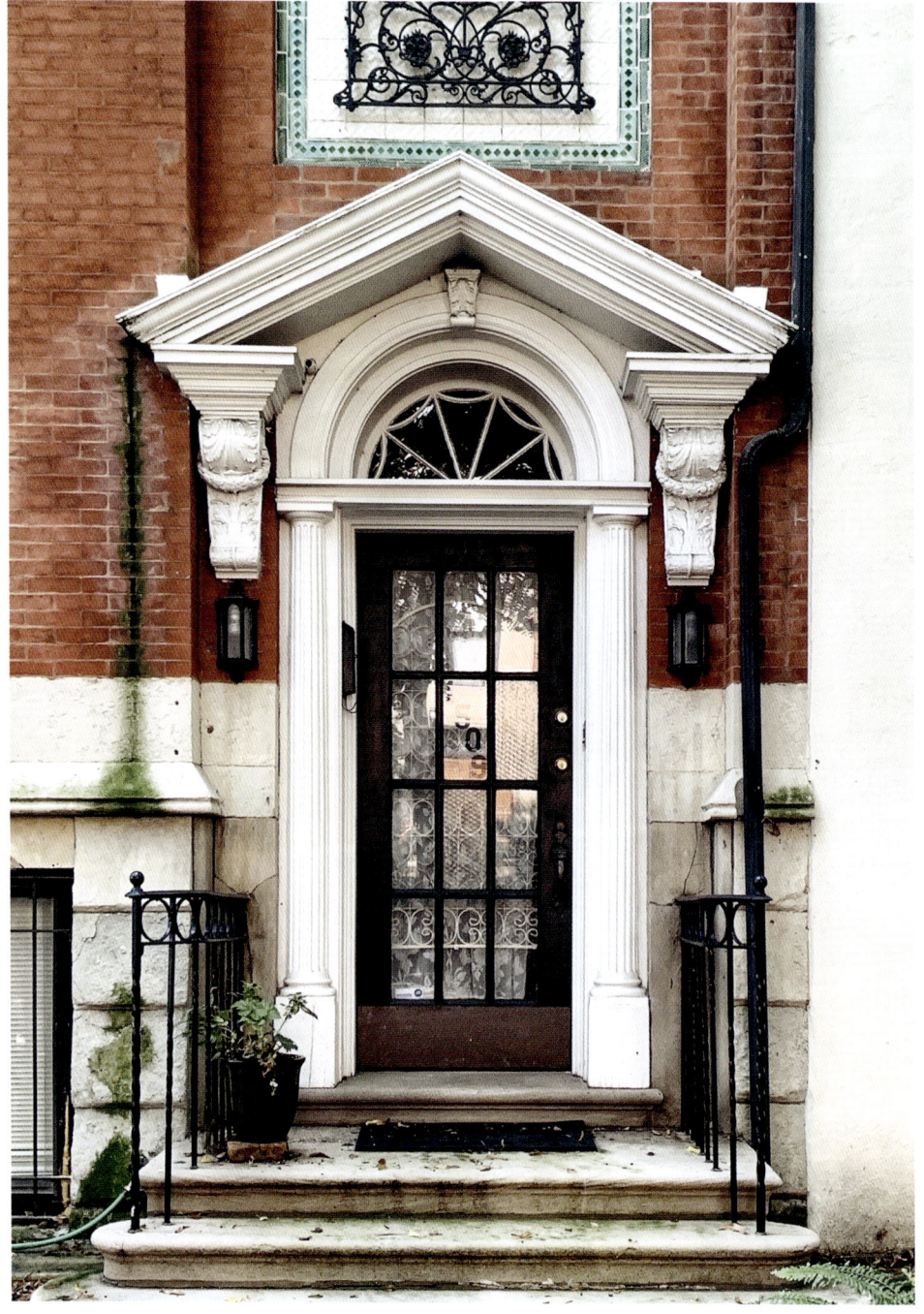

WEST LOOP

Residential

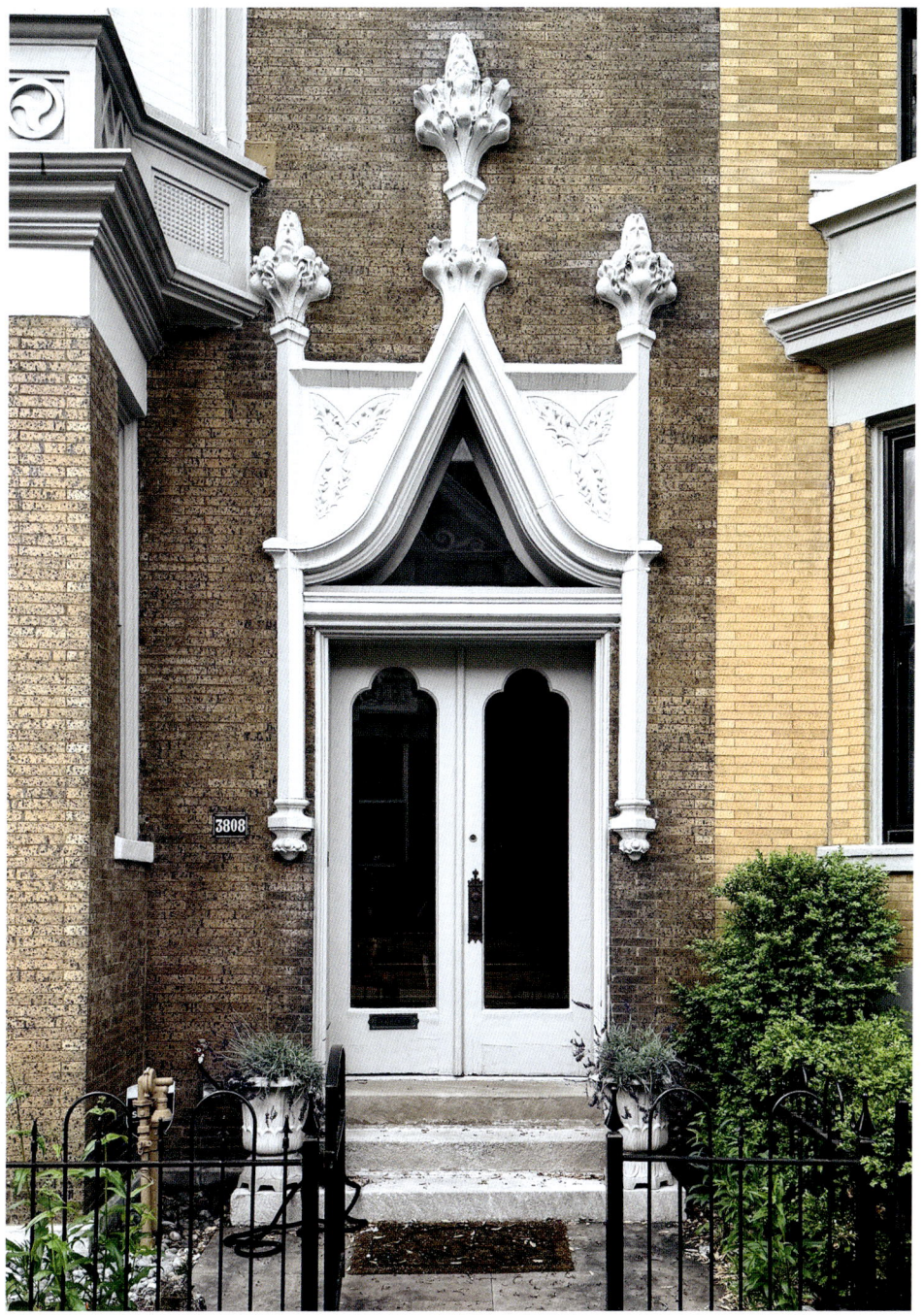

WRIGLEYVILLE

Residential

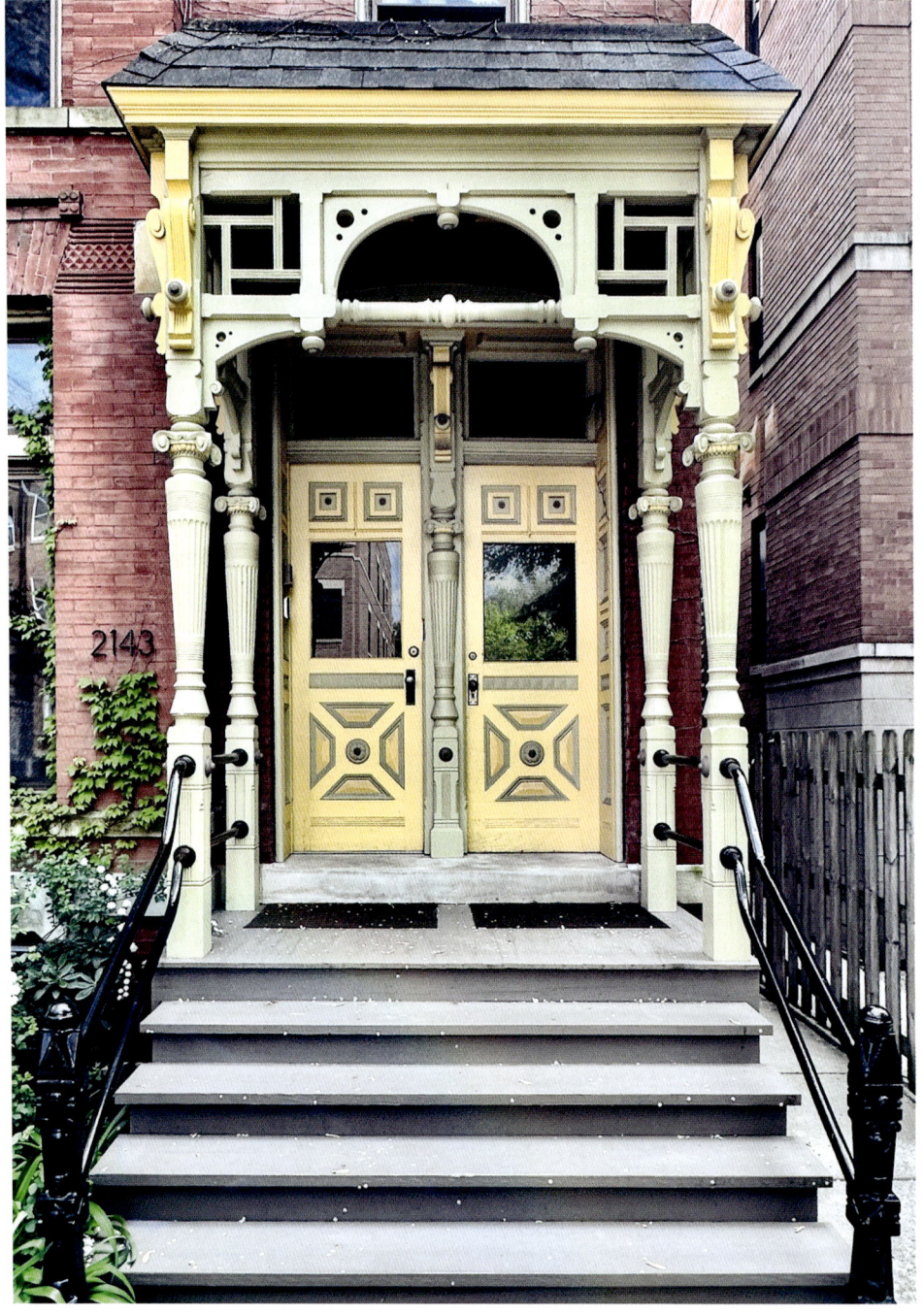

WICKER PARK

Residential

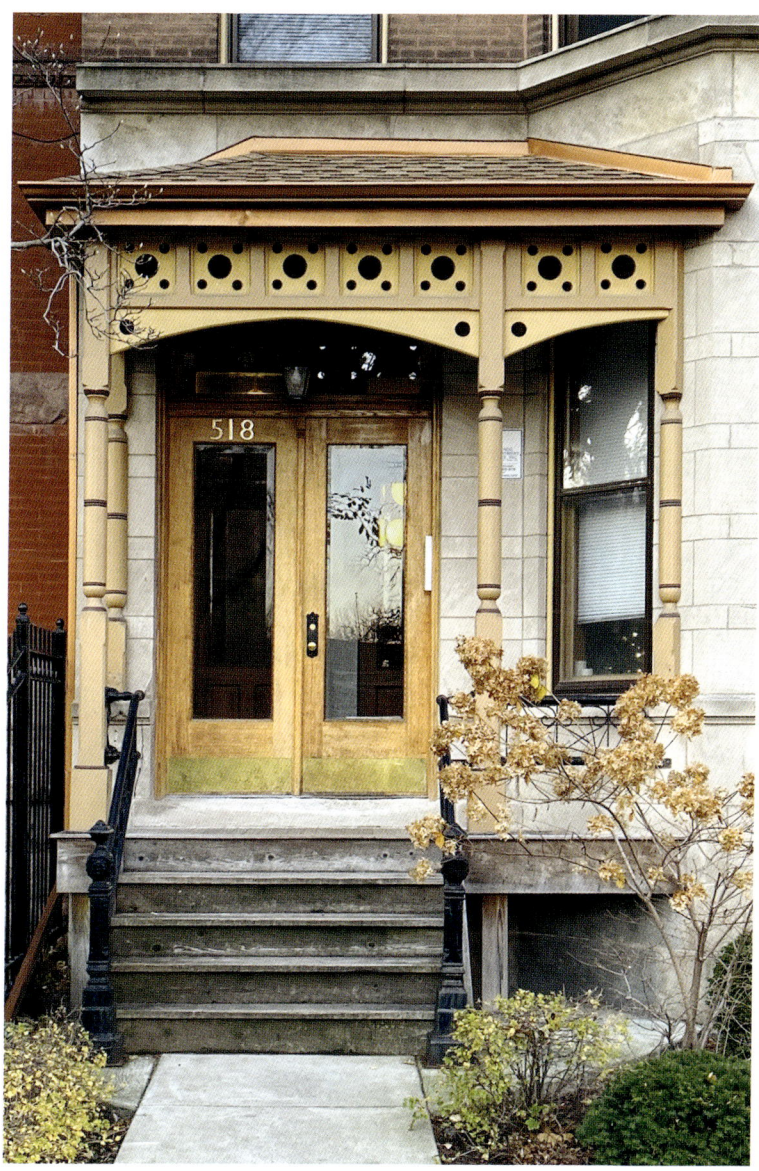

LINCOLN PARK

Residential

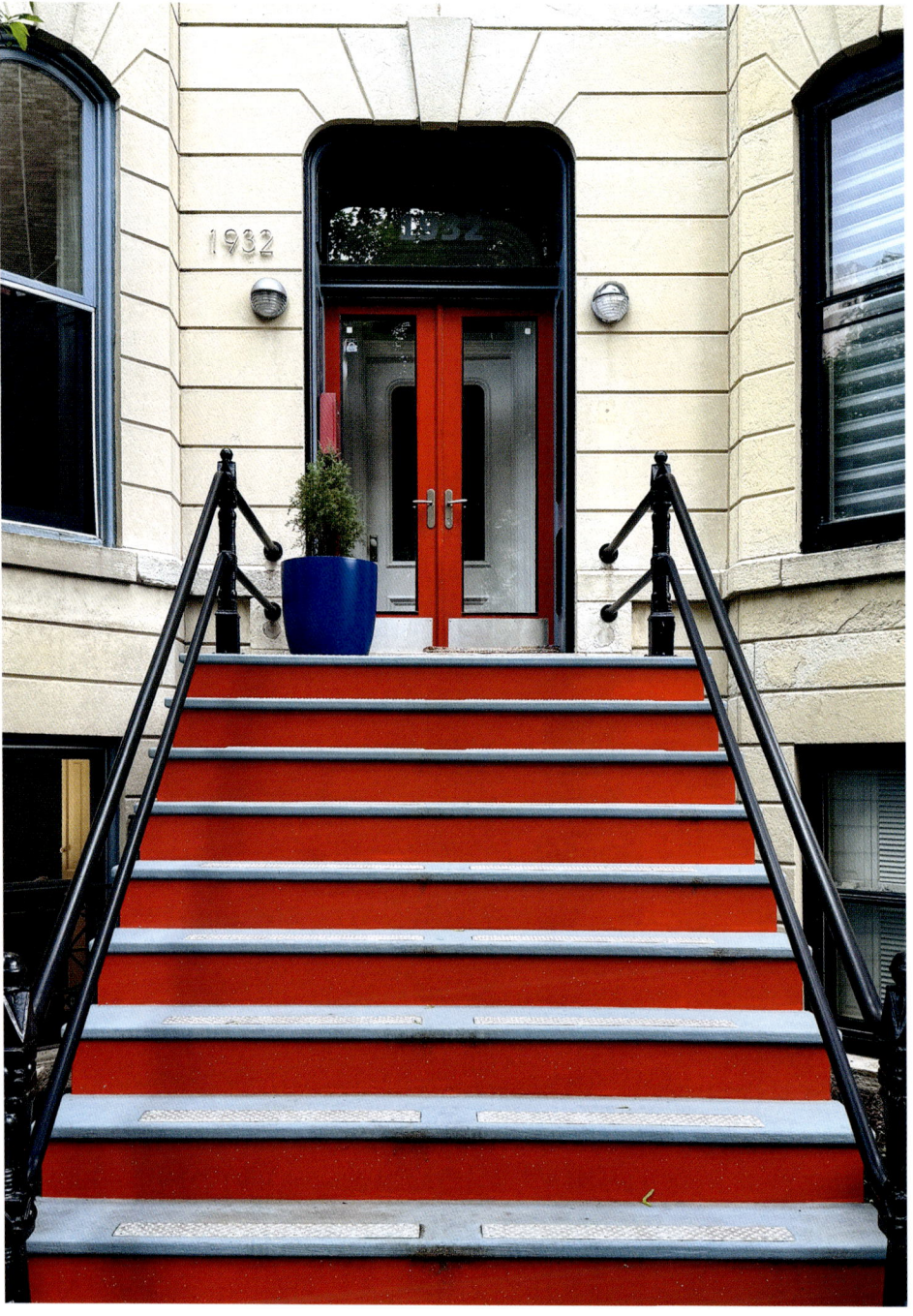

OLD TOWN

Residential

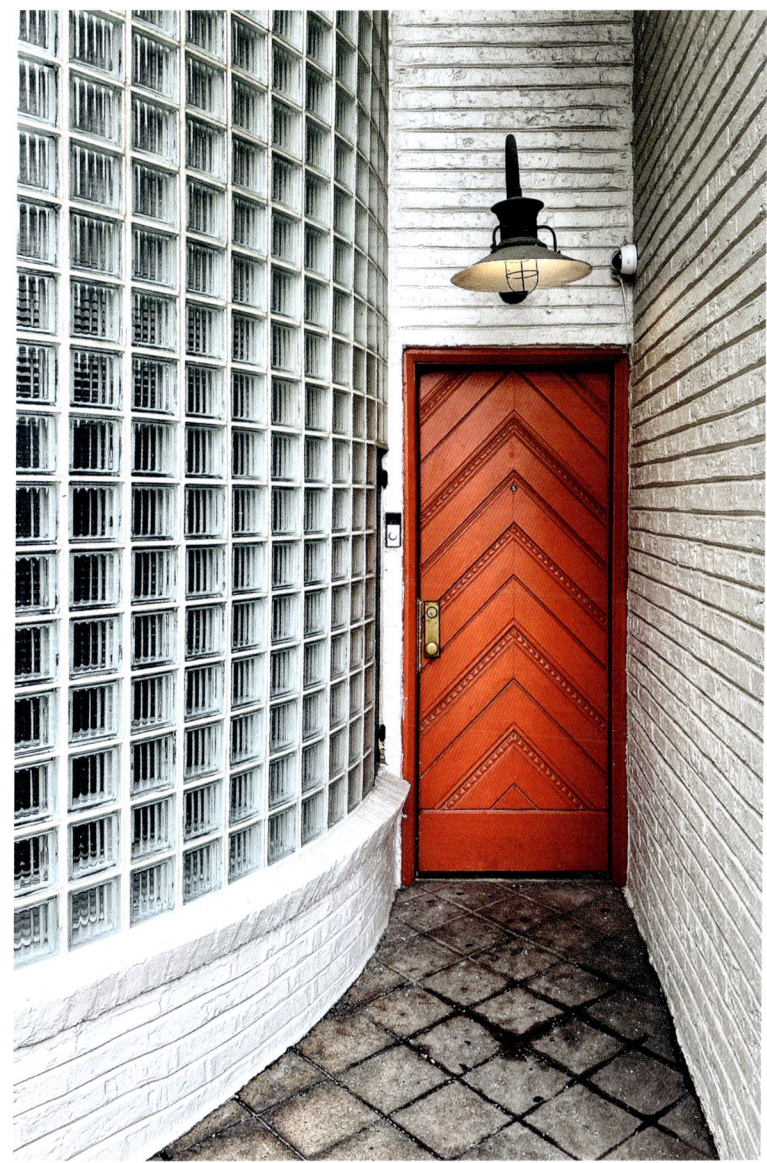

GOLD COAST

Residential

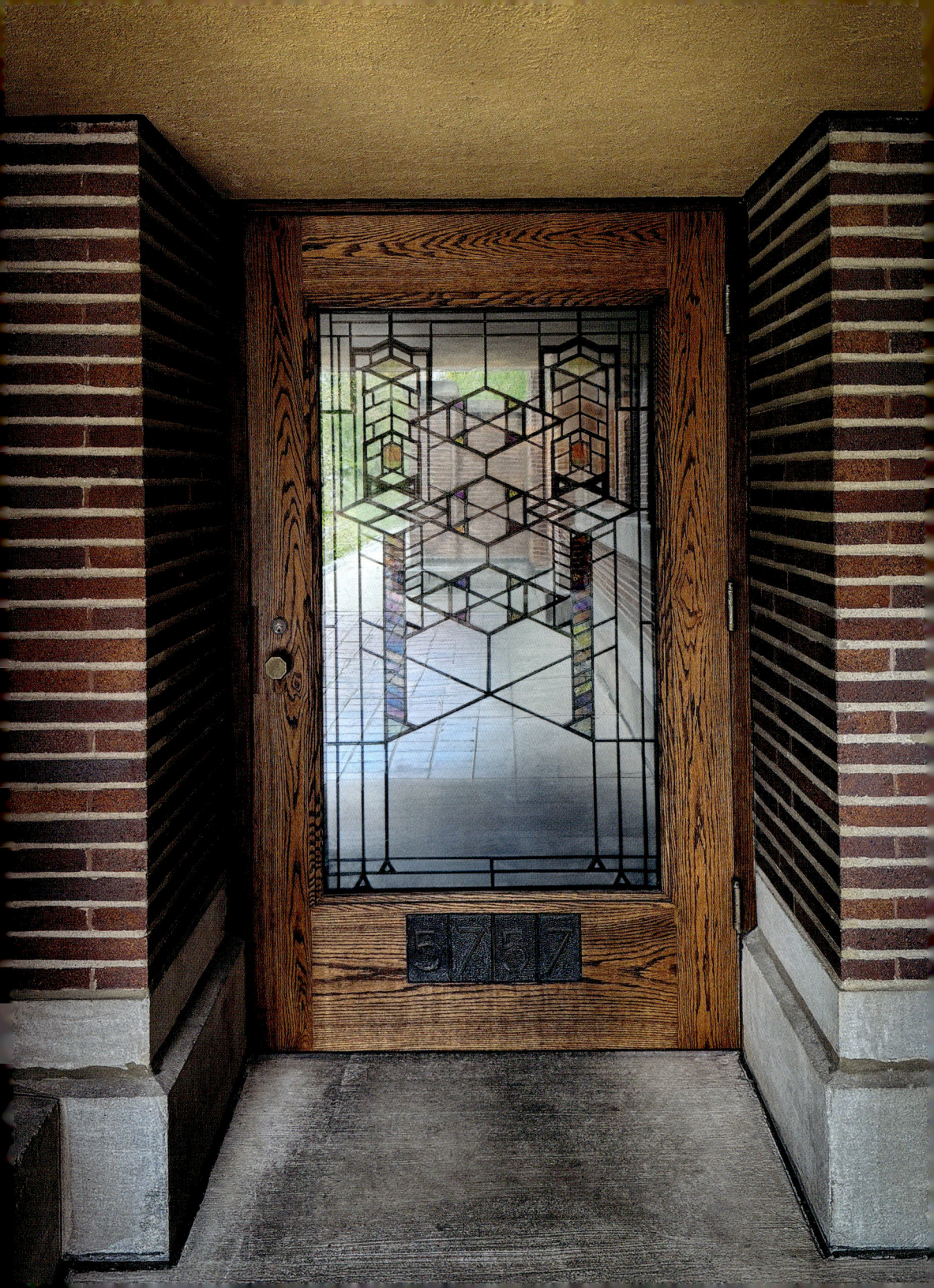

FREDERICK C. ROBIE HOUSE

Architectural Style: Prairie Style | Year: 1910

It's impossible to tell the story of Chicago architecture without mentioning Frank Lloyd Wright. A prime example of the Prairie style Wright developed in his early work, the Robie House in the Hyde Park neighborhood stands almost as a manifesto of his artistic philosophy.

As the first uniquely American architectural style, Prairie style responded to the expanse of American plains by emphasizing the horizontal rather than the vertical. The long, narrow lot bought in 1908 by bicycle manufacturing executive Frederick Robie was the perfect canvas.

Despite his enthusiasm for the project, Robie's time in the house was short-lived due to financial difficulties. After being sold 14 months after its completion, the house served as a private residence until 1926 when it was bought by the Chicago Theological Seminary for use as a dorm. With the threat of demolition looming, a 90-year-old Wright toured the house in 1957 and campaigned for its preservation. Thankfully, the house was purchased and then donated to the University of Chicago, subsequently being designated a National Historic Landmark in 1963.

The building itself is organized like two rectangles sliding alongside each other, slightly overlapping. The brick and limestone façade anchor the horizontal structure, accompanied by a dramatic overhanging roof. The open floor plan of the main room feels expansive and modern. Stained glass doors and windows channel sunlight into the house, blurring the boundaries between exterior and interior. A masterwork of the Prairie style and a forerunner of modernism in architecture, the Robie House lives today, fully restored and open to visitors.

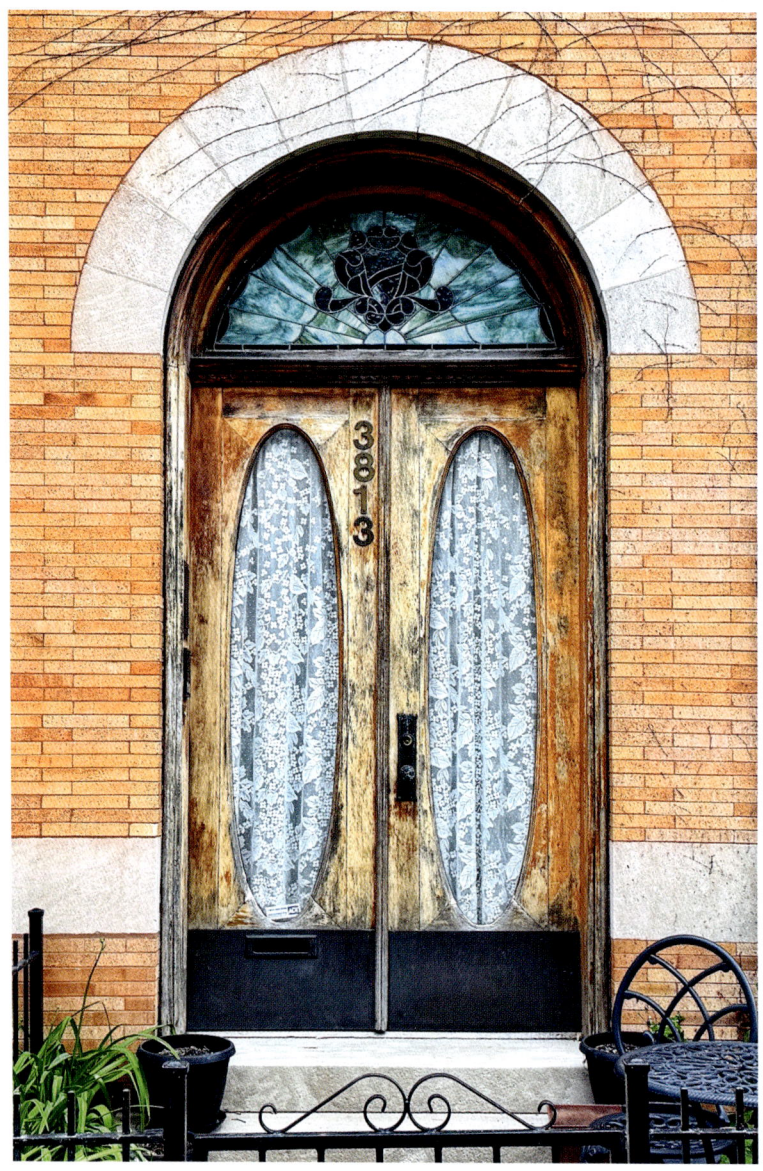

WRIGLEYVILLE

Residential

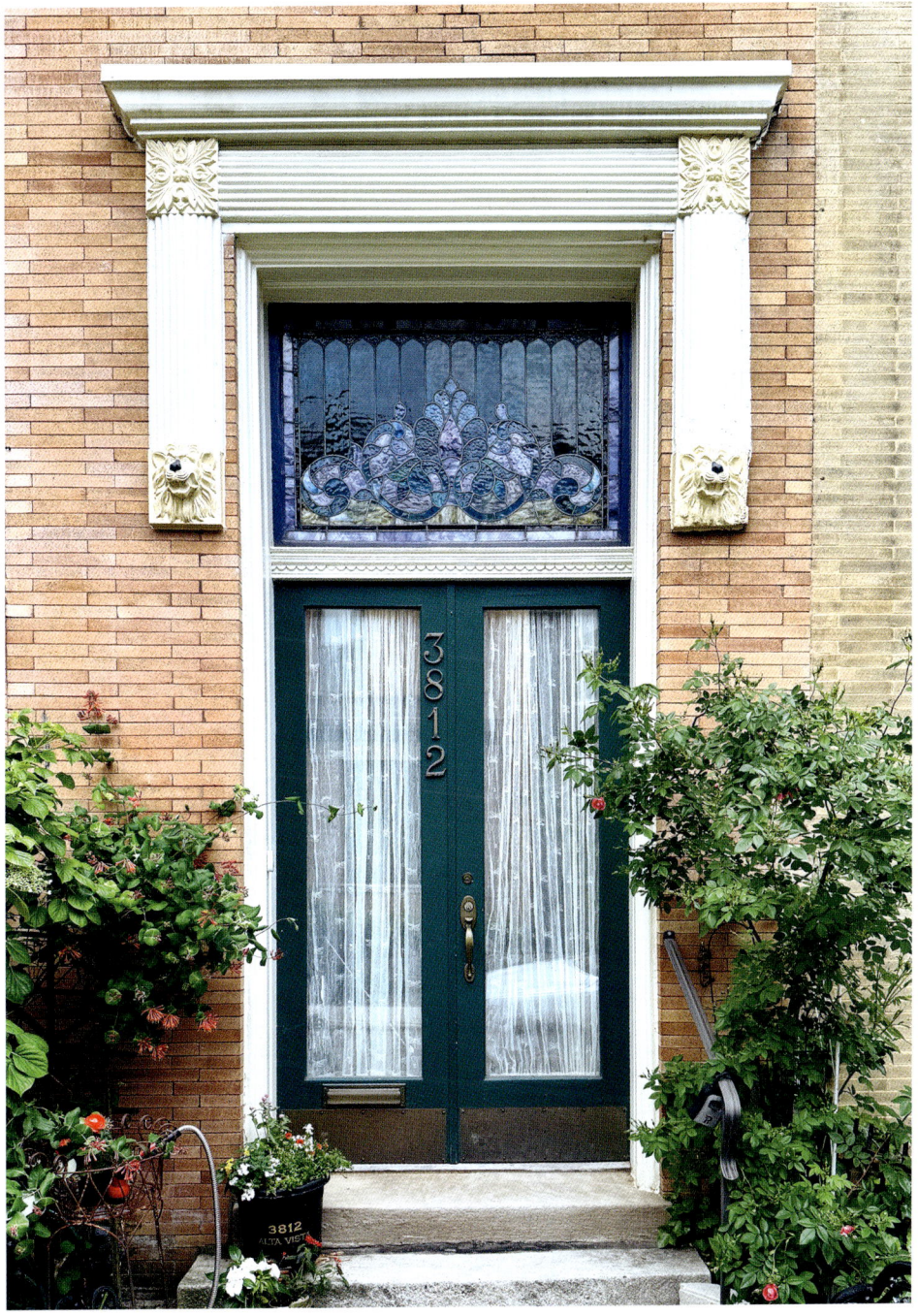

WRIGLEYVILLE

Residential

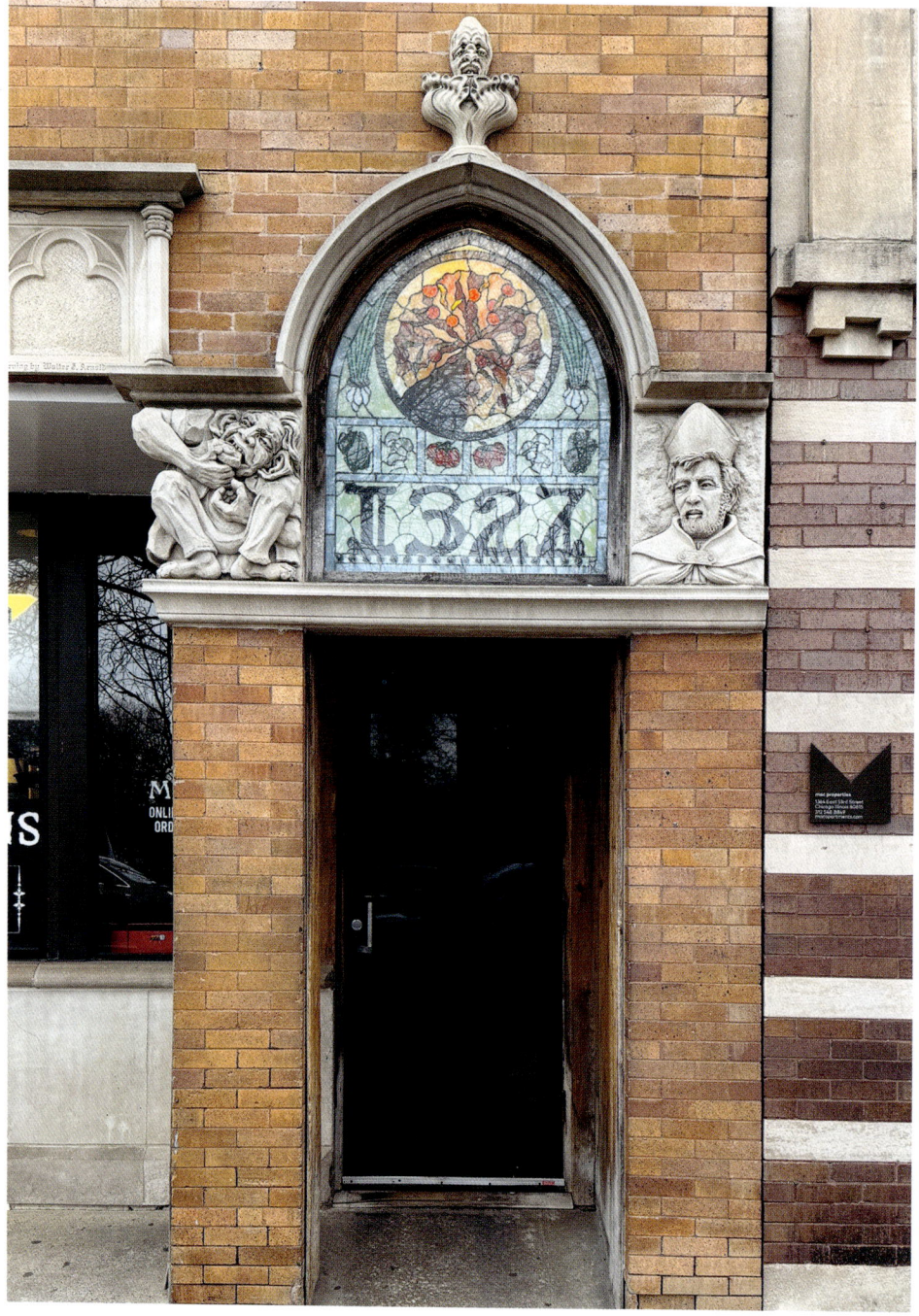

HYDE PARK

Restaurant

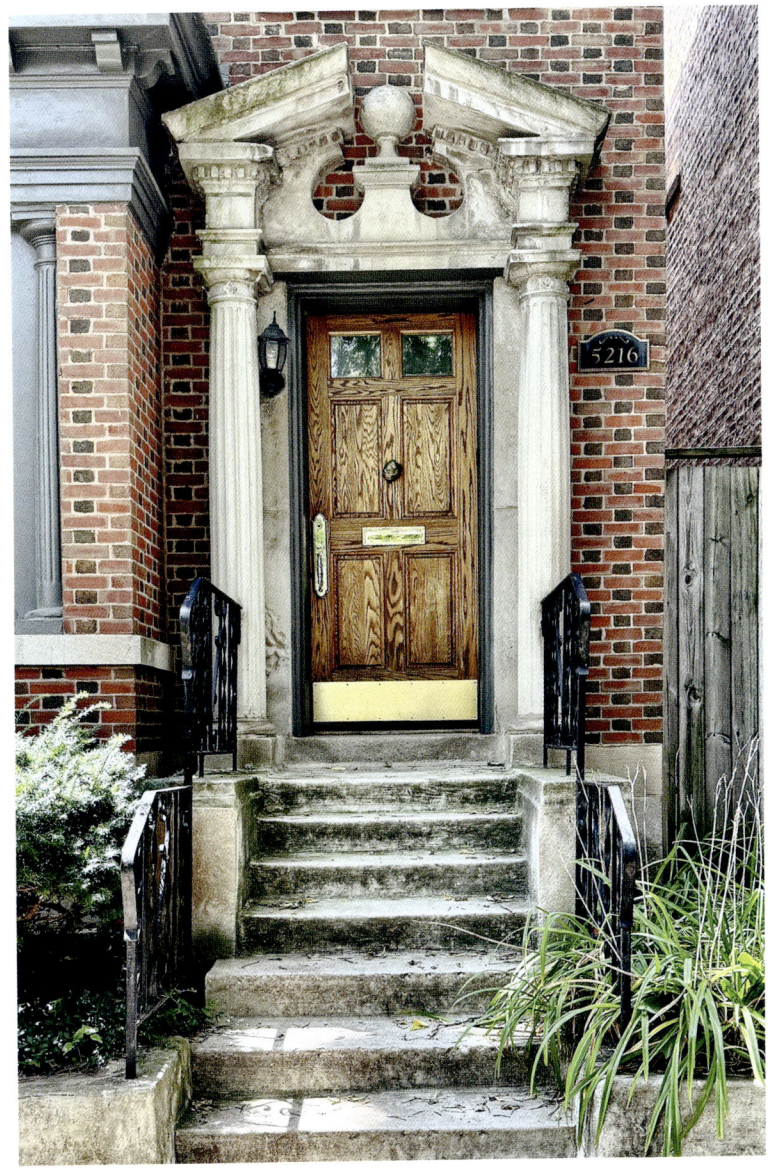

HYDE PARK

Residential

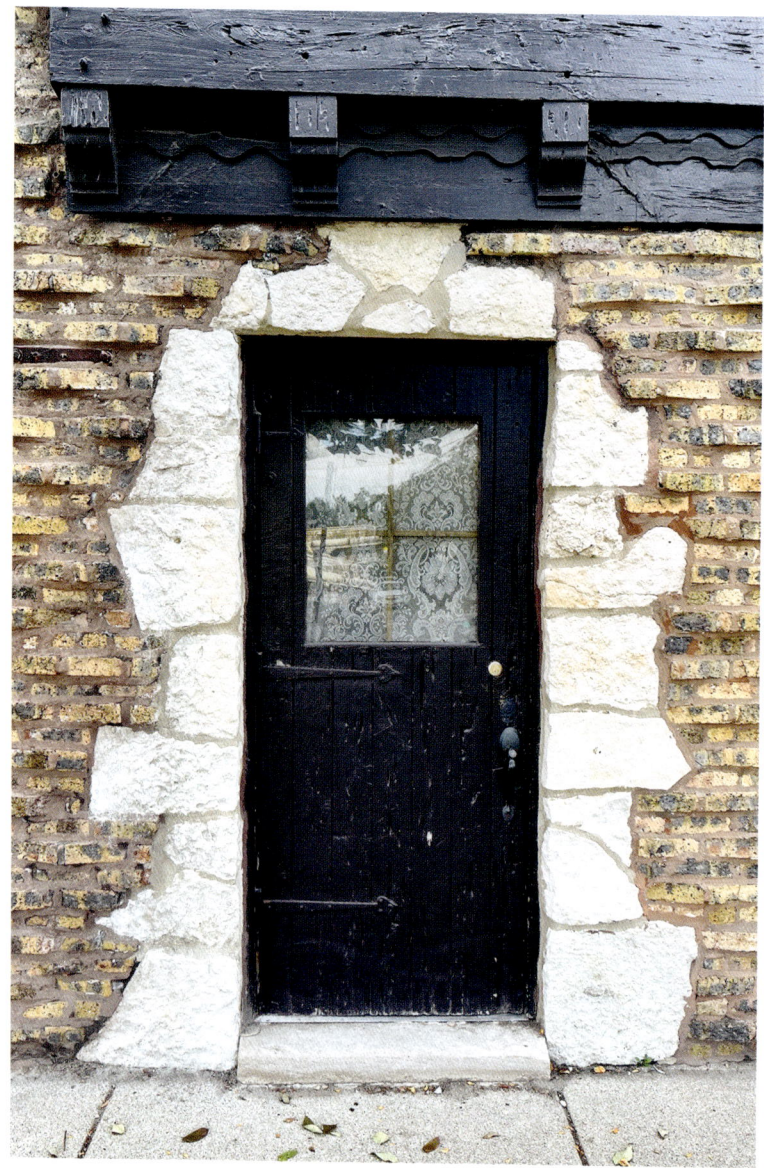

UPTOWN

South-East Asia Center

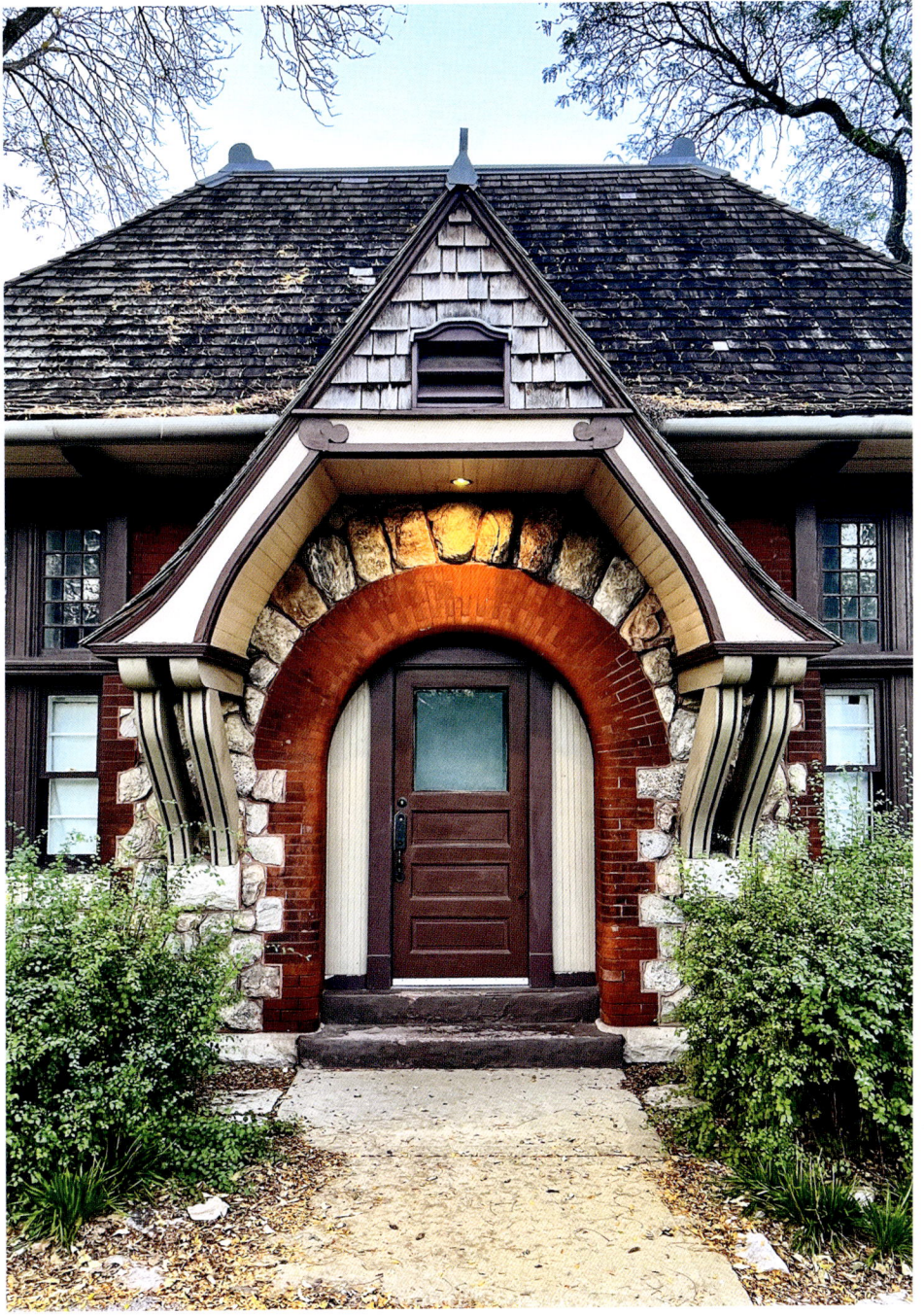

LINCOLN PARK

Carlson Cottage

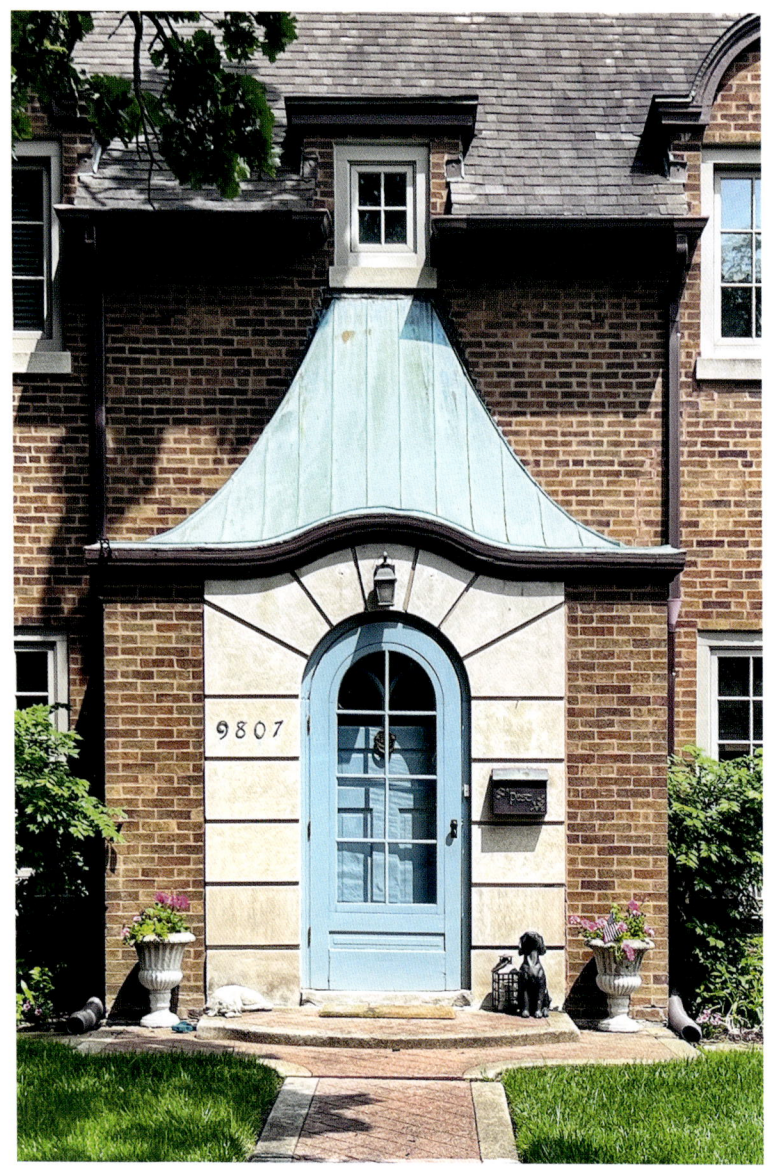

BEVERLY

Residential

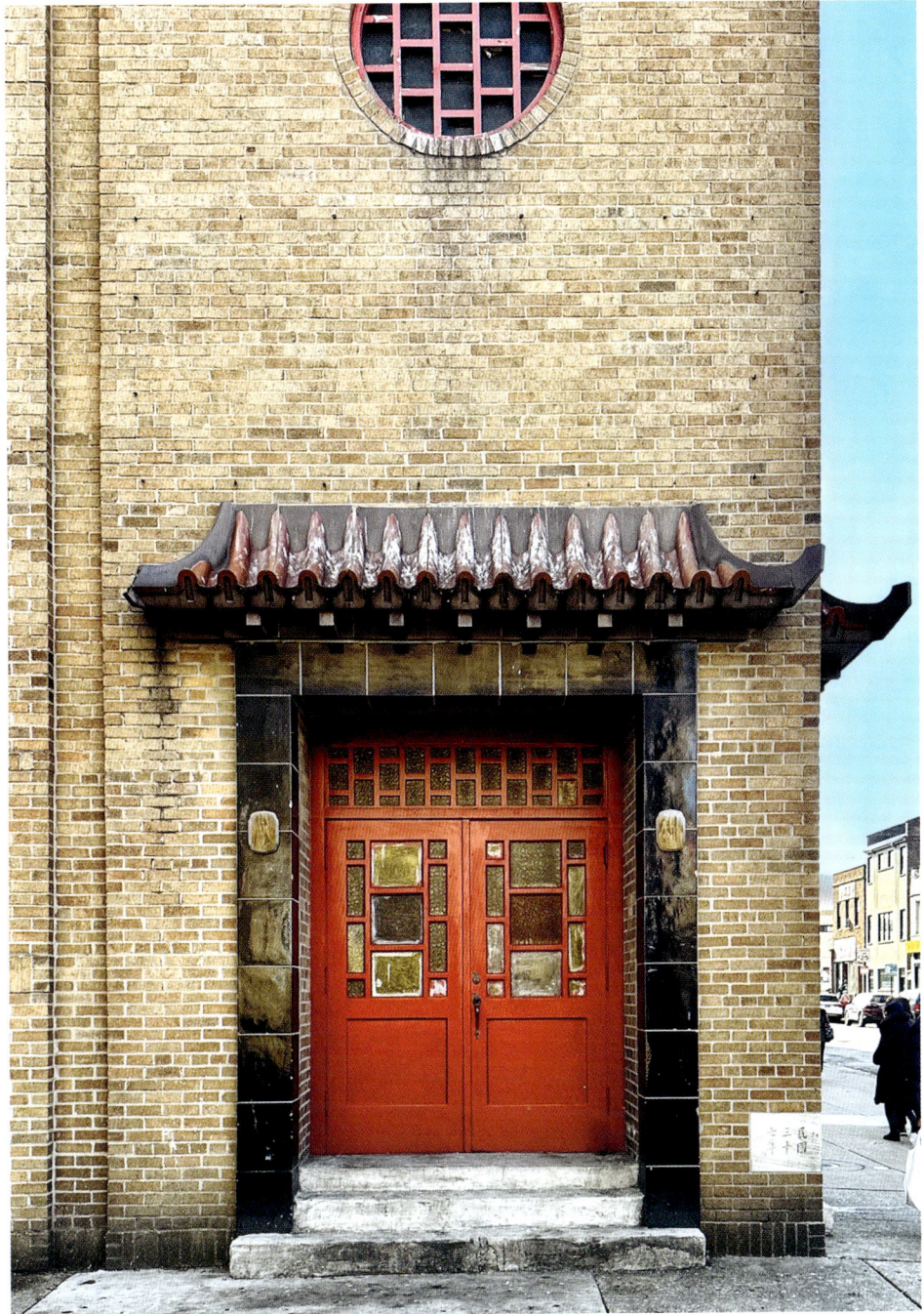

CHINATOWN

Chinese Christian Union Church

PUI TAK CENTER

Architectural Style: Orientalism | Year: 1928

Pui Tak Center has been standing in Chicago's Chinatown since it was established in the 1920s following the relocation of many Chinese businesses to the area. Originally built for the On Leong Merchants Association, it was considered Chinatown's unofficial city hall, buzzing with community life and cultural events.

As there were no licensed Chinese architects in Chicago at the time, the building was designed by Norwegian-American duo Christian Michaelsen and Sigurd Rognstad, who filtered traditional Chinese design through a Western lens. A prime example of Orientalism architecture, the building's design was derived from the architecture of the Kwangtung district of China, the ancestral region of many of Chinatown's early residents. This influence is evident in the green clay roof tiles, twin pagoda towers, and terracotta ornamentation. The side entrances, pictured here, are framed in jewel-toned tiles, guarded by imperial terracotta lions, and drenched in elaborate patterns.

After a federal raid in the late 1980s, the building fell silent until the Chinese Christian Union Church purchased it in 1993. It was renamed Pui Tak Center, meaning "to build character" or "cultivate virtue," and was reestablished as a hub for education, culture, and community. After winning a grant from the National Trust for Historic Preservation in 2007, the building's interior and exterior was restored and repaired. Preservation work on the building's exterior continues to this day.

Today, Pui Tak Center continues to offer religious services, educational programs, immigrant assistance, and more, and is the only officially designated Chicago Landmark in Chinatown.

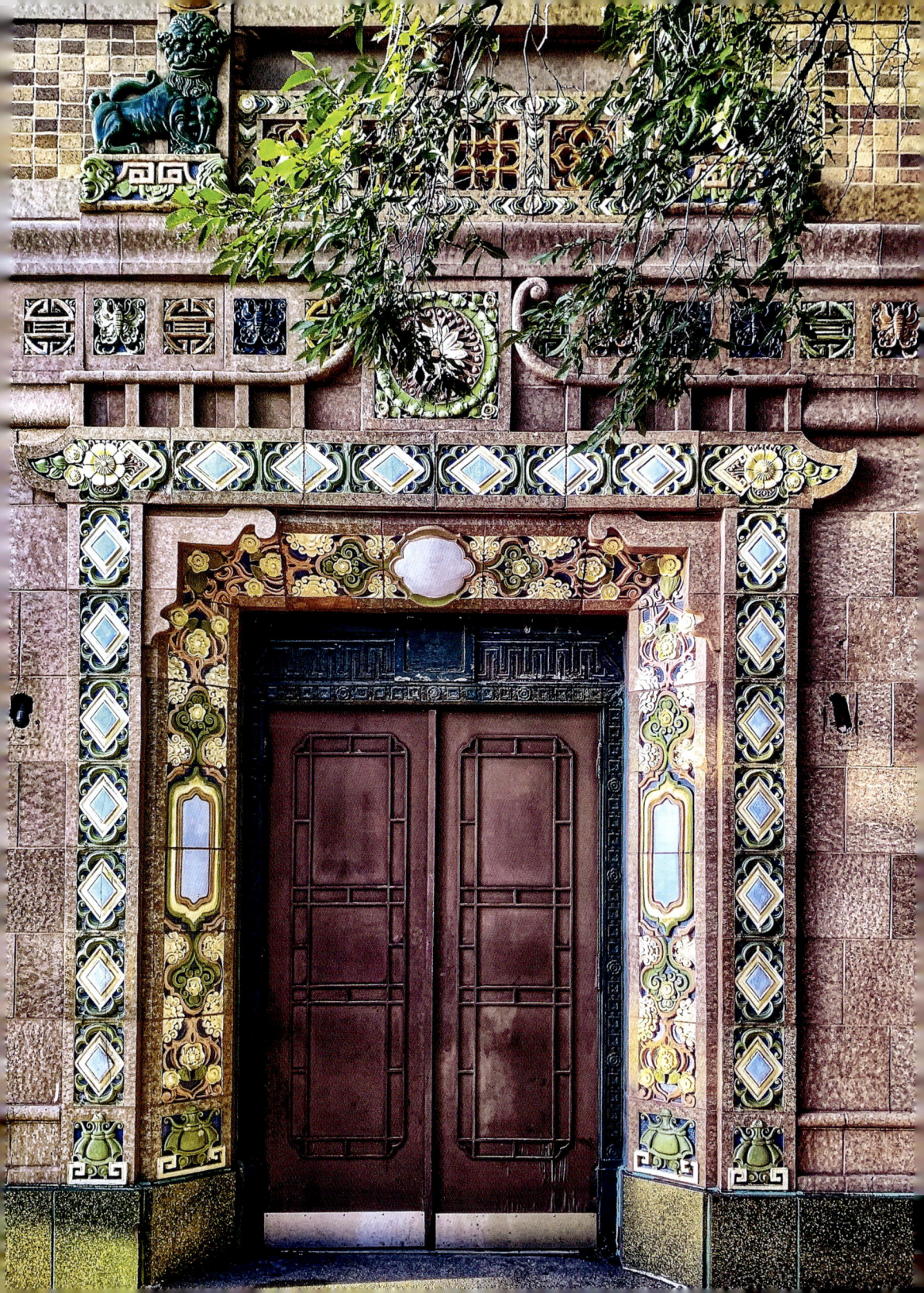

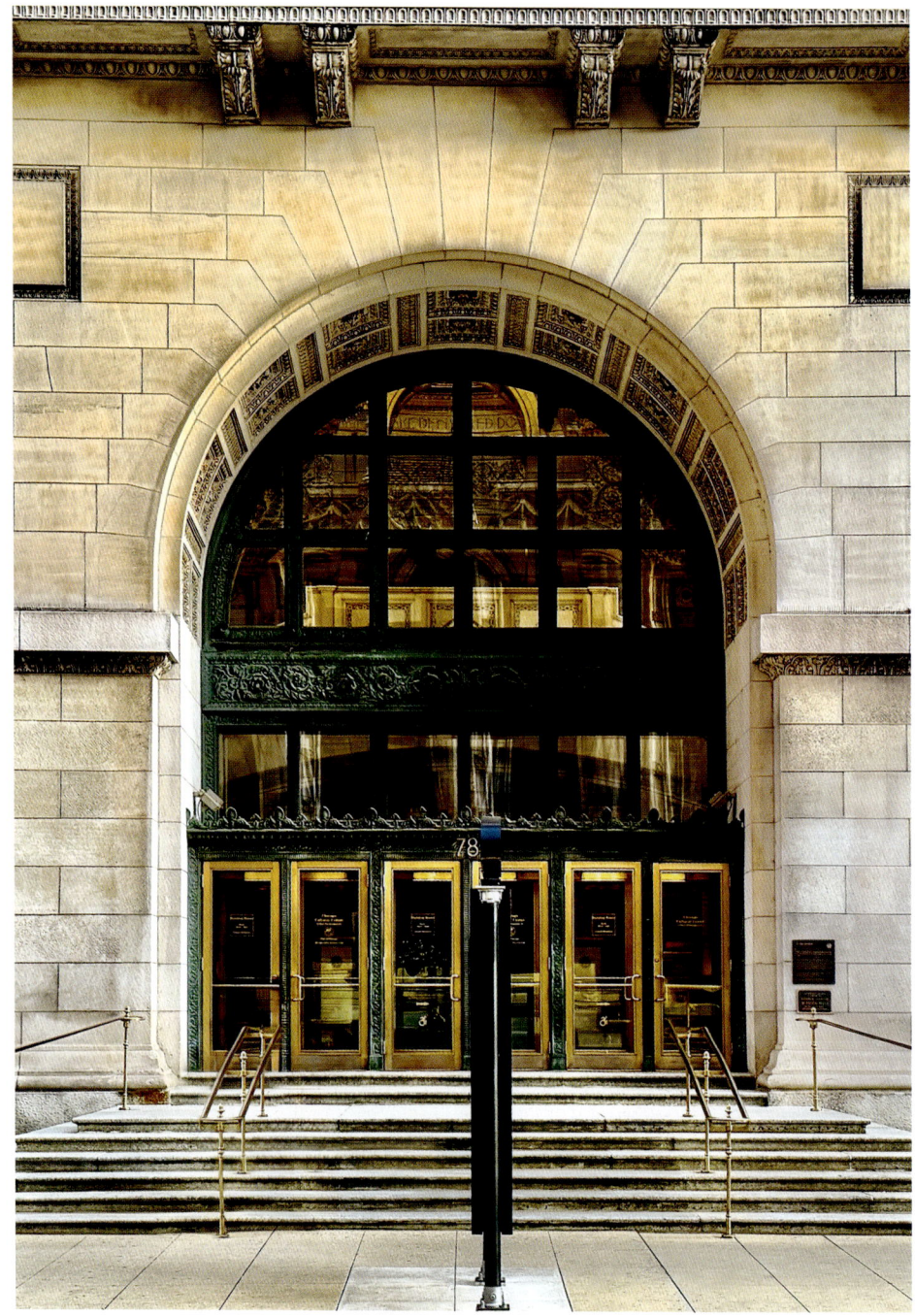

THE LOOP

Chicago Cultural Center

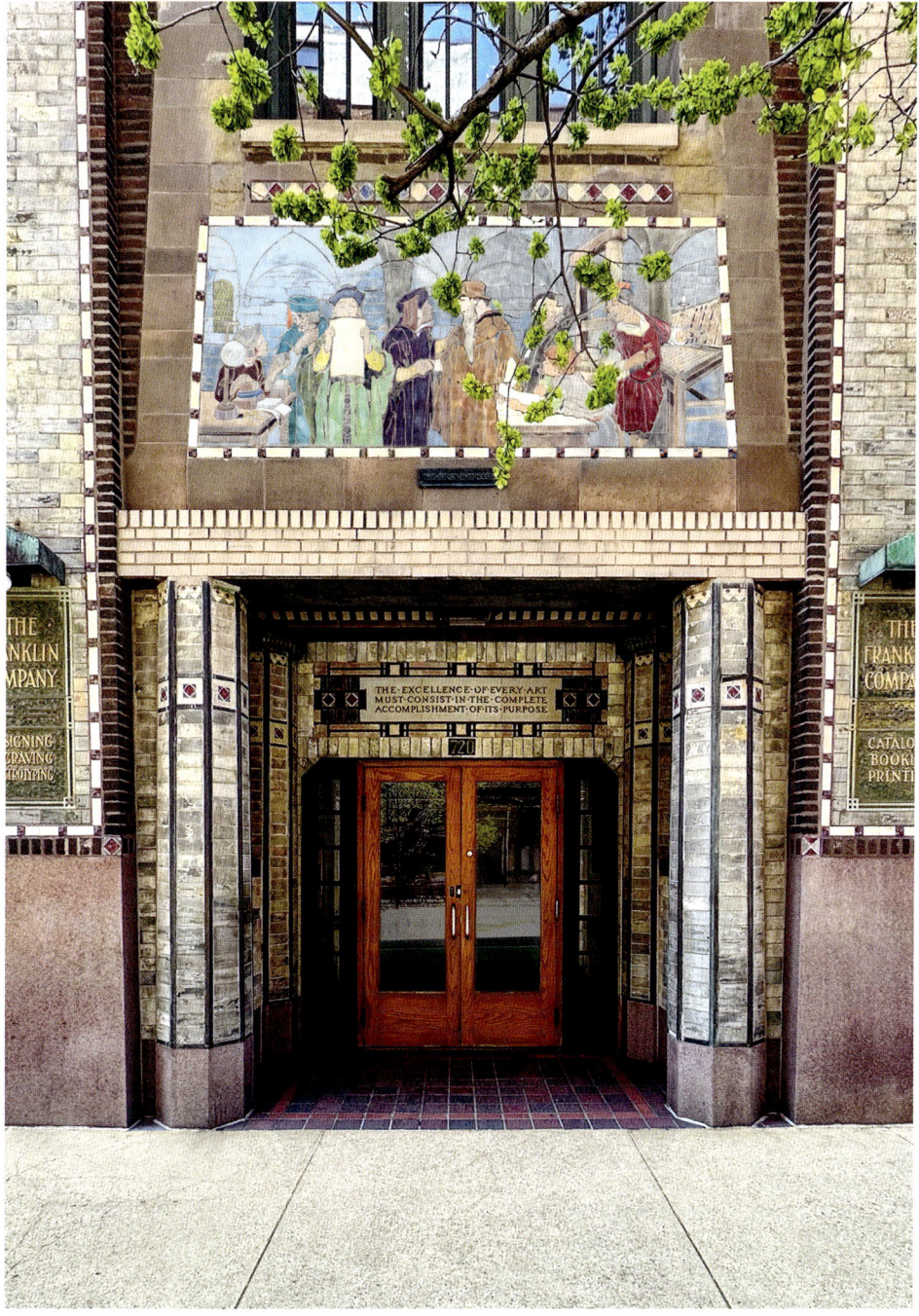

PRINTER'S ROW

Franklin Building

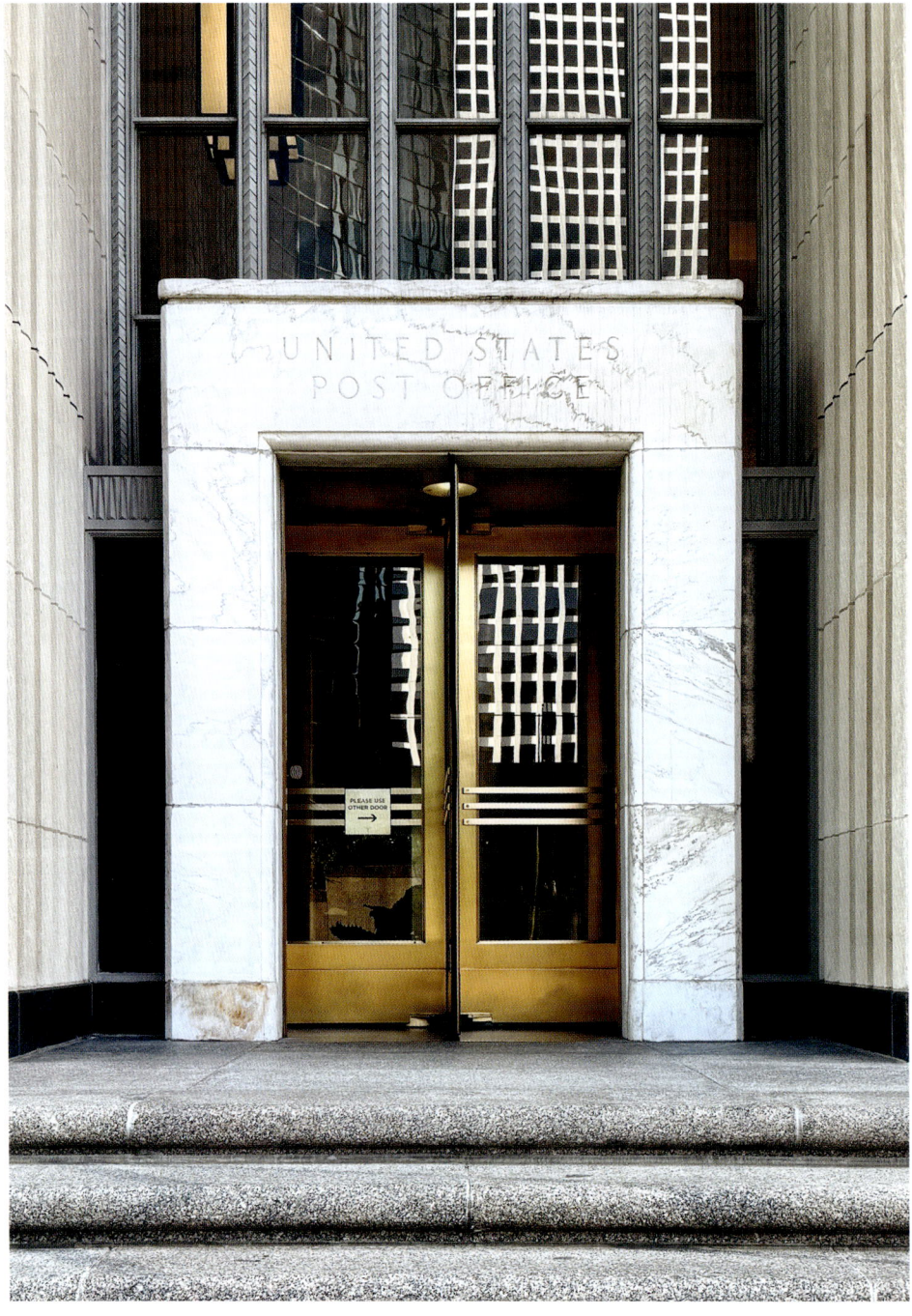

WEST LOOP

The Old Post Office

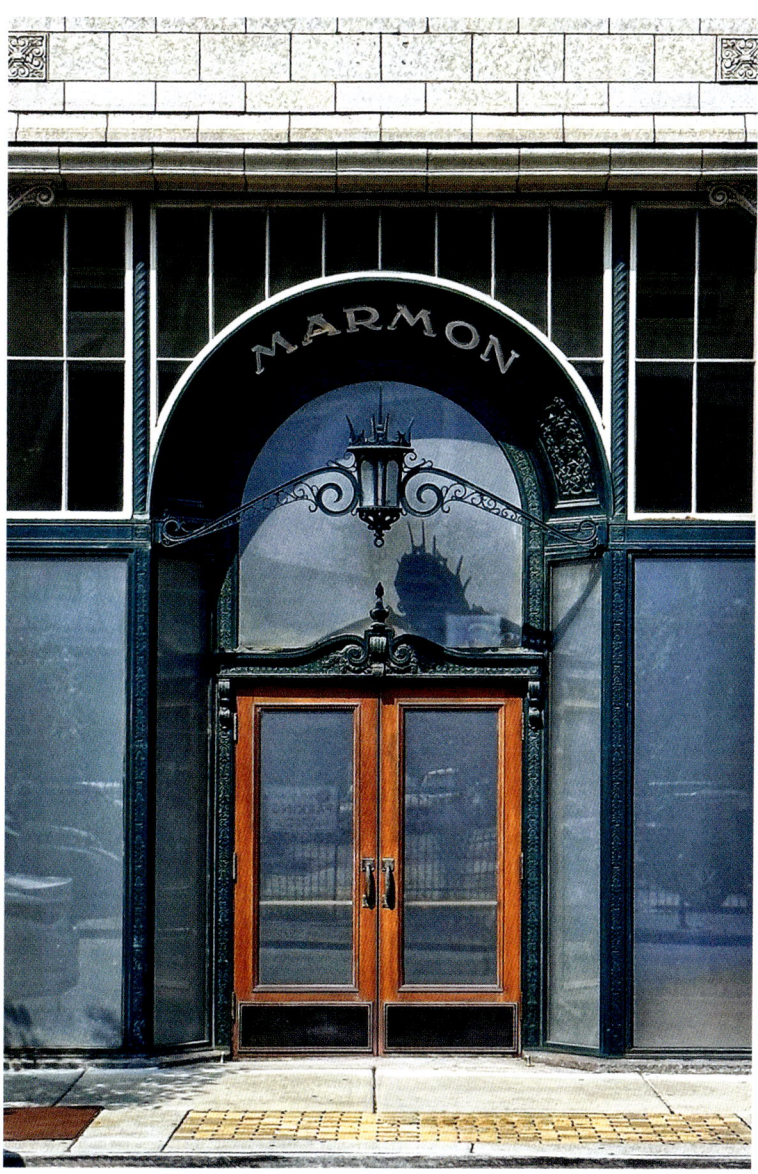

SOUTH LOOP

The Marmon Building

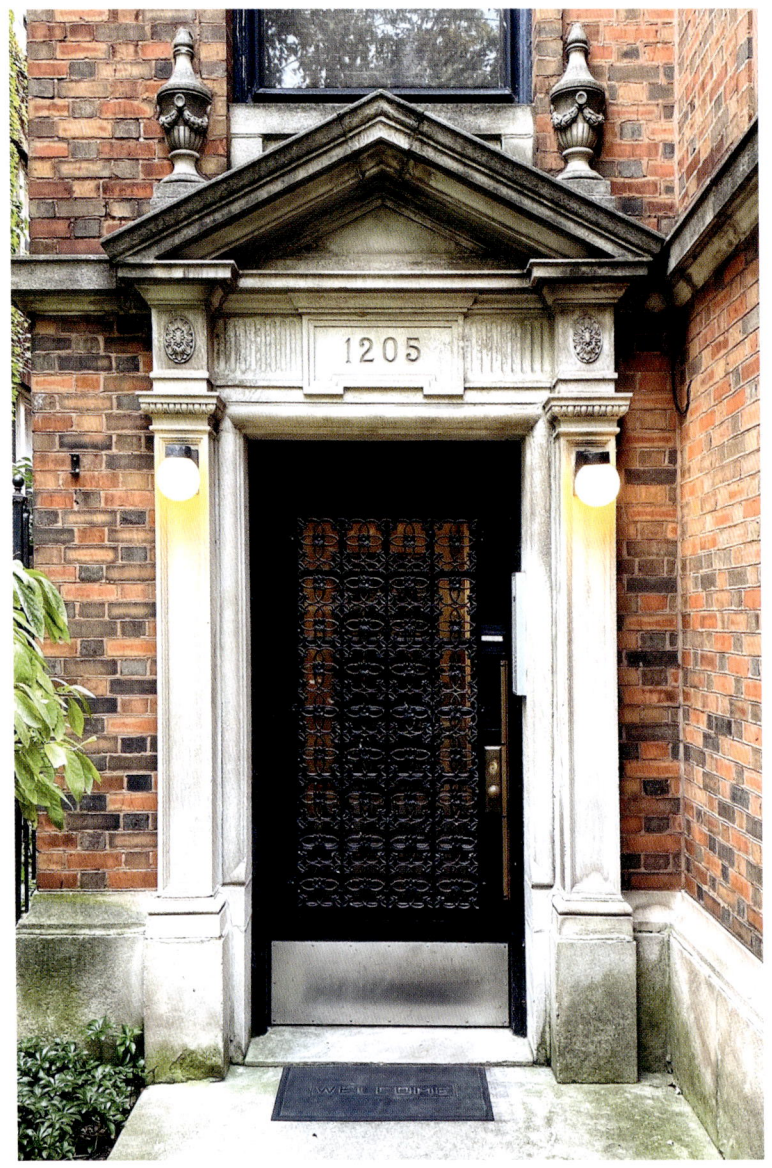

KENWOOD

Residential

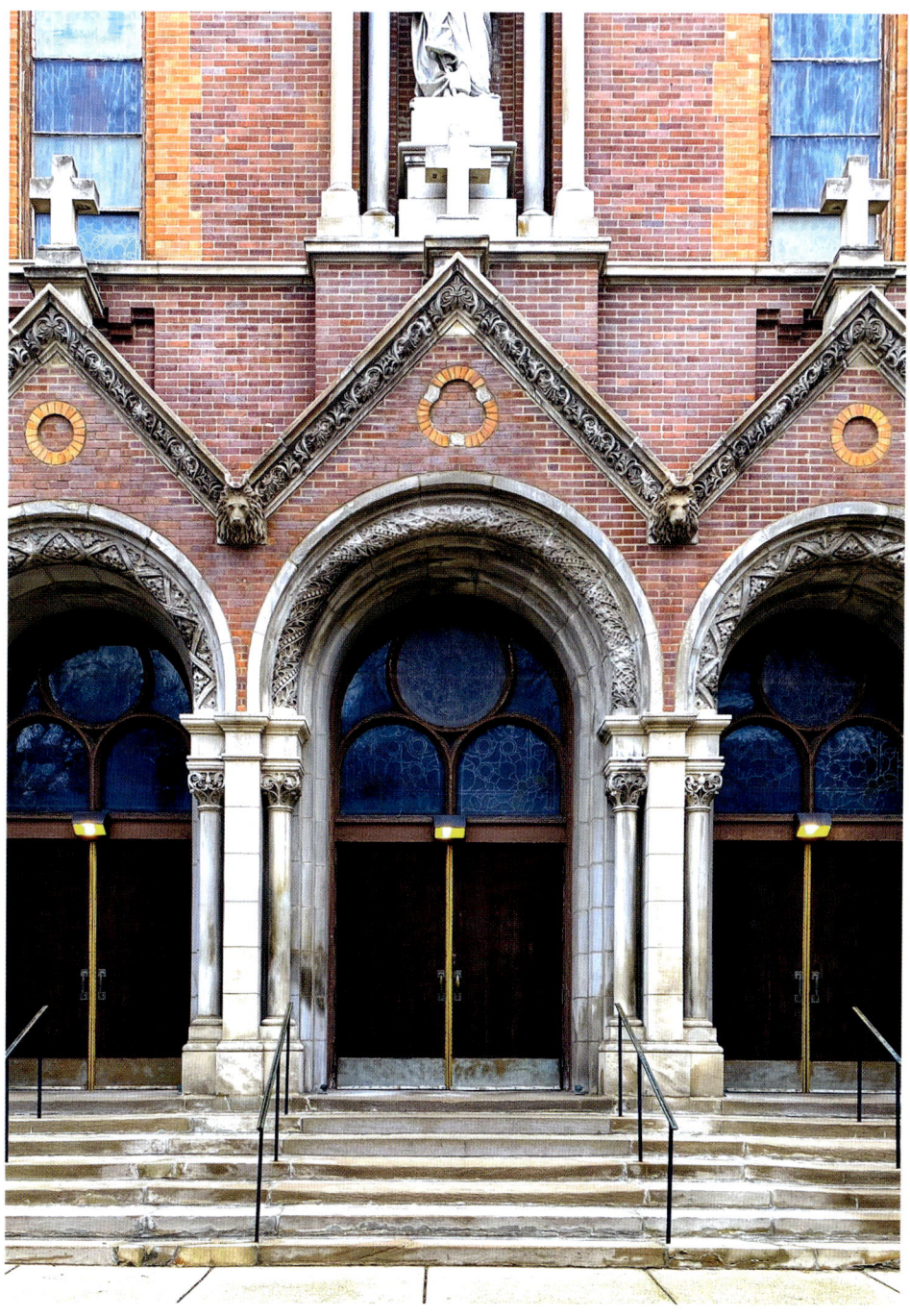

LINCOLN SQUARE

St. Matthias Church

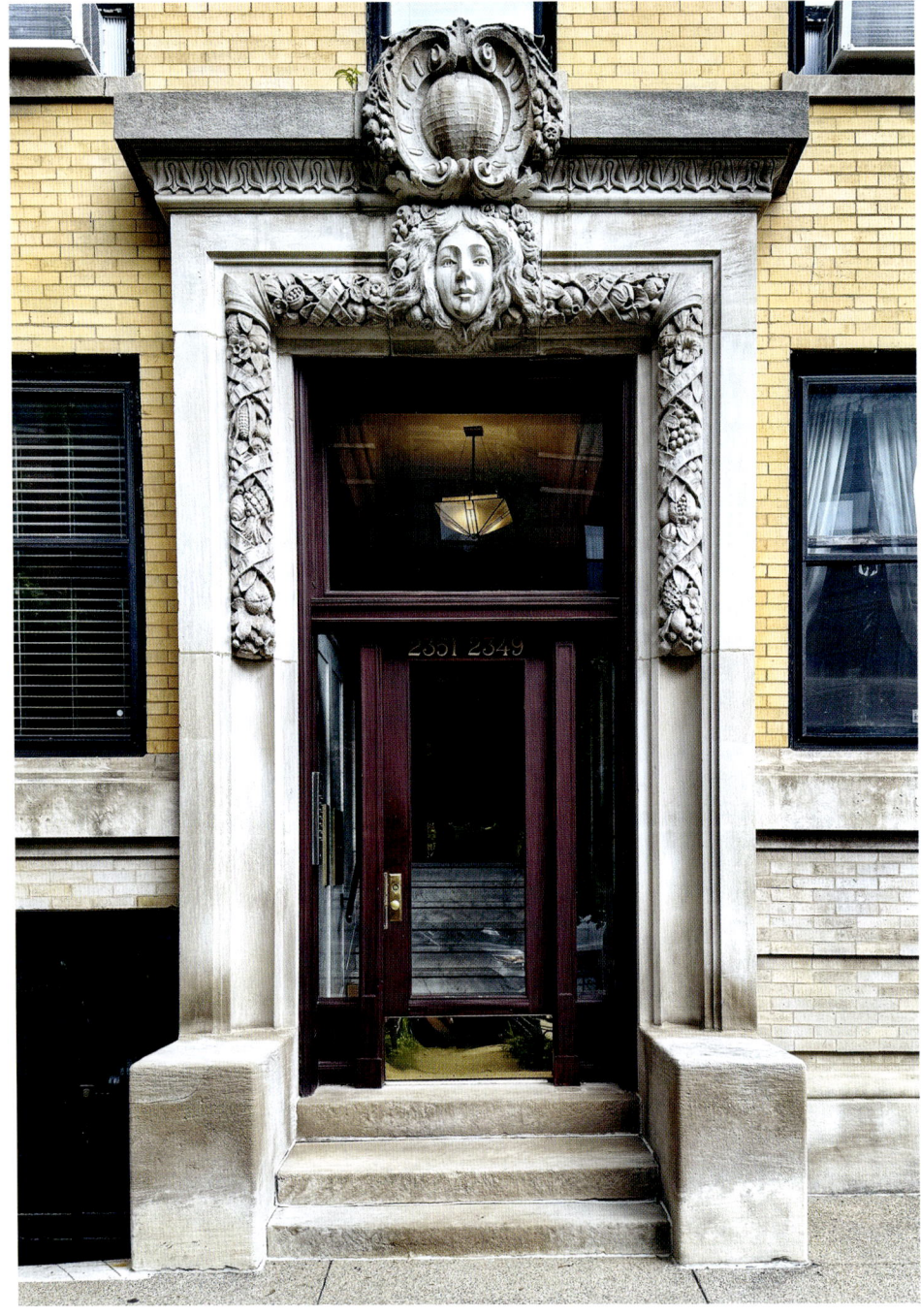

LINCOLN PARK

Residential

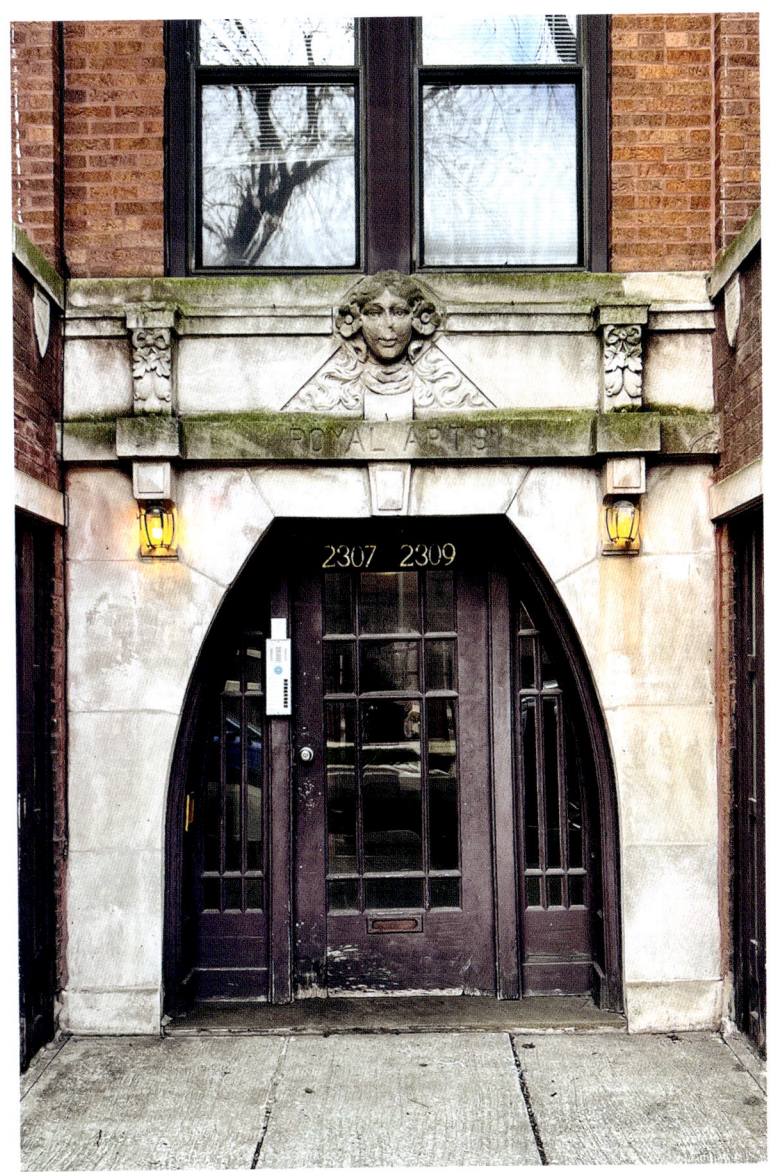

UKRAINIAN VILLAGE

Residential

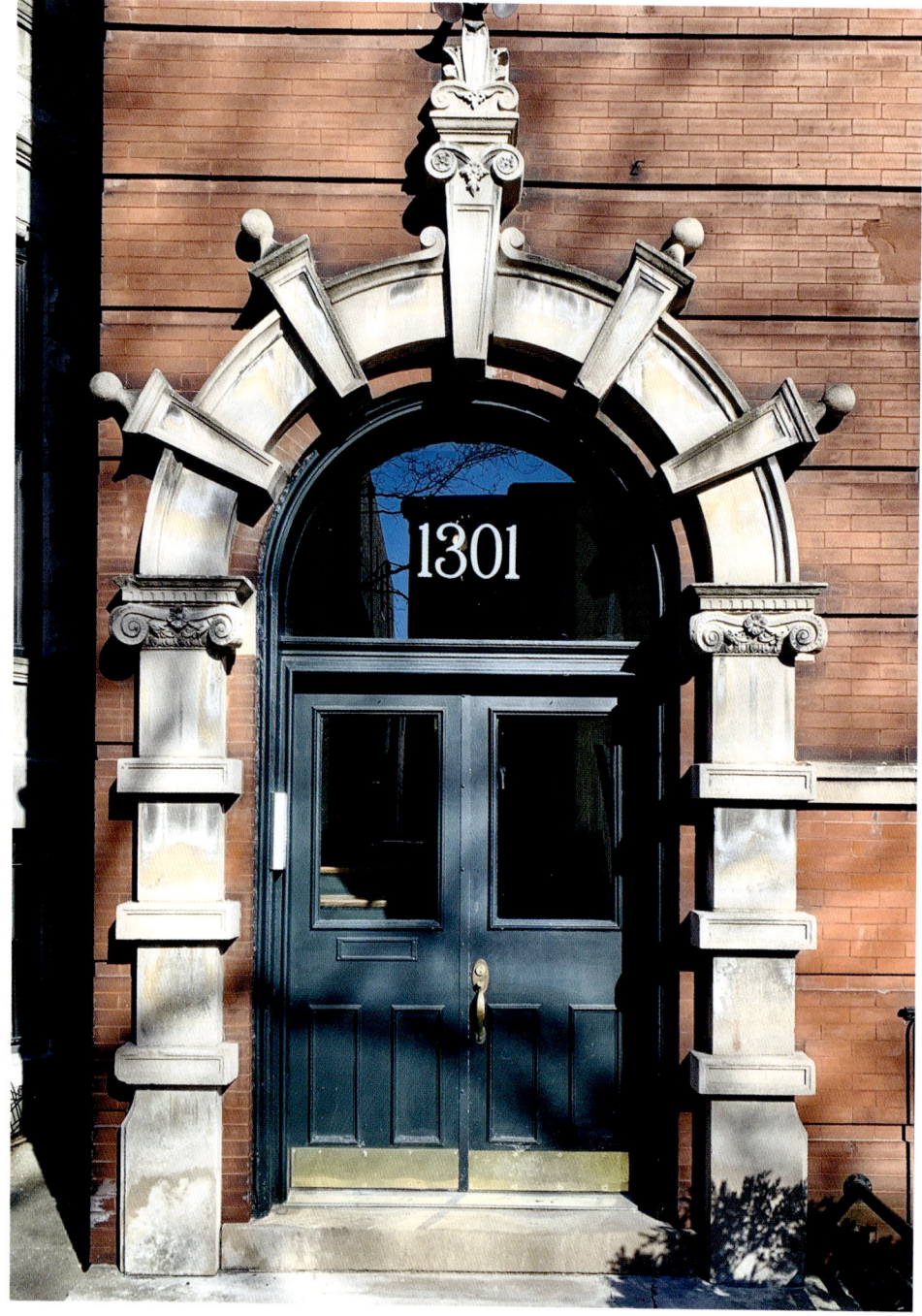

WICKER PARK

Residential

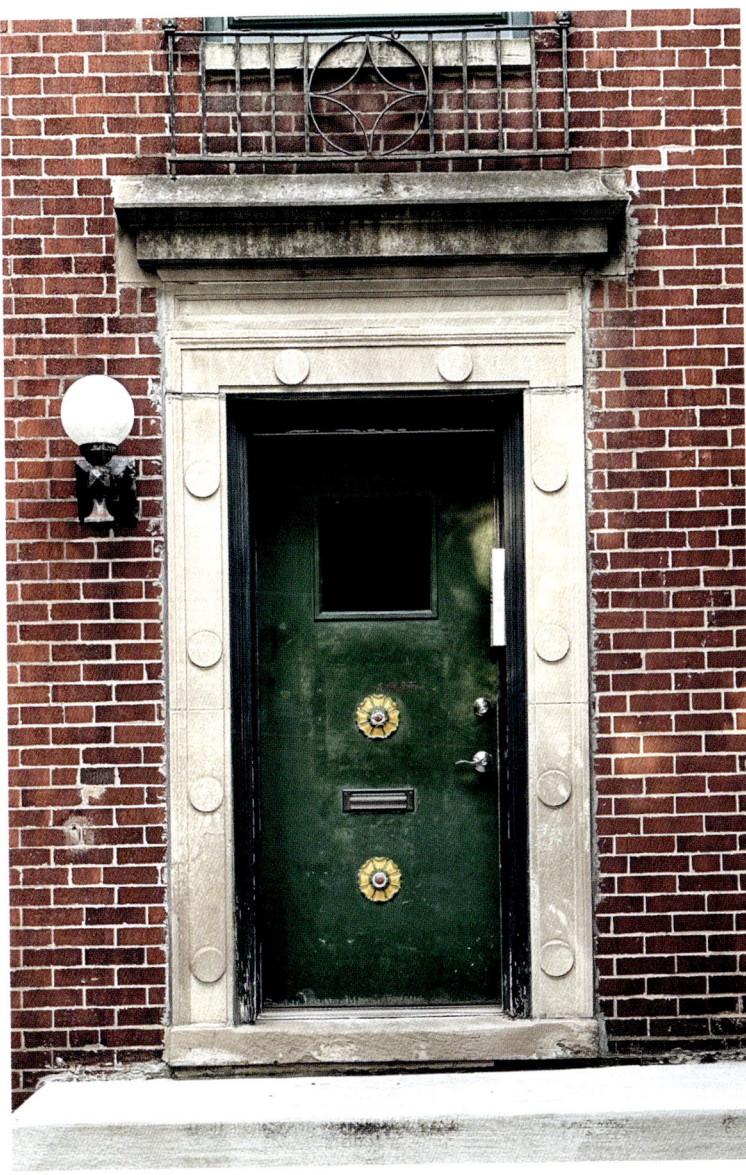

ROGERS PARK

Residential

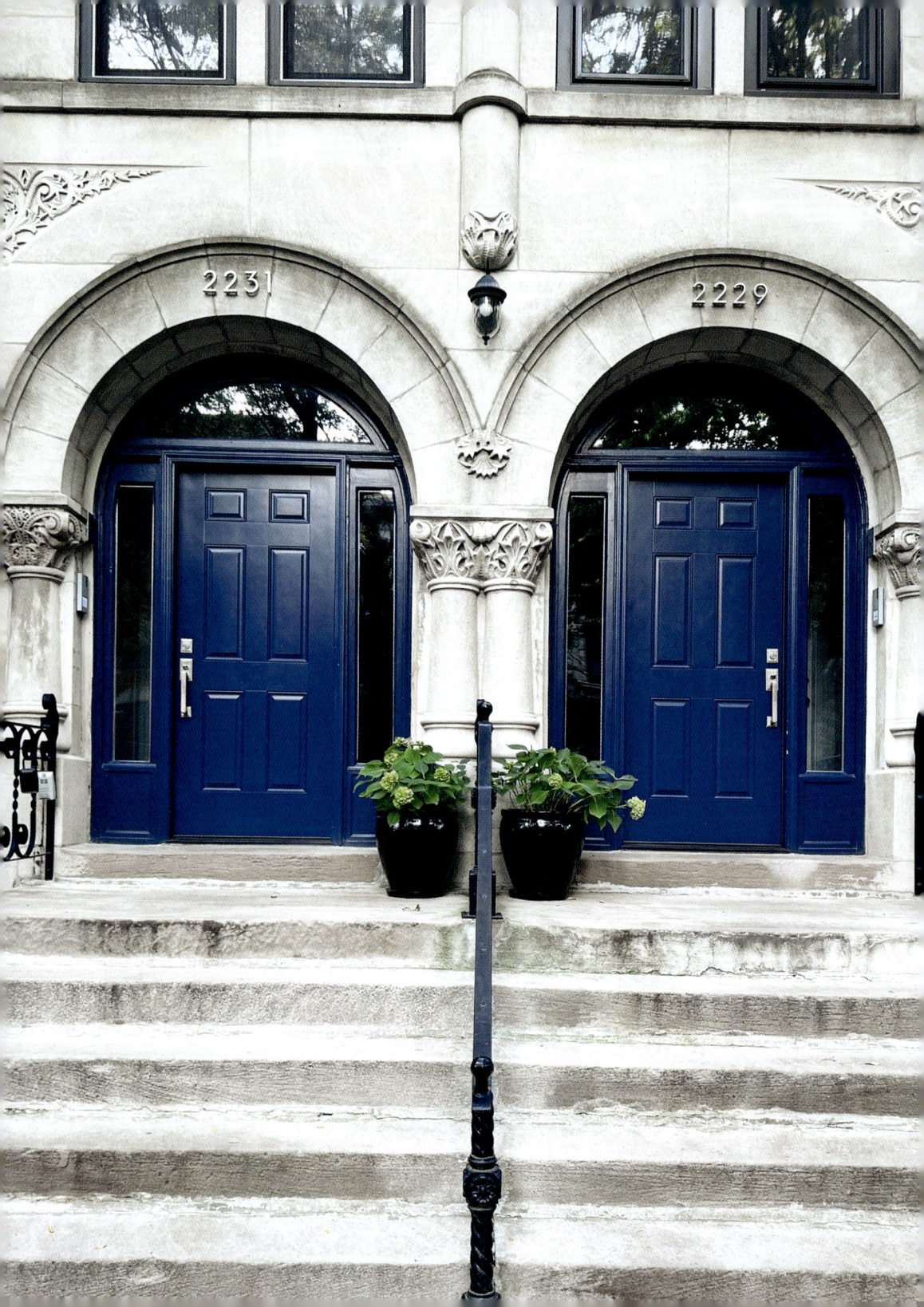

ACKNOWLEDGMENTS

I am deeply grateful to the many people who have walked this journey with me and encouraged me along the way. To my late dad, whose best advice was to make my hobby my career, and to my mom, who fostered the creator in me and never looked down on my "crazy" ideas. To my sister Julee, whose thousands of remarkable photographs inspired me to pursue my own. To my daughter Ariel, for her constant encouragement and the game-changing advice to buy my own printer, and to my son-in-law Matt, for reminding me how special it is to influence my grandson Oscar and show him he can do anything he dreams of.

To my friends: Laura, who, upon hearing I was considering a space in the Fine Arts Building, immediately said, "You HAVE to do this!"; Daniel, whose countless hours of help made my studio space possible and who continues to be constant support; Katie, who never stops gushing over my work and shares the best adventures with me; Chris, who insists he can't ask anyone if they've heard of *Doorways of Chicago* without getting a yes, and who has been a steadfast cheerleader for what I'm building; and my late roommate and best friend Laurie, who saw all of this before I did.

To my Instagram community, who show up time and again to remind me how important this work is; my clients, who support me through social media partnerships and by purchasing photography prints and cards; and my tour attendees, who have booked tour after tour and left the most flattering reviews.

Special thanks to RuPaul Charles, whose reminder to ignore my inner saboteur has made a lasting impact.

And finally, to my beloved city of Chicago, the best city in the world, thank you for the endless supply of architectural inspiration and fabulous doorways to discover. To all of you reading this, thank you, and maybe I'll see you out on the trails!

ABOUT
THE ARTIST
Ronnie Frey | @doorwaysofchicago

Ronnie Frey is the creative visionary behind the popular Instagram account @doorwaysofchicago, a visual archive that elevates the mundane into the magnificent. With a keen eye for detail and a deep love for Chicago's layered architectural history, Ronnie captures more than just doors and buildings; he captures atmosphere, memory, and soul. From the gritty to the pretty, nothing is too ordinary to capture his attention.

While doors are at the heart of his work, the @doorwaysofchicago project has naturally evolved. His feed now highlights architectural gems, neon and ghost signs, murals, and sculptures—anything vintage that tells a story. Planes, trains, and automobiles roll through as well; after all, they have doors too. And when Ronnie travels, the focus stays the same, seeking out geometry, detail, and quirk wherever he goes.

As a walking tour guide and historic storyteller, he brings this same passion to the streets of Chicago, leading groups through neighborhoods like Wicker Park, the Loop, and Old Town, sharing architectural history with humor, heart, and happiness.

Now based in a studio inside the landmark Fine Arts Building, Ronnie draws inspiration from his surroundings—a place where artistry, legacy, and creative energy meet. His work is a meditative practice, an act of urban preservation, and a joyful celebration of the beauty hiding in plain sight.

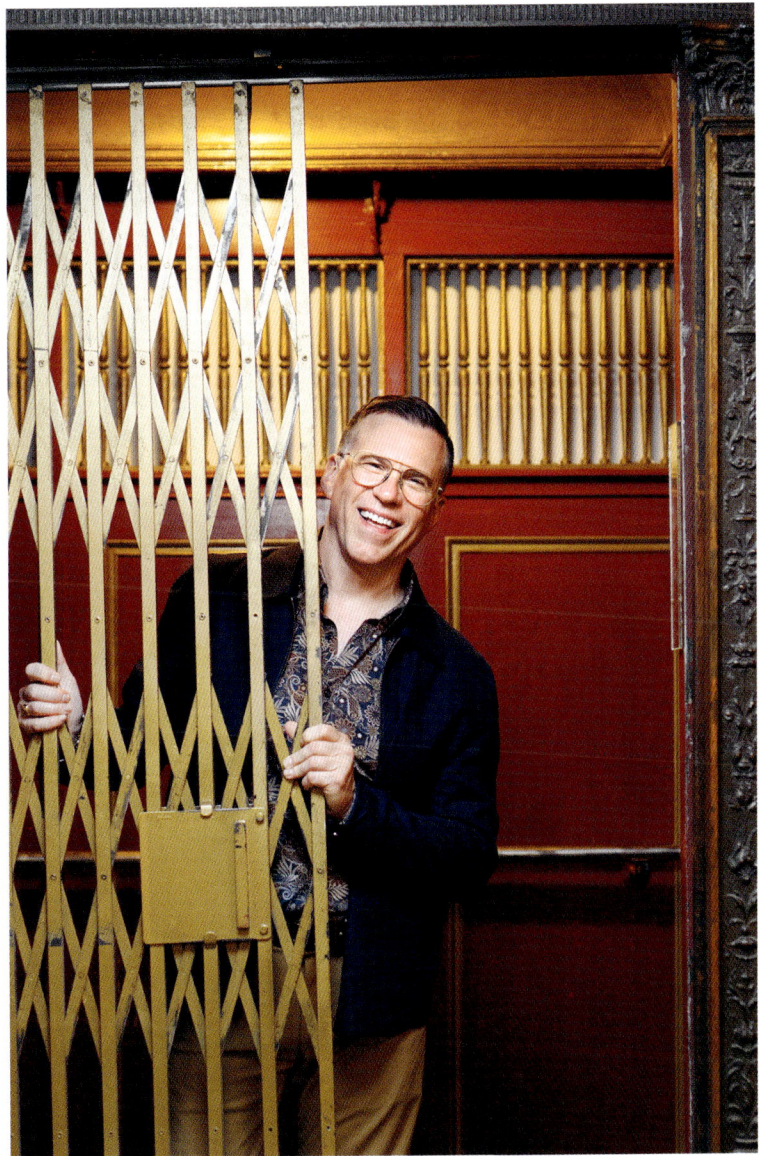

©2026 Photographs and text
by Ronnie Frey

Author photograph on page 159
courtesy of Garret Buckley,
Skyline Headshots

ISBN: 978-1-951963-56-9

Trope Publishing Co.
Chicago, Illinois

Printed in China
First printing, 2026

+ INFORMATION:
For additional information
on our books and prints,
visit trope.com

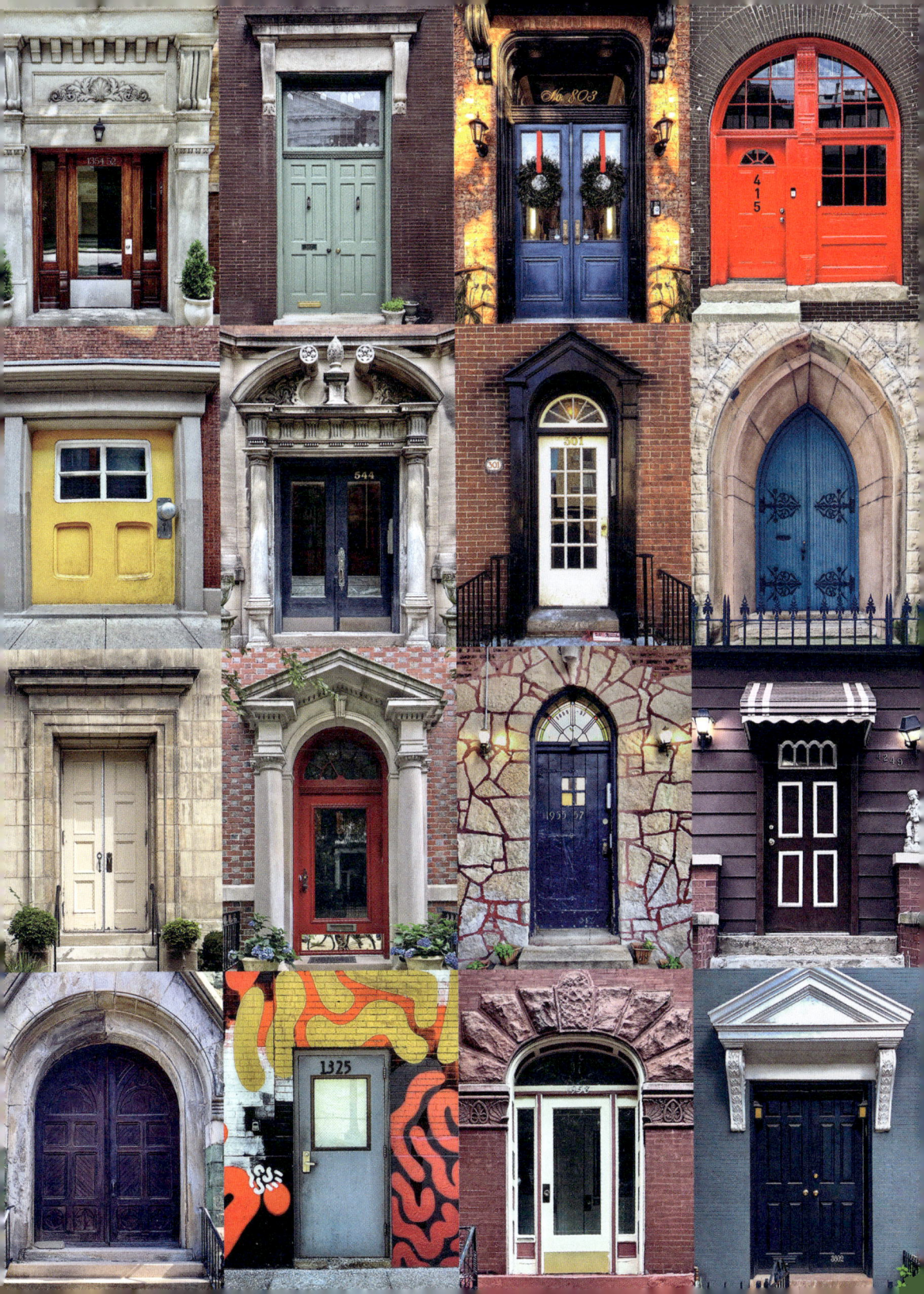